The Body and the Song

Ad Feminam: Women and Literature
Edited by Sandra M. Gilbert

Christina Rossetti
The Poetry of Endurance
By Dolores Rosenblum

Lunacy of Light
Emily Dickinson and the Experience of Metaphor
By Wendy Barker

The Literary Existence of Germaine de Staël
By Charlotte Hogsett

Margaret Atwood
Vision and Forms
Edited by Kathryn VanSpanckeren and Jan Garden Castro

He Knew She Was Right
The Independent Woman in the Novels of Anthony Trollope
By Jane Nardin

The Woman and the Lyre
Women Writers in Classical Greece and Rome
By Jane McIntosh Snyder

Refiguring the Father
New Feminist Readings of Patriarchy
Edited by Patricia Yaeger and Beth Kowaleski-Wallace

Writing in the Feminine
Feminism and Experimental Writing in Quebec
By Karen Gould

Rape and Writing in the Heptaméron of Marguerite de Navarre
By Patricia Francis Cholakian

Writing Love: Letters, Women, and the Novel in France, 1605–1776
By Katharine Ann Jensen

The Body
and the Song
Elizabeth Bishop's Poetics

Marilyn May Lombardi

Southern Illinois University Press
Carbondale and Edwardsville

Illustration on title page, "Elizabeth Bishop by a Stone Wall." Courtesy of Special Collections, Vassar College Libraries.

Library of Congress Cataloging-in-Publication Data

Lombardi, Marilyn May.
    The body and the song : Elizabeth Bishop's poetics / Marilyn May
Lombardi.
       p. cm. — (Ad feminam)
    Includes bibliographical references (p.) and index.
    1. Bishop, Elizabeth, 1911–1979—Criticism and interpretation.
    2. Body, Human, in literature. 3. Poetics. I. Title.   II. Series.
PS3503.I785Z76 1995
811'.54—dc20   94-10653
    ISBN 0-8093-1885-7   CIP

For my husband, Julian

Contents

Ad Feminam:
Women and Literature

Ad Hominem: to the man; appealing to personal interests, prejudices, or emotions rather than to reason; *an argument ad hominem.*
—*American Heritage Dictionary*

Until quite recently, much literary criticism, like most humanistic studies, has been in some sense constituted out of arguments *ad hominem*. Not only have examinations of literary history tended to address themselves "to the man"—that is, to the identity of what was presumed to be the *man* of letters who created our culture's monuments of unaging intellect—but many aesthetic analyses and evaluations have consciously or unconsciously appealed to the "personal interests, prejudices, or emotions" of male critics and readers. As the title of this series is meant to indicate, the intellectual project called "feminist criticism" has sought to counter the limitations of *ad hominem* thinking about literature by asking a series of questions addressed *ad feminam:* to the woman as both writer and reader of texts.

First, and most crucially, feminist critics ask, What is the relationship between gender and genre, between sexuality and textuality? But in meditating on these issues they raise a number of more specific questions. Does a woman of letters have a literature—a language, a history, a tradition—of her own? Have conventional methods of canon-formation tended to exclude or marginalize female achievements? More generally, do men and women have different modes of literary representation, different definitions of literary production? Do such differences mean that distinctive male- (or female-) authored images of women (or men), as well as distinctly male and female genres, are part of our intellectual heritage? Perhaps most important, are literary differences between men and women essential or accidental, biologically determined or culturally constructed?

Feminist critics have addressed themselves to these problems with increasing sophistication during the last two decades, as they sought to revise, or at times replace, *ad hominem* arguments with *ad feminam* speculations. Whether explicating individual texts, studying the oeuvre of a single author, examining the permutations of a major theme, or charting the contours of a tradition, these theorists and scholars have consistently sought to define literary manifestations of difference and to understand the dynamics that have shaped the accomplishments of literary women.

As a consequence of such work, feminist critics, often employing new modes of analysis, have begun to uncover a neglected female tradition along with a heretofore hidden history of the literary dialogue between men and women. This series is dedicated to publishing books that will use innovative as well as traditional interpretive methods in order to help readers of both sexes achieve a clearer consciousness of that neglected but powerful tradition and a better understanding of that hidden history. Reason tells us, after all, that if, transcending prejudice and special pleading, we speak to, and focus on, the woman as well as the man—if we think *ad feminam* as well as *ad hominem*—we will have a better chance of understanding what constitutes the human.

Sandra M. Gilbert

Acknowledgments

My first debt is to Stephen Yenser for introducing me to the skein of voices in Elizabeth Bishop's poetry. I am grateful as well to the scholars who have taken the time to listen to those voices, which was doubtless a labor of love: to Lloyd Schwartz and Sybil Estess for their collection, *Elizabeth Bishop and Her Art*; to the late David Kalstone for the depth of understanding he displays on every page of his biographical study, *Becoming a Poet*; to Bonnie Costello whose *Elizabeth Bishop: Questions of Mastery* is consistently illuminating; to Lorrie Goldensohn for her eloquent perspective on Bishop's life and art in *Elizabeth Bishop: The Biography of a Poetry*, and for her valued friendship; to Brett Candlish Millier for the scholarly dedication evident in her biography of the poet, *Elizabeth Bishop: Life and the Memory of It*; to Joanne Feit Diehl, Lee Edelman, Bonnie Costello, Thomas Travisano, Jeredith Merrin, Jacqueline Vaught Brogan, Barbara Page, Victoria Harrison, and Brett Candlish Millier for their insight as well as their eagerness to form a community of scholars for the advancement of Bishop studies. I also found three recent critical studies by Victoria Harrison, C. K. Doreski, and Joanne Feit Diehl to be enlightening and provocative, although they appeared after this book was completed.

In shepherding this study to publication, several colleagues made a gift of their time and expertise. I thank Lee Zimmerman for reading a portion of chapter 1 and helping me coax it into shape and Alan Shapiro for his encouragement in the early stages when my love for the subject was strong but my impressions amorphous. My greatest debt is to Thomas Travisano, not only for his pioneering critical study, *Elizabeth Bishop: Her Artistic Development*, but for his support and generosity in reading the manuscript at a crucial point in its life and for helping me to articulate the core of my argument. While rummaging through Bishop's archives, I received invaluable assistance from Nancy MacKechnie, curator of Special Collections at Vassar College Libraries. Ultimately, this study would not have been possible without the help and good wishes of Bishop's executor, Alice Methfessel, and the support of my family. My deepest thanks go to Julian Lombardi for his joking voice and Darien David Lombardi, who kindly waited until this study was finished to be born.

I gratefully acknowledge permission for quotations as follows:

Permission for the quotations from Marianne Moore's unpublished letter has been granted by Marianne Craig Moore, Literary Executor for the Estate of Marianne Moore. All rights reserved.

Quotations from unpublished letters of Elizabeth Bishop and Robert Lowell are used by the permission of the Special Collections of Vassar College Libraries; Houghton Library, Harvard University (bMS Am 1905); the Princeton University Libraries; and the Washington University Library; and Frank Bidart, Literary Executor for the Estate of Robert Lowell.

Excerpts from other unpublished writings of Elizabeth Bishop are used with the permission of the Special Collections of Vassar College Libraries and the permission of her Estate, copyright © 1995 by Alice Helen Methfessel. All rights reserved.

Excerpts from *The Collected Prose* by Elizabeth Bishop. Copyright © 1984 by Alice Methfessel. Reprinted by permission of Farrar, Straus and Giroux, Inc.

Excerpts from *The Complete Poems, 1927–1979* by Elizabeth Bishop. Copyright © 1979, 1983 by Alice Helen Methfessel. Reprinted by permission of Farrar, Straus and Giroux, Inc.

Excerpts from Elizabeth Bishop's letter to Marianne Moore. Courtesy Rosenbach Museum and Library.

Portions of chapter 1 were published under the title " 'The Closet of Breath': Elizabeth Bishop, Her Body and Her Art" in *Twentieth Century Literature* 38.2 (Summer 1992): 152–75, copyright © 1992 by *Twentieth Century Literature* (reprinted by permission of William

McBrien and *Twentieth Century Literature*) and also in *Elizabeth Bishop: The Geography of Gender* (Charlottesville: UP of Virginia, 1993.) 46–69 (reprinted by permission of the University Press of Virginia).

Abbreviations

CP   *Elizabeth Bishop: The Complete Poems, 1927–1979*
CProse *Elizabeth Bishop: The Collected Prose*
HL   Bishop-Robert Lowell Correspondence, Houghton Library, Harvard University, Cambridge, Mass.
KW1   Key West Notebook 1
KW2   Key West Notebook 2
PU   Bishop-Ilse Barker and Kit Barker Correspondence, Elizabeth Bishop Collection, Princeton University Library, Princeton, N.J.
RM   Bishop-Marianne Moore Correspondence, Rosenbach Museum and Library, Philadelphia, Pa.
VC   Elizabeth Bishop Collection, Vassar College Libraries, Poughkeepsie, N.Y.
WU   Bishop-Anne Stevenson Correspondence, Washington University Library, St. Louis, Mo.

The Body and the Song

Introduction

woe is translatable
to joy if light becomes
darkness and darkness
light, as it will.

—*William Carlos Williams,*
"Light Becomes Darkness"

Elizabeth Bishop stares back at me from a grainy, age-flecked photograph. It is 1954; she is forty-three years old and living in Brazil. Sitting on the ground, cradling her legs, she looks girlish and just as James Merrill remembered her: "The whitening hair grew thick above a face each year somehow rounder and softer, like a bemused, blue-lidded planet, a touch too large, in any case, for a body that seemed never quite to have reached maturity" (6). Even as an adolescent, Bishop was known for her startling appearance. To schoolmate Frani Blough Muser, "she looked remarkable, with tightly curly hair that stood straight up, while the rest of us all had straight hair that hung down. . . . We called her 'Bishop,' spoke of her as 'the Bishop,' and we all knew with no doubt whatsoever that she was a genius" (introduction, *CProse* xii–xiii). From first to last, "the Bishop" hated being photographed and rarely let herself be caught looking directly into a camera. Most snapshots show her in profile or three-quarter view, looking off into some incalculable distance. Aloof or shy—it's difficult to tell. And in the back of my mind I hear the rustling of an untethered phrase from one of Bishop's most well-known letters, words of advice for anyone sinking or sliding into the unknown terrain of a poet's life: "Catch a peripheral vision of whatever it is one can never really see full-face but that seems enormously important" (Stevenson 66).

Bishop's classmates at Vassar would remember that the young woman with unruly hair spent a great deal of time in a darkened room lying down or sitting with her feet elevated, suffering from an attack of asthma. They may have also caught a whiff of the Roquefort cheese she kept in a drawer by her bed and would nibble each night (with the understanding that it would somehow enliven her dreams) or may have shared a sip from a bottle of illicit liquor she hid among her books and papers. The drinking that began as a common collegiate expression of daring and insouciance became a full-fledged addiction from which she was never to recover.

Like her castaway in the late poem "Crusoe in England," Bishop often resorted to "home-brew" when the burden of registering the flora and fauna of her world grew too great, the demands of the eye too tyrannical (*CP* 164). Her eyesight was almost preternaturally acute, and she could spot objects at great distances. She was usually depressed by foggy weather or mountain ranges that obscured or blocked her view, much preferring the "bright, detailed flatness" of Key West, Florida, where she lived on and off for a decade during and after the Second World War (travel diary: 26, 10 August 1940, VC). If her blue eyes were hyperopic, however, they could also focus with rare microscopic intensity on all the assorted minutiae that gave her immediate surroundings their distinctive texture. "I would like to have had [Bishop's] quiddity, her way of seeing that was like a big pocket magnifying glass," Mary McCarthy once confessed, before quickly adding the caveat, "Of course it would have hurt to have to use it for ordinary looking: that would have been the forfeit" (267).

Bishop coped fitfully with the "forfeit" of having to look minutely on matters close to home. When her friend, the scholar Joseph Summers, described Marianne Moore's "meticulous attention" as a "method of escaping intolerable pain," Bishop found this an "awfully good" explanation of her early mentor's visionary precision (letter to Summers, 19 October 1967, VC). Leaving unspoken the reasons for her own endless, heroic observations, Bishop confides to Summers that his insight into Moore was "something I've just begun to realize myself—although I did take it in about Marianne Moore long ago. (It [is] her way of controlling what almost amounts to paranoia, I believe—although I handle these words ineptly)" (19 October 1967). Toying with the vocabulary of psychology (which she viewed with a mixture of interest and suspicion), Bishop raises questions central to her own experience: questions of control, or mastery, that extend into all aspects of her life as an artist and a woman.

Raised within a family and a social class that insisted on a code of self-discipline and reserve, Bishop became intent on expelling "morbidity" from her mind and body. On the subject of her unorthodox private life and her struggles with alcohol, she enjoined her friends to silence. There is always something troubling about revealing the fissures in a reputation so carefully managed, but there is evidence that Bishop had reconciled herself to the inevitable disclosures that would come following her death. Friends preserved her letters and deposited them in libraries for future scholars, while the poet herself went to the trouble of preparing her papers for the archives. Nine years before her death, Bishop confided to a close friend that her life had been "pretty darkened always by guilt-feelings" about her mother's mental collapse and her own "unstable personality" (letter to Dorothee Bowie, 16 June 1970, VC). She closes on a practical note and with a touch of bravado: "Maybe I should write an autobiography, telling ALL, right away—then ther-e'll be nothing to dig up and reveal. I don't care in the slightest at this point in my affairs." Bishop's typewritten letters (some a full five pages, single-spaced), travel diaries, and unpublished work must ultimately supply the place of the promised autobiography that was never written.

The poet demanded a strict code of silence from her intimate companions, and the mystery surrounding her personal life lasted for almost a decade following her death. But with the passage of time came the arrival of a freer atmosphere in which to discuss and evaluate the impact formerly closeted subjects had had on the poet's artistic principles. A number of biographically slanted studies of Bishop have appeared, beginning in 1989 with David Kalstone's *Becoming a Poet: Elizabeth Bishop with Marianne Moore and Robert Lowell* and continuing with Lorrie Goldensohn's *Elizabeth Bishop: The Biography of a Poetry* (1992), Brett Millier's *Elizabeth Bishop: Life and the Memory of It* (1993), Victoria Harrison's *Elizabeth Bishop's Poetics of Intimacy* (1993), and *Elizabeth Bishop: The Geography of Gender* (1993), my edited anthology of critical essays by leading scholars in the field. These studies firmly place the poet's silences and evasions within the context of the era in which she came of age as an artist, while drawing on the insights of current gender theory to expand our appreciation for this complex and unconventional woman.

The current state of Bishop studies has prepared her readers and admirers for a searching analysis and articulation of Bishop's poetics based more on her fugitive writings than on her published masterpieces. This fresh approach is especially important in Bishop's case because she left behind no comprehensive and explicit statement of her artistic theories. It is possible now, as it would not have been earlier when so many of her private papers were still inaccessible to scholars, to read the poet from the inside out, piecing together her underlying poetic principles from material she deemed inappropriate for publication either because she found it to be unworthy of her exacting poetic standards or too personally revealing. Given the sheer scale of the poet's manuscript writings (her letters, diaries, working notebooks, and drafts) and the fact that much of her most confessional work remained hidden in this cache of private papers, a case can and must be made for applying a special hermeneutics to Bishop's published canon.

A Special Hermeneutics

I argue that Bishop's poetry, like all narrative, is founded properly and necessarily on secrecy or parable, simultaneously proclaiming and concealing truth in order to preserve within the structure of the work a quality of transmutable meaning. Each work contains levels of manifest and latent meaning. In Bishop's case, relevant diary entries and early drafts, often far more forthright than the final, enigmatic version of the poem, unveil the flesh-and-blood author behind the poetic personae. Though it might come as a surprise to readers familiar with her poems in print, Bishop did indeed write (or attempt to write) explicitly about her chronic illnesses, her homosexuality, her alcoholism, and her abiding fear of mental instability. The poet's decision to suppress these confessions was not only a choice forced upon her by the social constraints and audience expectations of a less-tolerant age. It had as much to do with her own estimate of superior and satisfactory writing and how much greater an impact she might have as an artist if she were to withhold work that she believed would only encourage prurient rather than sympathetic interest. Delving into potentially damaging matters the poet would just as soon have kept to herself, Bishop's recent biographers necessarily tread the fine line between scholarship and gossip, raising certain ethical dilemmas that need not have worried their more circumspect predecessors. To console myself, I read in Bishop's decision to sell her papers to the Vassar College Libraries tacit approval or, more likely, resigned acceptance of the more probing inquiries that would follow her death.

My aim in this study is to trace the somatic imagination of a deeply private woman. The body and its impact on the poet's artistic preoccupations is an overlooked subject in Bishop's studies, largely because little was known about its significance until the availability of her unpublished writings revealed her surprising, and long-standing, attraction to metaphors drawn from carnal desires, impulses, and aversions. I choose to focus attention on the poet's translations of physical weakness into artistic strength because for far too long Bishop has been treated as something of a disembodied voice, in keeping with her own efforts to minimize or obscure the material circumstances of her life as an orphan, an eternal émigré, a lesbian, and a woman.[1]

While mapping her somatic history and telling much of the story in Bishop's own words, I candidly discuss the poet's asthma, alcoholism, and sexuality, their hold over her imagination, and their impact on her response toward poetic form, its pleasures and restraints. I argue that Bishop draws a rich cache of enabling metaphors from the realm of the body—metaphors that help her describe and enact her sense of the world. And the dialogue between her suppressed and her published poetry draws attention to the anatomy, the morphology, of her famous landscape poems, where the world spread out before the poet's eyes takes on the qualities of a generalized human body. Breathing from a "rib cage of giant fern," pulsing along veins of water, charging through a nervous system of live wires, the poet's message sings, flows, crackles through the magnified world body and the living integument of the poem.

Bishop's private papers reveal the poet's enduring interest in the relation between her own physical and creative drives. Her voluminous notes and letters clash with her spare poems, her detailed confessions of weakness reveal a morbid streak to her imagination that is judiciously suppressed in her public persona—and not without great effort, as the poet's unfinished drafts, with their moving cries from the heart, make apparent in unexpected ways. The stillborn poems carefully nurtured but finally suppressed, the voices of depression or disbelief or self-recrimination that surface in the pages of her private journals amid all the painstaking observations of the natural world, speak to an inner life at odds with the poet's wry, uncompromising public persona. Although many of Bishop's diaries and travel journals inform this study, two notebooks written while the poet lived in Key West, Florida, are especially important for their imaginative preoccupation with the flesh. Recently recovered from Brazil, where they lay in a shoe box since the poet's departure from her adopted country, these small blue binders are a diary of Bishop's daily struggle to discipline her body while composing her mind. They confront sensual excess and delight with a surprising, and unstinting, candor.

A cornerstone of this study is the poet's intense thirty-year correspondence with her personal physician, Dr. Anny Baumann (to whom she dedicated her second volume of verse). One of Bishop's most sustained correspondences, these letters to her New York doctor do not simply record her private medical concerns, although in them, the letter writer sometimes does resemble the "finical, awkward" bird in her poem "The Sandpiper," sifting through the symptomatic evidence, obsessively looking for something, something, something "in a state of controlled panic" (*CP* 131). They also testify to the poet's fascination with medical science; she had once considered giving up writing to become a doctor, until her mentor, Marianne Moore, struck the thought from her mind. As a respected friend, confidante, and surrogate mother, Dr. Baumann helps Bishop trace the tangled relations that existed in her life between psychosomatic illness and early maternal deprivation. Bishop's letters to Baumann reveal that the poet's equivocal experience of mother-love continued to haunt her adult sexual relationships and to influence her view of the ambiguous bond between poet and reader.

"Felt in the blood, and felt along the heart"

Although the imagery of Bishop's poems can be traced to the material circumstances of her life, pathology is neither the originating nor the final word on poetic creation, and writing is more than mere therapy.[2] Bishop often argued for the evanescence, the immateriality of creative stirrings. Though artists come into this world with a different way of seeing, genius for her does not hinge on the introversion or extroversion of the temperament, the myopic or hyperopic shape of the eye. Genius has more to do with an indefinable combination of anger and plasticity, wistfulness and rigor, impatience with things as they are and a willingness to pause over life in all its astonishing detail, and perhaps above all, a healthy dose of what Diane Ackerman calls "lidless curiosity" (270).

Still, even Arnold Hauser, Bishop's favorite authority on the subject of psychology and art, allowed that much could be gained from an inquiry into "the function of art in the life of those who produce or enjoy it" and "the reasons why a person has become an artist, why he gave way to the urge of creation as a solution to his problems, why his difficulties and conflicts called for a solution by art, and art alone" (85). When we proclaim that a writer lives on in his or her work, we customarily refer to these emotional touchstones, the private preoccupations that surface within, and between, the lines on the page.

Bishop herself looked for these moments of self-disclosure in the writing she most admired. Reading Darwin, for instance, she realized that a burden (in the sense of an accompanying voice) ran like an undercurrent of sound through his prose. Opening our eyes to the garden of the world, he opens them as well to the mysteries of human personality and individual choice. The path he had chosen for himself was a strange and a lonely one as Bishop realizes: "Reading Darwin one admires the beautiful solid case being built up out of his endless, heroic observations, almost unconscious or automatic—and then comes a sudden relaxation, a forgetful phrase, and one feels" the young man behind the prose who "fix[es] his eyes on facts and minute details" to fend off vertigo as he sinks "giddily off into the unknown" (letter to Anne Stevenson, 8 January 1964, WU). Bishop's Darwin is a young man who captures the particular in all its peculiarity and its beauty as though his observations were a way of centering his own sense of himself. It is Darwin's somatic imagination to which Bishop is drawn rather than some disembodied state of mind. Living on in a writer's work—more than moods and obsessions—is the life of the senses.

Writing offered Bishop, I argue, a second proprioceptive sense. In the body, this orienting sense tells us where to locate each part of our body at any moment of the day, enabling us to move through space, to know what it is that touches us and where we have been touched. Like a sensory handrail, Bishop's art supports and guides her through an ever-changing world. Inasmuch as the poet's sense of life is intimately tied to her corporeal senses—and to the body that converts sensation into dynamic energy—that body and those sensations are invariably the stuff of art. Tracing the "natural history of the senses," Ackerman identifies smell, touch, taste, hearing, and sight as "emotional steppingstones that lead through [artists'] lives" (209). Bishop may be gone, but her sense of life at that moment lives in her poems "at this moment, at any moment" (209). Poems transcribe sensations, both sweet and painful, "felt in the blood, and felt along the heart," as Wordsworth knew them to be ("Tintern Abbey," l. 28, *Poetical Works* 2.260).

Poems are also bodies themselves, suspended in the white space of the page. Like our own architecture of flesh, the body of the poem is a transducer (from Latin, *transducere*, "to lead across, transfer"), a device that translates. As Ackerman explains, we touch the soft petal of a rose and our receptors "translate that mechanical touch into electrical impulses that the brain reads as soft, supple, thin, curled, dewy, velvety: rose-petal like" (307–08). The poet's song effects yet another conversion of energy, since we know the mind does not dwell in the brain alone. From mechanical sense to electrical impulse, the rose is led across into the prism of the poem, where its energy and motion are organized. In a letter to Anne Stevenson, Bishop wrote of her attachment to organized form not simply as an expression of a partially satisfying (if imaginary) order but as a declaration of courage in the face of implacable, eroding time: "It seems to me that in the world of hate and horror we all inhabit that contemporary artists and writers, some of the 'action painters' (although I like them, too), the 'beats,' the wildest musicians, etc.— have somehow missed the point—that the real expression of tragedy, or just horror and pathos, lies exactly in man's ability to construct, to use form. The exquisite form of a tubercular Mozart, say, is more profoundly moving than any wild electronic wail (& tells more about that famous 'human condition')" (23 March 1964, WU).

"The exquisite form of a tubercular Mozart"—Bishop's poetics of translation hinge on the "exquisite" nature of impressions converted into the ratio of music, a language whose logic is itself keyed to the body's central nervous system, and to the rhythms and arrhythmias of the human heart. Bishop sings of the body, perhaps not with the sheer expansiveness of Whitman but with his precision and the "prudence suitable for immortality" (a phrase she underlined in her personal copy of *Leaves of Grass*). The translation of physical weakness into poetic strength, the conversion of symptomatology into "exquisite form," were more than passing interests for Bishop; transduction of this kind became a linchpin in holding together the elements of her complex aesthetic.

The work of translation can be seen clearly in David Wagoner's homage to the poet, "Poem about Breath (*a memory of Elizabeth Bishop, 1950*)." Wagoner recalls Bishop's mental process as she worked on "O Breath," a cryptic poem built on interstices, long pauses for air that fracture the poetic line. Wagoner traces Bishop's somatic imagination, describing her body's journey through language. He tells of how she searched for the proper punctuation (ellipses, blank spaces, double colons, or Dickinsonian dashes) "for catching her breath, for breath catching / Halfway in her throat, between her straining breastbone / And her tongue, the bubbly catching of asthma." His poem captures her reasoning as she tries to find a form that simulates the problem shared by writers and asthmatics:

> Each breath turns into a problem like a breath
> In a poem that won't quite fit, giving the wrong
> Emphasis to a feeling or breaking the rhythm
> In a clumsy way, where something much more moving
> Could happen to keep that poem moving and breathing.

In the end, Wagoner leaves us with an image of Bishop's impishness, her gallant resolve to find a "style" of breathing and writing differently, with a good-humored acceptance of life's discomforts. She curls her tongue back and unfolds it slowly, balancing a gleaming bubble of saliva on its tip, which she puffs "with her lightest breath" until it takes flight, floating through the "late-summer light": "Then she bent over and over, choking with laughter."

A poem must be kept aloft, she once said, like a balloon, a bubble, defying gravity with ebullience and laughter: "I don't like heaviness—in general, Germanic art. It seems often to amount to self-absorption—like Mann, & Wagner. I think one can be cheerful AND profound!—or, know to be grim without groaning" (letter to Anne Stevenson, 8 January 1964, WU). Her resolve was tested by a lifetime of loss. Her father died (from Bright's disease) when Bishop was barely eight months old, a shock from which her mother never recovered. Gertrude (Bulmer) Bishop was left a widow after just three years of marriage. She suffered a series of "nervous breakdowns," for which she was hospitalized in Boston and then in Nova Scotia. Finally in 1916, she was placed in a sanitarium where she remained until her death in 1934. The year of her mother's death, Bishop graduated from Vassar College to face an uncertain future. For the next three years, more or less, Bishop traveled in Europe, buoyed financially by a trust fund from her father's estate but emotionally untethered. She spent the war years in Key West, Florida, where she led a life of determined vagrancy and ripened as a poet despite continued attacks of asthma and unnerving spells of alcohol abuse, diseases to which she may have inherited a genetic susceptibility. Then beginning in 1951, she took up residence in Brazil, living for eighteen years in Rio de Janeiro, Petrópolis, and Ouro Prêto with Lota de Macedo Soares, the Brazilian woman she loved, until Lota's death by suicide in 1967. Bishop spent the last decade of her life teaching part-time at Harvard, but Lota's breakdown left her with a deep sense of guilt and depression and reawakened memories of earlier losses.

With this history of emotional uncertainty and dislocation, Bishop might well have turned for relief to the palliatives her culture provided. And indeed, her writings engage in a dialogue with devotional and romantic traditions of transcendence that speak of the spirit's "translation" or rapturous separation from the body. But Bishop's longing for some unifying vision was chastened by her unflinching encounters with a volatile and stubbornly "untidy" world. If translation traditionally entails a movement upwards, an etherealizing movement that transforms the carnal into the spiritual, the vulgar into the idealized, then Bishop's efforts of translation are often alchemical changes in reverse. In "Seascape," for instance, green leaves become illuminated letters outlined in silver "bird-droppings" (*CP* 40). Pivotal moments of moral choice—Peter's denial of Christ and the Prodigal Son's decision to return home—are conjured under inauspicious circumstances: in "Roosters," high biblical drama follows close upon the description of a cockfight that leaves one combatant dead, his body buried in dung; the prodigal's moment of illumination takes place in a barn with a rotten floor next to a sty "plastered halfway up with glass-smooth dung" (*CP* 71). In Bishop's poetry, the world remains, for the most part, cheerfully, even barbarically, rude. And yet more barbaric still to her mind is the artist who prophesies mightily but lacks the humbling gift of quiet, "self-forgetful" observation.

Singing the Body

Drawing on hitherto unknown or obscure sources, I place Bishop's aesthetic within a set of literary and sociocultural traditions. Throughout the book, I emphasize the body in relation to other bodies—whether human, natural, or geographical—as I follow the poet in her progress through the dangerous shoals of intimacy. The book's first three chapters are linked to one another through their shared concern with the representation of female sensuality. I begin by discussing the most long-lived of Bishop's physical burdens, her asthma, and its impact on the poet's writing style and on her view of the pleasures and forfeits of love. Personal relationships also form the backdrop for chapter 2, which concentrates on the representation of homoerotic desire. While Bishop's unpublished writings initially embody "queer" desire in the figure of the vampiric lover, the poet more typically relies on the figure of the hermaphrodite to subvert the sexual norms of her day. A suppressed love poem in which Bishop compares the female breast to the androgynous "rock rose" serves as the point of departure for the discussion in chapter 3 of the poet's response to two conflicting aesthetic philosophies: the romance or romantic tradition (emblematized by the rose) and the high modernist poetic (figured in the rock crystal).

Although Bishop's art is generally perceived to be calm, ironic, detached (despite the powerful current of pathos running through it), Bishop's life was often marred by her impulsive, erratic behavior, making this dichotomy between life and art a central feature of her mystery as a poet. Chapter 4 focuses on Bishop's cruelest problem, her physical addiction to alcohol, and the way it brought her into creative contact with Edgar Allan Poe and with the *poète maudit* tradition, against which she would come to define her own clear-eyed poetic.

As a poet who eschewed the morbid self-absorption of neoconfessional poetry, Bishop parted company with her dear friend and literary rival, Robert Lowell. She also distrusted Lowell's appropriation of experiences that were not his own and his cannibalizing of other lives in the service of his art. As my fifth chapter suggests, the body's impulse to feed itself at the expense of others becomes Bishop's principal metaphor for the artist's predatory potential. Chapter 5 follows Bishop from Florida to Brazil, where the country's brutal history of European invasion and commercial exploitation reminds the poet uncomfortably of her own poetic enterprise as a consumer and translator of the Brazilian landscape, literature, and culture. Her Brazilian-inspired writing and literary translations revolve around images of feasting and fasting; the world they reflect is darkened by the threat of predation but lit by the promise of crossbreeding or communion. Bishop's translations from the Portuguese conscientiously preserve the body of the original text while exploring the possibilities for kinship, drawing on the same qualities of humility and forbearance she valued in her own poetic.

The last three chapters of this study show the widening range of Bishop's art as she gradually opens her poetry up to greater personal revelation. While the book's opening chapters concentrate on the poet's body, its desires and disabilities, the concluding chapters focus on Bishop's responses to her mother's body lost in time and memory. The elegiac poems and stories that come with increasing frequency during the Brazilian years and in the last decade of her life are traced back to earlier, unpublished experiments and to the poet's long-standing habit of investing talismanic bodies, souvenirs, or found objects with the uncanny power to evoke the absent mother and the inexpressible pain of her loss. In the course of this discussion, Bishop's poetics of the souvenir is contrasted with the surrealist aesthetic and compared to the more companionable art of the postimpressionist, Édouard Vuillard.

This book's discussion of the relation between soma and psyche in the framing and fashioning of Bishop's poetry draws to a close by focusing on the most ancient trauma in the poet's life, her mother's madness. In chapter 7, my reading of "In the Village" pursues the relation between writing and the symbolic body language of the hysteric. Chapter 8 argues that Bishop saw her literary mission as a salvaging operation modeled after Dorothea Dix's work on behalf of the shipwrecked and the insane. The possibility of creating an asylum or sanctuary from mental and physical pain sounds a tonic chord throughout *Geography III*, her last, and warmest, collection of poems.

Bishop's history of accumulated loss and her aging, ailing body never let her forget those forces of time and circumstance to which she must resign herself as an artist and as a woman. A youthful diary entry confirms that this had been her tough-minded philosophy all along:

Anyone who can learn really to "face the facts," as they say, should have much more to write about—have hundreds of fresh things to say. It is because you don't, can't, won't, admit many unpleasantnesses, recollect them or see them at present, that you occasionally feel that there is nothing to be said. Think: if you were to resurrect any one year or week of yourself at any past age and be quite honest with it—how awful you were, how awful all those people were, what things really looked like—there'd be enough there for many poems. This holds true for the *smallest* impression as well as "morals." That's where a foolish passion for order, getting every-thing to fit, would be all wrong for anyone who wants to write poetry. You're bound to have to fix things a little if you insist on order, just as "social *orders*" have to use "propaganda." ("Recorded Observations," 1934–37: 25, VC; Bishop's emphasis)

Providing the frame of reference for my whole discussion, this passage is one of Bishop's earliest articulations of her core poetics, with its resolve to confront her own emotional, intellectual, and physical frailties. In her distinctive voice and in her own well-chosen range, Elizabeth Bishop strove to "face the facts" and sing the body electric.

1 *"O Breath"*
Asthma and Equivocality

In 1937, when Elizabeth Bishop was only twenty-six, she discovered the wilds of Florida on a fishing expedition and fell in love with the swamps and palm forests of a state that was still a North American wilderness. When the poet and her friend Louise Crane came to live in Key West the following year, their response to the tropical *Cayo Hueso*, known as the "Bone Key," was severely colored, however, by the tragic six-month stay in Europe that intervened between Bishop's first ecstatic visit to Florida and her return.[1] Bishop and her close friends Crane and Margaret Miller had been traveling from Burgundy back to Paris when their car was forced off the road and flipped over. Miller, a painter, was the only one seriously injured. Her arm, partially cut from her body when she was thrown clear of the car, eventually had to be amputated to the elbow.

If we look at Bishop's life and work during her time in Florida, we find that her imagination is understandably haunted by this maiming of her intimate friend and fellow artist. The tragedy brought into terrible focus preoccupations already troubling the young poet—chief among them, the artist's relation to her own body, to its passions and its vulnerabilities. In one of a series of notebooks kept during her years in Key West, Bishop describes the automobile accident that severed Miller's arm from her torso: "The arm lay outstretched in the soft brown grass at the side of the road and spoke quietly to itself, 'Oh my poor body! Oh my poor body! I cannot bear to give you up.' " But the detached limb's desire to be quickly reunited with its body soon gives way to another

thought: "So this is what it means to be really 'alone in the world!' "
(KW1 59). Bishop clearly identifies with the lonely arm—the analytic
arm of the artist detached from the woman and from the sensual
memories that a woman's form retains. Like the acutely conscious
arm speaking to itself by the side of the road, Bishop was drawn
to and yet alienated from the unconscious life of her own body,
which she comes to view with a mixture of fascination, embarrass-
ment, and pity (KW1 12).

During the years in Florida, Bishop suffered from almost nightly
attacks of debilitating asthma and recorded her dreams and anxieties
in a set of small notebooks that have only recently been made
available to scholars. In the seclusion of these private journals, she
turns with uncharacteristic forthrightness to the subject of the flesh,
its pleasures and its torments. She jots down plans to develop plays
and poems about the physical afflictions of Job, Jonah, St. Teresa,
and St. Anthony and appears especially preoccupied, for very per-
sonal reasons, with the fate of St. Sebastian. Repeatedly referred
to in the Key West journals, he figures prominently again in an
unfinished essay entitled "A Little About Brazil," where the poet
explains her fascination with him: "St. Sebastian protects Rio de
Janeiro and perhaps that is the reason why the people are all crazy
about hypodermic injections" (box 74, folder 6, VC). An asthmatic
forced to inject herself with cortisone, Bishop sees Sebastian's mar-
tyrdom, his body pierced by arrows, as a reminder of her own
intimate relationship with the hypodermic needle.

The poet's asthma and allergic inflammations—her most chronic
physical ailments—are the primary focus of her lengthy letters to
her New York doctor, Anny Baumann, during the years in Key
West. These letters along with other private correspondence and
notebook entries reveal that the poet's early, ambivalent experience
of mother-love exacerbate her illness, continue to haunt her adult
sexual relationships, and influence her view of the ambiguous bond
between poet and reader.

Bishop's published work, though, rarely speaks about her illnesses
directly. In her poetry, she refuses to allow herself, her body, and
her experience to be contained within any culturally prescribed
notion of gender or sexual orientation. She chooses instead to cloak

and recloak her own flesh, to cross-dress, displace, or otherwise project her most intense feelings onto a variety of poetic protagonists in order to escape stifling categorization and conventional definitions of identity. Still, Bishop's imagination continually pursues the implications of her private battle for breath. As a poet, she transmutes the symptoms of her asthmatic condition into a rich cache of metaphors that help enact her sense of the world: for Bishop, human interaction takes place within a set of smothering categories (a series of waiting rooms) that enforce a kind of artificial intimacy among their occupants—an intimacy that often fails to respect the uniqueness and the privacy of each human soul.[2] While asthma is not the central subject of poems like "In the Waiting Room," "O Breath," and "The Riverman," knowledge of Bishop's condition opens up new ways to approach crucial images of respiration, suffocation, and constriction in each work—images that draw attention to the equivocal reality of human relationships.

"The Family Voice"

For much of Bishop's life, her body registered emotional distress in painful ways. The poet's allergic inflammations were responsible to some degree for perhaps the most important personal and professional decision of her life—to remain as a permanent resident in Brazil. In November 1951, she set out on a trip to South America. Stopping to visit friends in Rio de Janeiro, Bishop ate the fruit of the cashew and experienced a violent allergic reaction that prevented her from continuing on to the Strait of Magellan. After recovering, she decided to stay on in Brazil. From her new home near the mountain resort of Petrópolis, she wrote a series of letters to Dr. Baumann describing the onset of her ailments: "That night my eyes started stinging, and the next day I started to swell—and swell and swell; I didn't know one *could* swell so much" (8 January 1952, VC).

Taking 15 ccs of calcium and 7 or 8 ccs of adrenaline in the vein each day to bring her swelling down, Bishop was suffering simultaneously from a "very bad" recurrence of her childhood eczema, an inflammatory condition of the skin characterized by oozing lesions that become scaly, crusted, or hardened: "Before this started," she writes her doctor, "I had noticed my mouth got sore from eating, I thought, too much pineapple." Her "ears [swollen] like large red hot mushrooms," and her asthma as bad as ever, Bishop writes to Baumann with frustration and a hint of justifiable self-pity: "I finally got sick of being stuck with so many things [to reduce the swelling, and felt] like St. Sebastian" (8 January 1952, VC). She proved allergic to the new "wonder drug" penicillin, and her infected skin glands formed localized inflammations, or boils. Writing about the episode to her favorite relative, Aunt Grace, she remarks, "When someone is allergic like me, you never know what may happen, apparently" (16 July 1956, VC). Even when she was singing the praises of cortisone, an anti-inflammatory drug that left her in a state of euphoria and heightened creativity, she worried about still another form of swelling: "It's amazing how energetic it makes one feel although also I'm afraid it has a tendency to make one get even fatter" (letter to Baumann from Samambaia, 28 December 1952, VC). Weight gain had been a worry for many years; she had been taking thyroid pills daily to control her weight while in Washington, D.C., in 1949: "If I don't, I just keep getting fat no matter what I eat" (letter to Baumann, 12 December, VC). Like a latter-day St. Teresa, whose *Way of Perfection* became a permanent part of Bishop's private library, Bishop tests her own strength by a "fastidious" disciplining of her wayward, expanding flesh (KW2 23).

Of all her inflammatory reactions, however, bronchial asthma was the most chronic. Asthma is an allergic response to foreign substances that generally enter the body by way of the air breathed or the food eaten. In response to the foreign substances, the mucous membranes of the respiratory system secrete excessive amounts of mucus and the smaller bronchial muscles go into spasms. This narrows the passageways, making it difficult to expel air. Bishop's wheezing lungs prevented her from taking up a comfortable and lasting residence in the places she loved, contributing to an already intense feeling of homelessness. To Anny Baumann she confides that asthma had become the single most frustrating impediment to her happiness. "As soon as I get to a place I like best of all it starts again," she writes from Key West, Florida, on 30 December 1948

(VC). Earlier that year, she writes to Baumann from Stonington, Maine (5 August 1948, VC), where her asthma and a variety of other acute allergic reactions made it impossible for her to sleep and the almost hourly injections of adrenaline she took to regulate her breathing left her nauseated and dizzy: "For the past eight or nine years I have had asthma about every day and night." Awarded the first Lucy Martin Donnelly Fellowship from Bryn Mawr College in 1951, Bishop finds by February 1952 that the "bounty [from the fellowship] has gone mostly for adrenaline" (letter to Baumann, 10 February 1952, VC).

The period covered by the Key West notebooks became a time of psychological investigation for Bishop. Her remarks to Baumann make it clear that she had come to regard her doctor as a psychiatric adviser. From Stonington, Maine, she wrote Baumann that she was concerned with the state of her mind and its impact on her physical condition: "Every magazine or paper I pick up has an article proving that asthma is psychosomatic, everyone now thinks it is almost entirely, if not entirely mental" (5 August 1948, VC). In a letter to Baumann from Yaddo dated 17 January 1951, Bishop describes bouts with asthma that leave her emotionally as well as physically exhausted, and she traces her "discouragement, panic, sleeplessness, nightmares" to the realization that she was "exactly the age now at which [her] father died." Her body's inflammatory reactions accorded somehow with what Bishop calls in yet another letter to Baumann, her "morbid swellings of the conscience"—lasting anxieties rooted in childhood sadness that rise up unpredictably to overwhelm her, like bad dreams. In her notebook she broods about "dreams that overpowered [her] / ("mugging") from behind" (KW2 141). Just above these observations, she scribbles three phrases in quick succession: "the fierce odors," "family mortality," "families of mortalities."

The central conditions of Bishop's childhood, her early orphaning and sense of maternal deprivation, left her with an acute sensitivity to the ways in which personal anguish and shame may be hidden from view. Her family corseted their emotions in a futile attempt to tame the brute world of pain and raise themselves out of lassitude. The effort drove them into a den of artificial innocence. Early on,

Bishop was initiated into strategies of evasion and indirection and a "Puritan outlook" with respect to the body and its "embarrassing" weaknesses that accompanied her on her travels and became the burdensome "inheritance" she carried with her to Brazil—an inheritance that set her apart from that country's more "tolerant" natives (letter to Baumann from Rio de Janeiro, 7 July 1954, VC).[3] Bishop considered herself allergic to the atmosphere in which she was raised, the "hypocrisy [that was] so common then, so unrecognized, that it fooled everyone," including the hypocrite himself ("Memories of Uncle Neddy," *CProse* 230). Hypocrisy reminded her of the molds and mildews that made her life so miserable; like the hypocrite, the "gray-green dust" is double in nature suggesting blooming life and its sooty shadow, "morbidity"—"or perhaps mortality is a better word." In her private notebooks she would call this hypocrisy the "fierce odor" of "family mortality" that surrounded her earliest years.

Though she had suffered from bronchitis in the first years of her life, the condition became much worse after her mother's final mental breakdown. She was staying with her mother's parents in Nova Scotia, but the arrangements did not suit her wealthy paternal grandparents, the Bishops, who took the girl ("unconsulted and against my wishes," as she later put it) to Worcester, Massachusetts: "The B's were horrified to see the only child of their eldest son running about the village in bare feet, eating at the table with the grown-ups and drinking *tea*, and so I was carried off (by train) to Worcester for the one awful winter that was almost the end of me. 1917–1918" (letter to Stevenson, 6 March 1964, WU). Elizabeth was given the impression that her New England relatives were "saving" her from a life of poverty and provincialism in Canada. As it turned out, her grandfather was frequently absent from the house, the aunt and uncle still living there were chilly toward her, and her grandmother's sensibilities were offended by a little girl who showed no interest in playing the piano, knitting afghans, or dressing dolls. Waited on by an impersonal staff of servants who spoke only Swedish, she was listless, bored, and surrounded by daily reminders of her earliest loss, the death of her father.

The Bishops kept their grandchild for only nine months, but it was enough to instill in Elizabeth a sense of self-consciousness that she would carry with her into adulthood. She learned to feel ashamed of her motherless existence, in a house where shame was endemic—even the pet Boston terrier displayed a "peculiar Bostonian sense of guilt" (*CProse* 21). And that feeling of worthlessness translated itself into a battery of physical symptoms. Feeling like a guest in the airless atmosphere of Worcester, expected to somehow intuit an unknown past that no one ever directly explained to her, Elizabeth experienced a combination of severe illnesses, including eczema, asthma, and symptoms of St. Vitus's dance. She ended up spending most of her time isolated, "lying in bed wheezing and reading" (Stevenson 34; Kalstone 27). These health problems only exacerbated her feelings of estrangement as she came to think of herself as odd and unconnected to others. Years later she would admit to her first biographer, Anne Stevenson, that she suspected her "hopeless shyness" was born one "awful day" in Worcester when she sent home from first grade because of her unsightly eczema sores.

In May 1918, Elizabeth went to live with one of her mother's sisters, Aunt Maud: "I couldn't walk and Ronald [the Bishops' chauffeur] carried me up the stairs—my aunt burst into tears when she saw me. I had had nurses, etc.—but that stretch is still too grim to think of, almost. My grandfather had gone to see my aunt M[aud] privately and made the arrangements—he said my grandmother didn't 'know how to take care of her own children,' most of them had died.—My aunt was paid to care for me—but she would have anyway, I imagine, if there'd been no money. She really devoted herself to me for years until I got better—She probably never slept for nights and nights, getting me injections of adrenaline, etc., etc." (letter to Stevenson, 6 March 1964, WU).

Her wheezing seemed to worsen as she felt herself being steadily drawn into a conspiracy of evasion concerning her father's death and mother's insanity. The female voices around her—grandmothers and aunts on both sides of the family—formed a "skein" in which she was "caught" (*CProse* 270). Although her mother's family seemed warm and attentive beside the Boston Bishops, with their stoical reserve, both sets of relatives shared a gift for evasion. "In the Village," Bishop's autobiographical account of her mother's final breakdown, describes the inscrutable adult world into which the six-year old Elizabeth felt herself being pulled "against her wishes" (*CProse* 17)—a world in which speech is always elliptical and secret shames are guarded even from the child that is most affected by them. Refusing to speak about her mother's embarrassing mental illness in anything but oblique terms in front of the child, Bishop's female relations became associated in her mind with the equivocal: Their speech was always subject to two or more interpretations, always generating misleading and confusing double meanings and puns. The young Elizabeth had difficulty with the word *mourning*, for instance, which she hears as "morning," a confusion that unsettles her: "Why, in the morning, did one put on black" (*CProse* 254). Apparently death—and in particular, her father's death—had never been explained to her.

Years later Bishop looked back on this period in her childhood as her initiation into the duplicity of speech and the suffocating constraints that propriety imposes on free expression. In her short memoir, "The Country Mouse," she remembers the hard lessons learned that winter with her paternal grandparents. First among these was the revelation that she was becoming "*one* of them" (*CProse* 33): rather than tell a playmate the shameful truth about her mother she lies, saying that her mother has died—a lie born out of a "hideous craving for sympathy" (32). The moment the lie leaves her lips she is gripped by her own capacity to be as "false" as any of her relations, to lie, that is, in the "family voice" (*CP* 161). In the "family voice"—strongly associated with the garrulousness and duplicity culturally ascribed to women—Bishop finds the tendency toward morbidity she would later attribute to confessional poets (especially women writers like Elizabeth Bowen). Throughout her life Bishop would grow irritated when she heard this tone of social obligation in the poetry of female contemporaries, the voice of "old silver," she called it (letter to the Barkers, 28 February 1955, PU): "They have to make quite sure that the reader is not going to misplace them socially, first—and that nervousness interferes constantly with what they think they'd like to say." Rather than reveal their true experience, women who employ the voice of "old

silver" want to "show that they are 'nice' and lead beautifully pol-
ished lives 'even when they aren't' and even when they don't." To
her close friends Ilse and Kit Barker, she explains her distrust of the
woman writer's concern with social standing and taste: "I suppose it
is at bottom a flaw in reality that irritates me."

The family voice Bishop ascribes to women in general works
against the fidelity to facts that she hoped to make the hallmark of
her art. In one of her Key West notebooks, she records a scrap of
verse that defines the problem succinctly (KW2 47):

> speaking
> It is an adaptation   or
> social obligation of some sort
> the real thrilling   beautiful voice
> is off somewhere else singing loudly
> fully
> in clear choir.

The "social obligation" imposed on women of a certain era, class,
and situation to speak in well-modulated tones and corset unseemly
emotions exacted a dreadful price on Bishop's own family—and
especially on her mother whose "real thrilling beautiful voice,"
stifled by grief and convention, became in the end a terrifying
scream.

Long into adulthood Bishop is haunted by nightmare images of
dark, shrouded, caterwauling women whose grating voices threaten
to invade and animate her own body, and whose intrusive presence
she attempts to expel: "In a black sedan with high windows, a tall
woman, Aunt Florence, only I knew it wasn't really Aunt Florence,
stood outside, wanting to get in talking, talking. I screwed up the
window, hurriedly and caught the tips of her gloved fingers in the
crack at the top. She kept on talking, talking, begging me to let
her in the car, and I felt nauseated. She was dressed all in black,
with a large black hat, the gloves were soiled gray" (KW1 38).

Any reader of the late poem "In the Waiting Room" will recog-
nize in this Key West nightmare both Aunt Florence (who is con-
cealed behind the name "Aunt Consuelo" in the poem) and the
powerful sensations and images that this vision describes. Florence
Bishop was the aunt who still lived in the Worcester mansion when

Elizabeth came to stay there as a child. She appears as Aunt Jenny in Bishop's memoir, "The Country Mouse," which concludes with the definitive episode in Florence's relationship with Elizabeth: her visit to the dentist. In "The Country Mouse," she is characterized as a "tall and flat" woman who is not "particularly glad" to see her young niece arrive from Nova Scotia (*CProse* 19). Within moments of their meeting, Jenny suggests that Elizabeth accompany her to the barn where her Buick is housed. Throughout the story, Jenny (or Florence) is associated with her "lady-like car" (19), her bad driving, and her distant, ironic attitude toward the displaced Elizabeth. Bishop's relationship with her aunt would always be strained and dutiful, a fact that troubled her and apparently became conjoined in her imagination with their first experience of thwarted intimacy, that short car ride to the house in Florence's Buick.

Ultimately, Bishop denied her aunt entry into her own tall-windowed, black sedan—her own private world. In the dream, the poem, and the short story that were all inspired at least in part by her relationship with Florence, the aunt's voice induces nausea in her niece and threatens to invade the sanctuary Bishop has provided for herself. The black sedan of Bishop's Key West nightmare cannot help but call to mind the "armored car of dreams" she speaks of in her poem, "Sleeping Standing Up" (*CP* 30). With its window-like "mouth," the sedan seems an extension of the dreamer's own body. Breathing in the fierce odor of her aunt's frantic desperation "to be let in," Bishop responds violently by closing this one avenue of access and figuratively biting the hand that reaches out to her.

Significantly, Bishop's single most vivid memory of her mother, which she recounts in an interview with Elizabeth Spires, parallels the narrative of this Florida nightmare. Her mother, dressed incongruously in the mourning clothes required of a widow "in those days," sits with the three-year-old Elizabeth in a swan boat on a Boston lake. A real swan comes up to the boat. Her mother "fed it and it bit her finger," splitting the black kid glove and the skin beneath ("The Art of Poetry" 74). The mother's gloved hands suggest the extent to which her illness became a barrier to intimacy; the child of such a mother might well harbor an unacknowledgeable desire to bite the hand that failed to feed her. In a recent tribute to Bishop, Elizabeth Spires speaks of having seen the poet's drafts and notes for a poem about the swan boats. It was, as Spires suggests, "a subject fraught with so many explosive associations for her it proved impossible to write" ("Elizabeth Bishop: 'The Things I'd Like to Write' " 66). And yet tantalizing fragments remain, scattered phrases: "dead water where the live swan paddles"; "My mother's hand proferred [proffered] a peanut from the bag"; "Ungracious, terrifying bird!"; "the whole pond swayed"; "madness and death"; "I saw the hole, I saw the blood"; "amniotic flood." Approaching these images with her customary sensitivity, Spires writes: "Unconsciously perhaps, there is a pairing and juxtaposition, even in this roughest of drafts, between fearful opposites: life and death, predictability and madness, a white swan and a mother in black. The terror in the memory lies in the child's inability to read the situation, to know if these opposites will cancel one another, and who—swan or mother—is the dark force" (66).

Bishop's asthma recurred most violently at points in her adult life when she was forced to consider the potentially suffocating nature of maternal love. She succumbed to an acute attack, for example, when Margaret Miller's mother arrived from America following the car accident in France. Bishop began to feel her carefully cultivated independence and emotional control breaking down in the presence of the older woman's devotion and solicitude. The surge of vulnerability she experiences when Margaret's mother appears lands Bishop in a hospital herself. Writing to her longtime friend Frani Blough Muser, she points to her deep discomfort with disarming flippancy: "Mother-love, isn't it awful. I long for an Arctic climate where no emotions of any sort can possibly grow, always excepting disinterested 'friendship' of course" (9 August 1937, VC). For Bishop, mother-love would always wear a threatening aspect. The imaginary iceberg of emotional detachment she conjures in her letter to Frani would remain a strongly appealing fantasy throughout her life.

Bishop's mother, an equivocal woman in black, reappears in her daughter's Key West nightmare, transposed but still powerfully present in the guise of Aunt Florence. "In the Waiting Room" shows that the peculiar tension between Bishop and her Aunt Florence has a long history, precisely as long a history as Bishop's asthmatic condition. Whether or not a poem like "In the Waiting Room" is intended as a serious attempt to describe the psychogenesis of Bishop's lifelong asthma, it does link a traumatic childhood confrontation with a woman to the onset of intense physical distress: in the poem, as in the dream, Bishop chokes on the "cruel conundrums" of shared female experience (CP 73).

It seems right to suggest, as Alicia Ostriker does, that "In the Waiting Room" is a poem Bishop "waited a lifetime to write" and that, "in some sense, [the poet] has never left the room it describes" (72). But if this is the case we had better not sanitize the meaning of what takes place there. The child protagonist of the poem, just shy of seven years old, does not simply become alive for the first time to her identity with others of her gender in the waiting room of a dentist's office, rather the reality of womanhood is rammed down her throat and she chokes on it. The central moment of the poem occurs when Elizabeth hears a cry of pain that disorients her because it seems to come from two places at once—literally from two throats at once, her Aunt Florence's and her own. In the instant her "foolish, timid" aunt screams (CP 160), Elizabeth is invaded and possessed from within by what she describes as "the family voice." She feels herself caught in an enmeshed community. A distaff chorus seems to rise up out of the pages of the *National Geographic* and shoot straight through her own body. Feeling her own singular sense of herself crowded out by the presence of the collective, the child Elizabeth drowns under wave after black wave as she falls into "cold, blue-black space" (CP 160); in other words, she experiences the dizziness that always accompanied one of Bishop's asthmatic attacks.

We have become accustomed of late to certain metaphors drawn from the processes of breathing and speech that are used to celebrate the bond between mother and child and the unconstrained female voice. When Hélène Cixous speaks to us of the woman artist who opens herself up to her maternal muse, never defending herself against possession by other "unknown women" but welcoming all the multiple "streams of song" that issue from her ecstatically crowded throat, it is perhaps a disappointment to then enter the claustrophobic atmosphere of Bishop's waiting room. When the aunt's cry of pain makes what Cixous might call a "vertiginous crossing" into the body of her young niece, Elizabeth derives no pleasure from the "identificatory embrace" that results (259–60). The effect is indeed "vertiginous" but only in the worst possible sense; the ground gives way beneath the young girl as her old sense of herself collapses. She is not empowered but emotionally and ontologically battered by the initiation rite. In "The Country Mouse," Bishop is far more explicit about the "great truth" she learned waiting for her aunt to emerge from the dentist's office. Elizabeth feels the full force of being "tricked into a false position" (*CProse* 33). Not only is she trapped forever within her "scabby body and wheezing lungs," but she will grow to resemble the woman who sat opposite her in the dark room, the woman "who smiled at [her] so falsely every once in a while," a disturbingly willing slave to social etiquette and a censorious world.

It is no accident that the child's disorienting experience is triggered by grotesque images that focus her attention on the cruel conundrums of mother-love.[4] The multiple and contradictory meanings that seem to attach to the maternal body and the conflicting emotions that the maternal presence evokes in Elizabeth push against each other in the child's throat, swelling up behind her voice and pitching her into a new world without clear dimensions or comforting boundaries. Like the volcanoes that the child finds pictured in her magazine, Bishop's own mother threatened to erupt in unpredictable ways; emotionally numb one moment, she would spill over in rivulets of fiery, hysterical emotion the next. Elizabeth, who we know is feeling the loss of her own mother, studies the pages of the *National Geographic*; her attention is understandably drawn to the photographs of mothers and children as she turns the pages of the magazine: black, naked women, their necks strangled, "wound round and round with wire," hold babies whose malleable heads have been "wound round and round with string." A mother's "awful hanging breasts"—so "horrifying" in their power to excite longing and betray trust—are pictured in unbearable proximity to her infant's distorted head caught in its terrible vise of wire.

The black woman captured by the Western photographer's shutter and trapped in the grip of her own culture passes a legacy of submission on to her infant. By manipulating her infant's skull, she reinforces the very codes of beauty and sexual attractiveness that have delimited her own life, and we begin to wonder how fully the mother is implicated in her culture's campaign to mute individuality and enforce conformity. This compression of the baby's head also reminds the reader of a scene from Bishop's "In the Village," the extraordinary story of her mother's final breakdown. Elizabeth sits in her grandmother's kitchen in Great Village, Nova Scotia, being force-fed a bowl of porridge by her mother who struggles to maintain her mental balance by repeating mechanically the primal gestures of maternal love. Then, seeing how tall her child has grown in her absence, the mother impulsively lays her hands on her daughter's head, pushing her down—hoping to bring back the paradisiacal time of her daughter's infancy and bring the shrill tone of their relationship back down to a safer pitch. The child of "In the Village" quickly "slides out from under" the mother's oppressive hands, but she grows up to be the Elizabeth who cannot escape the lessons of the waiting room—the heavy emotional legacy that may be passed from mother to daughter through the laying on of hands (*CProse* 261). "Sliding beneath a big black wave," the walls of the waiting room seem to dissolve around the child who undergoes the kind of a disillusionment Bishop describes elsewhere in "Napoleon & Hannibal," an unpublished poem (KW1 199): "The delightful kindergarten, the garden of the world, is shown growing on the hollow soil of a volcano." The acute question of "In the Waiting Room" proliferates helplessly across every Bishop poem concerned, however obliquely, with the dynamics of female connection. But the question is stated most explicitly in "Faustina, or Rock Roses." There, the "sinister kind face" of the black servant tending her white mistress evokes the "cruel black / coincident conundrum" of mother-love and female bonding darkened even further by the history of relations between the races: does woman-love offer "a dream of protection and rest" or the "very worst, / the unimaginable nightmare" (*CP* 73–74)?

Whatever happiness Bishop found with other women grew on the hollow soil of a volcano, since inevitably she carried her childhood experience of love's instabilities and betrayals into the world of adult relationships. Bishop's mature poetic style, known for its rich ambiguities and oblique approach to love and sexuality, stresses the emotional dislocation and instability in all efforts of affection. Oscillating between self-exposure and concealment, her poetry captures the approaches and withdrawals that mark any human relationship in which an individual's privacy is necessarily placed at risk. Settling on a poetic style that seems to give and take away meaning in the same motion, Bishop captures the quality of circumlocution that, as we have seen, she first found in the conversation of her grandmother and aunts. Irritated with her family's hypocrisy, she nevertheless recognizes that such duplicity is a part of the dynamics of human relations—and part of the very language we use as culturally circumscribed human beings.

Bishop's guarded style is attuned to the way parents and their children, poets and their readers, actually appear to one another: the way, that is, that they alternate emotionally between accessibility and obscurity. With the tenacity of the water spider that stays on the surface of the pool, Bishop holds to a poetry of ripples and verbal feints. But in generally refusing to speak directly about her personal tragedies, she would find herself struggling upstream against the currents of a new post-fifties generation of poets—writers like Anne Sexton who follow the example of Bishop's own dear friend Robert Lowell and plunge headlong into the river of self-reference, making rich use of the sorrow to be found there.

"A Hint of Morbidity"

In significant ways, Bishop's responses to trends in the poetry of her contemporaries are moored to somatic issues—dependent, that is, on what Bishop considers to be a crisis in the size and scale of personal ambition. Her notebooks show just how closely she tended to relate poetic control and a stoical and disciplined approach to physical discomfort. Indeed, once we fully appreciate the impact of the poet's allergic inflammations on her life—and her private struggle to bring her swollen body back down to the scale of human life—we gain a better understanding of why Bishop published only ninety-five poems in her lifetime, each one a model of leanness and restraint.

Bishop's personal code of ethics demanded such discipline, in art as well as in life. For this reason, her criticism of what she regarded as self-dramatizing confession and easy vulgarity in the work of certain younger poets is far more than the prudish response of a woman raised in an older decorum. The outpourings of Anne Sexton and W. D. Snodgrass raised grave suspicions in Bishop's mind because they struck her as "egocentric—simply that" (letter to Lowell, 19 May 1960, HL). She considered the general weakening of standards and the failure to discriminate between good poetry and mere self-promotion, a peculiarly "American sickness" (letter to Lowell, 5 March 1963, HL). Both the art and the culture that produced it had grown bloated, flaccid, infected with unoriginality—and needed a good lancing. Essentially she objected to the confessional poetry of her peers because its authors boasted about their private catastrophes so shamelessly and congratulated themselves so continually on their candor. To speak as though one were always in the throes of some intolerable crisis, Bishop explained in 1967, is "really something new in the world. There have been diaries that were frank—and generally intended to be read after the poet's death. Now the idea is that we live in a horrible and terrifying world, and the worst moments of horrible and terrifying lives are an allegory of the world. . . . The tendency is to overdo the morbidity. You just wish they'd keep some of these things to themselves" (Cory and Lee 69).

The key to Bishop's poetic style, its minimalism, deflection and hard-won moral vision, lies in her battle to rid her work of the excessive morbidity she recognized in the world around her. Morbidity, the body's susceptibility to disease and corruption, becomes Bishop's trope for moral as well as physical "weakness and acquiescence" spreading over the younger generation of poets like the sly growth of mildew. The molds and mildews that make her choke, swell, and violently shake were "just enough to serve as a hint of morbidity" (*CProse* 228) and reminded her of the "great American sickness" she diagnosed in a March 1961 letter to Robert Lowell: "Too much of everything—too much painting, too much poetry, too many novels—and much too much money. . . . And no one really feeling anything much" (qtd. in Millier, "Modesty and Morality" 47). Bishop believed that her ethical aversion to literary inflation distinguished her in an age that seemed to her to have lost its discrimination and restraint. A deeply reserved and subtle poet, Bishop would apply a cool compress to her poems at the first sign of inflated self-regard or swollen ego.

Objecting to the way confessional art transformed the poet into a diarist and the reader into a confidant or confessor, Bishop insisted that the actual bond between writer and reader was marked not by genuine intimacy but by distance and impersonality. Adrienne Rich once suggested that intimacy was altogether absent in Bishop's later work where the poet seems to examine, instead, the way people are distanced from one another by differences of class and race (16). But the effect of distance that Rich observes in Bishop's art may just as easily be seen as the poet's way of expressing her own experience of intimacy: the unyielding reality of loss, separation, even betrayal, that makes erotic and emotional connection "a billion times told lovelier" and "more dangerous," to borrow from Hopkins, one of Bishop's poetic masters ("The Windhover: To Christ Our Lord" ll. 10–11)

Finally, Bishop shows us that writer and reader are linked to one another not by imagined intimacy but by the bonds of a common language—a language that is never straightforward in its effects. "In the Village," as we have already seen, describes the poet's early awakening to the fact that language is equivocal, open to two or more possibilities, always hiding something in the process of revealing everything. Donald Hall was frustrated by this equivocal quality in the poetic language of Marianne Moore, which for him always appeared teasingly inaccessible—"giving as it takes away, folding back on itself the moment one begins to understand so that an exactly opposite meaning begins to seem plausible" (84–85). But it would seem that Bishop came to accept an ambiguity that once troubled her, transforming equivocation into a treasured artistic effect. The moments of apparent personal connection between the poet and her reader are immeasurably enriched by the understanding they share that each must finally remain a mystery to the other.

The mystery remains despite the efforts of literary interpreters to, as Bishop put it, "pretty up" the poet's work. "Poetry should have more of the unconscious spots left in," she writes as she distinguishes her own poetry from that of Wallace Stevens: "What I tire of quickly in Wallace Stevens is the self-consciousness—poetry so aware lacks depth" (KW2 89). It seems a mild irony that the richly ambiguous Bishop seems to make a model of clarity out of a poet famous for his own brand of obscurity. Her criticism of the poet is directed at the way he dissects his own psyche and deprives his reader of a distinct pleasure—the delight of speculation. In a fragment from the same notebook Bishop reminds herself that "art is never altogether pleasing unless one can suspect it of ulterior motive . . . of a 'secret confidence' " that the poet has reserved to herself. A fundamentally shy person, Bishop nevertheless accepts that the reader's pleasure lies in pursuing her maddeningly elusive presence in the poem. She does all she can to enhance the thrill of the chase through subtle indirection.

"O Breath" and Equivocality

Bishop obscured the shape of her personal life, of course, for other reasons as well, reasons having to do with the particular social and aesthetic conventions of her day.[5] Love and sexuality were threatening subjects for a woman with poetic ambitions, and doubly so for a woman of Bishop's sexual preference. Even in her late poems when she is no longer cloaking her own sexuality under the guise of animal courtship, her verse still dances around the subject of her homosexuality. Bishop's strategies of concealment resemble those of the female lizard she describes on a scrap of paper folded into the back cover of one of her notebooks (KW1 unnumbered): the lizard "hides . . . all her tail, all her tiny horny sides" while the males around her "blow out [their] beautiful rose balloon [for all] to see." The poet's imagination is distinguished by a desire to protect herself from everything that threatened either the borders of her own body or her uniqueness as a person and an artist, and her poems seem to expand outward in an intimate embrace of the world only to fold back on themselves and on the haven of the sole self.

Bishop's "O Breath" is one of her only published poems about the eroticized female body. At the same time, it is also one of the few poems in which she consciously and conspicuously turns her attention to the equivocal nature of her own poetic style. Moreover, here she uses asthma, the disabling condition that afflicted her, to describe the stifling pressures that impinge on her life as a poet. "O Breath" is a captivatingly ambiguous love poem that plays with the narrow passageway for authorized speech permitted a woman of her class and education in 1955. Beneath the poem's surface reticence, we sense something moving invisibly: a faint image of erotic coupling or its aftermath. All we do see clearly is the broken contours of this poem as it appears on the page—as though it were determined to speak though under enormous pressure to hold back. The poem's gasping, halting rhythms and labored caesuras mimic the wheezing lungs of a restless asthmatic trying to expel the suffocating air. In the struggle to breathe, each hard-won phrase wrested from silence arches over the negative troughs, the breaks, the white space left on the page. The poem's structure enables Bishop to "catch her breath" and give the agonies of asthma visible shape—the cradling and containing rib cage of words:

> Beneath that loved   and celebrated breast,
> silent, bored really   blindly veined,
> grieves, maybe   lives and lets
> live, passes   bets,
> something moving   but invisibly,
> and with what clamor   why restrained
> I cannot fathom   even a ripple.
> (See the thin flying   of nine black hairs
> four around one   five the other nipple,
> flying almost intolerably   on your own breath.)
> Equivocal, but what we have in common's   bound
> to be there,
> whatever we must own   equivalents for,
> something that maybe I   could bargain with
> and make a separate peace   beneath
> within   if never with.

> (*CP* 79)

We seem to have entered that ambiguous realm of address where two people have become one, yet remain irremediably distant from one another. One lover speaks fitfully between gasps for air as she watches the woman lying beside her "silent bored really." The difficulty and restraint associated with breathing and speaking in the poem suggests the ongoing constraints the poet labors under as a woman and a lesbian bound to leading a life of surface conformity and concealed depths.

When the speaker of the poem questions what lies beneath her lover's "celebrated" breast, she does so in a context that extends beyond this single lyric: "O Breath" is the last of Bishop's "Four Poems," a short cycle that concerns itself with the frustrating puzzle of "uninnocent" conversation between lovers—of exchanges that "engage the senses, / only half meaning to" until "there is no choice" and "no sense" or until the tension is relieved with an "unexpected kiss" (*CP* 76, 77). The poem sequence concentrates on images of the heart's helpless, bewildered imprisonment in miscommunication and its unanticipated release into authentic expression. In "Conversation," lovers obdurately hold to their positions, willfully misunderstanding one another, until the great cage of misconception breaks up in the air around them and they reach a point of understanding when "a name / and all its connotation are the same" (*CP* 76). In "Rain Towards Morning," an electrical storm suddenly ceases, its "great light cage" releasing a million birds from bondage, and the sky brightens like a face surprised by love (*CP* 77). With "While Someone Telephones," the cosmic is brought back down to the personal as the poet shifts from electrically charged wires of light to the crossed wires of lovers parted by distance and disconnection waiting tensely for contact and "the heart's release" (*CP* 78).

Like the protagonists of the other poems, the speaker of "O Breath" regards her companion with tender wariness. She lies awake, watching her lover's breast and the nine thin, black hairs surrounding the nipples—small, flying hairs that stir "almost intolerably" on the woman's "own breath." Aroused by the sight, she nevertheless seems shaken by her partner's apparent insularity, her self-absorption, the regular rise and fall of her breast. Such shallow breathing is almost intolerable to the speaker because she herself is forced to gasp for air. The placid lover remains to the poem's end an enigma whose motivations escape the speaker, though she hopes to find in her lover's heart an equivalent for her own tumult, her own anxious desire for the unexpected, releasing kiss.

"O Breath," like "Conversation" (the first of the "Four Poems"), gives expression to "the tumult in the heart" that "keeps asking questions" and then "stops and undertakes to answer" in the same mystified voice (*CP* 76). The speaker of "O Breath," however, seems to talk only with herself or with the reader. Since the true inner workings of her mate are invisible to her, the speaker can only project her own inner turmoil onto the other woman by way of analogy, of correspondence. Hoping that boredom is actually a mask for desire but unable to "fathom even a ripple" of her lover's motivations, the speaker has no recourse but to draw from her own experience of desire in describing what might live and move within the inaccessible woman breathing beside her. She imagines the force of desire within the body lying beside her as something moving invisibly—something caged within that body as surely as a clamoring heart or a pair of wheezing lungs. But when she stops and undertakes an answer to the proliferating questions of the heart, the reader cannot tell the difference between inquiry and resolution, and peace is still something to be negotiated once common ground is finally discovered. Like the bond between the two partners, the release obtained at the poem's end is uncertain, and as Bishop puts it, "equivocal."

"O Breath" focuses on the barely endurable proximity of the loved one's body, awakening a longing for still deeper contact that may not be achieved. This is no utopian vision of a lesbian continuum where lovers always feel easy in one another's presence, able to, as Cixous would say, "expire without running out of breath" (248). For Bishop, the urge to penetrate the deepest recesses of another person must be resisted for the sake of both people involved. The tactful poet or lover acknowledges the bounds as well as the bonds of love.

Mermaid Dreams

Given her ambiguous experience of home and the "efforts of affection" (*CProse* 121), Bishop had to reinvent her life before she could draw strength from the past and translate her body into song. This reinvention is apparent in a series of dreams Bishop recorded in her private notebooks—dreams that link the poet's own pursuit of "quiet breath" (*CP* 214) to the figure of the mermaid breathing effortlessly in amniotic seas. Ultimately, these dreams prepare the poet for her life in Brazil where she found, for a time, the happiness that had eluded her since childhood. Cradled by an "atmosphere of uncritical affection" in her adopted country, the poet would be able at last to navigate the waters of memory—and explore the remarkable powers of healing that lie within.[6]

In the first of these visions, a dying mermaid washed ashore and gasping for breath becomes an emblem of Bishop's own anxieties. Her estrangement as an artist and a lesbian finds expression in the foundering ocean woman exiled from her natural element. In a later celebratory dream, the mermaid is returned to the sea where her body feels exhilaratingly weightless. This vision of liberation prepares the way for the greater personal happiness and freedom of expression Bishop would experience during her first years in Brazil. Though the mermaid begins as a tragic figure, she eventually allows Bishop to navigate the dangerous shoals and eddies of a life spent in the body of a woman.

The mermaid first makes her appearance in a fearful dream Bishop had one night in Stonington, Maine. In a letter to Robert Lowell, she confesses that the vision left her shaken, suffering from "solitude & ennui": "That's just the kind of 'suffering' I'm most at home with & helpless about, I'm afraid, but what with 2 days of fog and alarmingly low tides I've really got it bad & think I'll write you a note before I go out & eat some mackerel. The boats bringing the men back from the quarries look like convict ships & I've just been indulging myself in a nightmare of finding a gasping mermaid under one of these exposed docks—you know, trying to tear the mussels off the piles for something to eat—horrors" (8 September 1948, HL).

As this letter suggests, Bishop is affected by the strangeness, the liminality, of the legendary sea creature. A siren with her sexuality muted and concealed, lost in the sleek lines of a fish's tail, the mermaid becomes a problematic fantasy image for Bishop in more

ways than one. Like the late poem "Crusoe in England," the mer-
maid image speaks to the limitations of homoerotic love and same-
sex friendship. Bishop's wish to "propagate [her] kind," expressed
poignantly through Crusoe's infertile love for Friday (*CP* 165), is
conveyed as well through the mermaid's eternally maiden status.
When Lowell, on the verge of proposing marriage, tried to capture
his complex feelings for Bishop, he incorporated her mermaid night-
mare into his poem, "Water." As David Kalstone rightly observes,
the early drafts of "Water" exaggerate the tone of hysteria in Bishop's
account of the dream (180–81). In the finished work, impersonality
replaces the initial sense of personal melodrama. The two friends,
who sat so long ago on a "slab of rock" overlooking the icy sea,
are seen now across an expanse of years. From this perspective,
their urge to immerse themselves in the dangerous element of love
appears tempered, just as Bishop's voice is muted, replaced by the
resigned, Arnoldian tones of the poem's male speaker. The work
is transformed from a poem about Bishop's "thwarted passion" to
a poem about their relationship as seen through Lowell's eyes and
the evanescence of desire in general (Kalstone 181):

> dozens of bleak
> white frame houses stuck
> like oyster shells
> on a hill of rock.
>
> (*Selected Poems* 99)

Resembling these calcified houses in Stonington, Maine, the lovers
are "stuck" in their respective bodies, slaves to their own incompati-
ble natures and to time itself.

While Lowell used Bishop's mermaid dream as a locus for his
own feelings and as a screen onto which he could project his own
personality (Kalstone 183), Bishop herself characteristically shied
away from the more histrionic implications of her fantasy self-image.
She was simply not willing to explore the connection between the
sterile mermaid and her own "thwarted passion" for Lowell or for
the children she would never have. Still, as an asthmatic, she had
other reasons for identifying so strongly with a mermaid washed
ashore or a fish held half out of the water. We see a partial afterimage

of the Stonington mermaid in her most anthologized poem, "The Fish," where she empathizes with the fish on her line "breathing in the terrible oxygen" (*CP* 42). The gills of a fish are equipped to obtain oxygen from water and not from air. They suffer when taken out of their natural element. Strictly speaking, Bishop might have said that air, and not oxygen, proves "terrible" for the struggling sea creature. For Bishop to link terror with oxygen instead, she would have had to first project her own fears onto this fish out of water, just as she had identified with the gasping mermaid trying to tear sustenance from an implacable world.

Like the mermaid, the poet feels herself to be unequipped to breathe the same air, to live by the same social strictures, as other beings whose natures are different from her own. The dream suggests that Bishop dreads the exposure of her unconventionality—of her body and her homosexuality. Ultimately, in the way it evokes feelings of freakishness and alienation, the nightmare of the dying mermaid recalls the pathos of "The Little Mermaid," the Hans Christian Andersen fairy tale that Bishop knew and loved so well. In the Andersen tale, the mermaid destroys herself in her futile attempt to cross over into the world of human (heterosexual) union. Seen in this light, Bishop's dream is a poignant reminder of the border crossings lesbians were forced to make in the forties and fifties—when so many felt compelled to conceal their desires and to publicly embrace the heterosexual erotic ideal.

If we look backward through even the earliest juvenilia, we see Bishop's struggling to avoid the horror of foundering and hear her yearning for a watery haven. In the 1928 poem "Sonnet," written while Bishop was still a schoolgirl in Massachusetts, she longs for the "subaqueous stillness of the sea" where she might find "a spell of rest, and quiet breath, and cool / Heart" (*CP* 214). At least fifteen years later, Bishop had a dream that returned her to the sea, where she enjoyed a rare moment of physical freedom and release. The beauty of the mermaid as an image of the poet is visible in a Key West notebook account of this utopian vision:

The fish was large, about 3 ft. long, large-scaled, metallic gold only a beautiful rose color. I myself seemed slightly smaller than life-size. We met in water the color of the water of the 3rd—clear, green, light (—more like

the cut edge of plate glass, or birch leaves in bright sun, than emerald.)
He was very kind and said he would be glad to lead me to the fish, but
we'd have to overtake them. He led the way through the water, glancing
around at me every now and then with his big eyes to see if I was following.
I was swimming easily with scarcely any motion. In his mouth he carried
a new, galvanized bucket. . . . He was taking them a bucket of air—that's
how he'd happened to meet me. I looked in—rough water had got in to
make the bucket of air a bucket of large bubbles, seething and shining—
hissing, I think, too. I had a vague idea they were to be used as decorations,
for some sort of celebration. (a "coronation"). (KW1 15)

Like the Stonington nightmare, this dream is intensely interested
in air and the mechanics of breathing underwater. In the "inverted"
world of sleep, the mortal dreamer seems to breathe effortlessly
beneath the waves while fish require life-giving oxygen from the
surface. The sea, which Bishop once described as a "dark deep . . .
element bearable to no mortal" but only "to fish and to seals" (*CP*
65), has become strangely natural to her. In these waters that make
mortal bones ache and hands and tongues burn, she is fantastically
and utterly free. Like the riverman in a later poem, Bishop commu-
nes with speaking underwater spirits, attending a subaqueous party
where beautiful rose-colored fishes gather to crown one of their
number with shining bubbles in "some sort of celebration." The
bubbles hiss like a community of whispering voices free to seethe
and shine and rejoice.

It is tempting to see the dream as Bishop's way of imagining a
time when she could swim the rough waters of intimacy with an
ease that had always escaped her. Like the "clear, gray, icy water" of
the northern seas she knew so well, the poet-dreamer is "suspended"
between air and land, impervious to suffering, poised indifferently
above the rocky breasts and cold, hard mouth of the world—and
the difficulties of love (*CP* 65). Rough water does not disturb the
dream's serene mood; instead it turns the air that has troubled
Bishop all her life into large shining bubbles—the poet's lifelong
metaphor for the buoyant spirit.

In sleep, Bishop could take on the sexual ambiguity and dazzling
versatility of the mermaid, a creature of the sea who breathes with
miraculous ease. At the end of her life, the true nature of the
yearnings expressed in the 1928 "Sonnet" are given fuller, franker

expression in a poem to which she gave the same name. In the 1979 "Sonnet," published posthumously, Bishop imagines what it would take to free the bubblelike spirit from the prison of social intolerance, liberate herself from the divided existence: but she cannot conceive of such a possibility, since the very laws of the physical universe would have to be broken. Only in the seclusion of her notebooks and her dreams did she dare to write unguardedly about love and sexuality. As she explains to Anne Stevenson in a letter dated 8 January 1964 (WU), Bishop thought of herself as being born into a certain era, situation, decorum, and for that reason, she could never truly breathe freely—or sing gaily in full-throated ease.

The poet's desire to make a separate peace with her own woman's body by finding some "pure elixir" (*CP* 109) of *amor matris*—until her arrival in Brazil, a desire reserved for the world of dreams—takes on a pleasing shape in *Questions of Travel*, the volume of poetry she dedicated to her Brazilian lover. There the poem "The Riverman" seems to resolve, or dissolve, fear and hope, mother and maid in the "watery, dazzling dialectic" of art ("Santarém," *CP* 185). When Bishop was readying her third volume of poetry for publication, she sent off a worried note to Robert Lowell about "The Riverman." Lowell calmed her fears by assuring her that this new book would be her very best and reminding her of a dream she once had: "I wouldn't worry about the Amazon poem—it's the best fairy story in verse I know. It brings back an old dream of yours, you said you felt you were a mermaid scraping barnacles off a wharf-pile. That was Maine, not Brazil" (28 April 1960, VC).

Astute as always about the psychic origins and ulterior motives of his friend's work, Lowell had made the connection between Bishop's dream and "The Riverman," the tale of a man who has been "singled out" by the natural spirits of the Amazon (*CP* 109), given the power of breathing underwater, and initiated into the rites of the shaman, or spiritual healer. Lowell is not deflected by Bishop's use of a male protagonist, recognizing at once that the apprentice shaman is a mask for the poet herself. He remembers Bishop's dream about the mermaid washed ashore and gasping for breath, a dream of extreme dislocation and deprivation, and sees that "The Riverman" is Bishop's transposition of her nightmare into a different key—into a vision of strength. Recognizing the personal origins of the poem, Lowell sees all that the new poem implies about Bishop's emerging poetic—a poetic of healing. Under the cloak of riverman, Bishop tests the waters of her Brazilian life and the haven of "uncritical affection" she had found there—and her capacity to draw from her own heart the remedy for her distress.

"The Riverman" is one of the few of her pieces that Bishop praises for not being literal or accurate—for being entirely a dream salvaged from her own psychic yearnings. At the time she wrote this poem about a river that "drains the jungle" and "draws from the very heart / of the earth the remedy / for each of the diseases" (*CP* 108), she had never actually seen the Amazon: "When I finally got to the Amazon in February and March [1960] I found I hadn't been too accurate at all, thank goodness" ("Recorded Observations," 1934–37, VC). Her Amazon, the river of her imagination, is not drawn from the immediate world that surrounded her as she wrote.

Her Brazilian home was the heart of her experience there and the source of her understanding of the unseen river. In July 1952, Bishop wrote Dr. Baumann to say that she had found in Brazil "a wonderful country" where "when you arrive the janitor and the porter and the cook all hug you tenderly and call you 'madame my daughter.' " At the time, her new "family" consisted of an assortment of Lota's friends, "2 Polish counts for a while, the architect over the weekends, etc., all a strange tri- or quadri-lingual hodge-podge that I like very much" (28 July 1952, VC). For her friend Robert Lowell, Bishop described Lota's Samambaia as "an ultra-modern house up on the side of a black granite mountain, with a waterfall at one end, clouds coming into the living room in the middle of a conversation, etc." (21 March 1952, HL). Bishop enjoyed the idea of living in the unfinished house as she had as a child in Nova Scotia, making do with "oil-lamps, no floors—just cement covered with dogs' footprints": "What I'm really up to is recreating a sort of deluxe Nova Scotia all over again in Brazil. And now I'm my own grandmother" (21 March 1952, HL). In a house of many voices, where "equi-vocality" is liberating rather than distressing,

Bishop learned to accept nurturance from the world around her: "I get up in the freezing dawns here and begin with all the confidence in the world—the mountains look exactly as if floating in *vin rosé* then, with a white bowl of milk down below us" (letter to Lowell, 20 May 1955, HL).

As she depicts it in "Song for the Rainy Season," the studio Lota built for her above the main house is bathed in a milky mist, cradled by a "private cloud" of vapor, and from this nest the poet can hear the "brook sing loud / from a rib cage / of giant fern" (*CP* 101). Safe in her aerie, the poet, like the riverman beneath the water's surface, can approach the "family of mortalities" that plagued her life (KW1 141), the choking web of voices she left behind in Great Village and Worcester—a "skein of voices" that she can now unravel (*CProse* 270); like the riverman traveling beneath the waters of the Amazon she glides "right through the wicker traps" of "Godfathers and cousins" who can "never, never catch" her now.

> When the moon burns white
> and the river makes that sound
> like a primus pumped up high—
> that fast, high whispering
> like a hundred people at once—
> I'll be there below.
>
> (*CP* 108)

The poet who wrote these lines had finally found her element—for as long as she could feel at home in her Brazilian haven. The river she imagines is no more, and no less, than her own studio, which she describes in a letter to Baumann as "one large room . . . away up in the air" containing a "kitchenette with a pump and a primus stove for tea" (28 December 1952, VC). The stove made the studio resound with the "fast, high whispering" of the hissing kettle. From her aerie she conjures the Amazon deep within her own interior and learns to practice the healing art of remembrance. In *Questions of Travel*, Bishop's imagination follows the stream of emotions that link the primus stove beside her as she writes and the Little Marvel stove in her grandmother's kitchen so many years ago. She hears in the Brazilian rain the sound of her grandmother's voice "talking to hide her tears" ("Sestina," *CP* 123). And so Bishop's travels take her back to herself—through the once-threatening, but now-delightful, equivocality of language: with a brilliant pun on her own family name, she escapes her fear of the vocal net created by the past. Safe in her Brazilian home, Bishop has become the "primus"—a choirmistress who untangles the aural web. From this time forward, she will conjure her haunting family voices and lead them in song.

2 "The Queer Land of Kissing"
Sexuality and Representation

In *The Genesis of Secrecy*, Frank Kermode wonders why narratives are basically obscure. He comes to the conclusion that all stories are properly and "essentially dark" (45), radiating only intimations of meaning. For Kermode, the greatest narratives operate on at least two levels simultaneously. They must "proclaim a truth as a herald does and at the same time conceal truth like an oracle" (47). Fiction that partially conceals its meaning in this way is filled with "inexhaustible hermeneutic potential" (Kermode 40). Narrative's highly functional ambiguity is the principle theme of Kermode's book on the art of hermeneutics—and the principle theme of this chapter, which will focus on the radiant obscurity of Elizabeth Bishop's love poetry and its "Hermetic ambivalences" (Kermode 47).

Bishop understood, long before Kermode, that the power of all narrative lay in secrecy or *parable* (the Greek word for "dark speech"). Speech that is too revelatory, too direct in its implications, necessarily limits the narrative's potential, encouraging weak readings that rarely rise above the apparent. Undisguised confession held little intellectual appeal for her, while its emotional impact proved facile and fleeting. Bishop avoided what she would have thought of as morbid or embarrassing sentiment by composing narratives of the kind Kermode might term "parables." Between "the maxim [or riddle] and the short story," Kermode reminds us, "there occur parables of varying degrees of 'narrativity' and varying degrees of opacity." Lying somewhere within this spectrum, the Bishop poem banishes "interpreters from its secret places" and relies on the evocative force of obfuscation (34).

David Kalstone once said of Bishop that she saw her principle task as being the conversion of "the descriptive poem into a narrative—while keeping it descriptive in nature" (252). Translating Kalstone's remarks into a slightly different register, I would say that Bishop strove to convert an external landscape into a narrative arena for the simultaneous proclamation and concealment of deeply felt truths. Her poems focus on the interplay between the described landscape and the implied inscape, the physically manifest and the emotionally latent, without offering the closure of a determinable moral perspective. In fact, Bishop's moral sense emerges in the very lack of closure that typifies her art. She feels morally obliged to accept the inconclusiveness and the varicolored senses latent in the world without and the world within.

Eventually, as James Merrill reminds us, Bishop's "lifelong devotion to narrative" (6), particularly to the parables of Chekhov, Kafka, and Babel, would bear fruit in the story poems that make up *Geography III*, her last and most autobiographical collection. But the years leading up to this final achievement were devoted to perfecting her parabolic approach to verse. Bishop's working notebooks chronicle the painstaking process of revision during which the private truth at the heart of each poem becomes more cryptic, less personally revealing, through a succession of drafts. The sheer volume of hidden manuscript material underscores the deliberately encrypted nature of Bishop's most familiar work. Her published poetry, with its cool surface and its secret recesses, therefore demands of its readers a special hermeneutics.

Bishop's interpreters would do well to consider the many advantages of parable, or "dark speech." Chief among them is the fact that a properly managed obscurity increases the reader's pleasure. The primary source of pleasure in poetry, for both writer and reader, resides in mystery—in the interpreter's "right to affirm, and obligation to accept, the superiority of *latent* over *manifest* sense" (Kermode 2; my emphasis). In approaching Bishop's intentionally self-concealing work, it is especially helpful to keep in mind the distinction Kermode draws between a narrative's "manifest" and "latent" meanings. Poetry that yields nothing beyond the level of the obvious will exercise only the smallest fraction of the reader's interpretive abilities, but "our divinatory powers grow," Kermode assures us, "as the primary reading, carnal, manifest—the most obvious to the first readers—loses its compelling force, its obviousness" (10). The poem's complexity should carry the reader beyond a "carnal" or literal level of interpretation toward a "latent" or hidden meaningbeyond the obvious to the obscure.

While Kermode certainly uses the term *carnal* in a special sense, the other, more common, connotation of the word lingers in the listener's mind. This is especially true given that a narrative's least-subtle or most-"carnal" reading (in the Kermodian sense of the word) so often limits itself to the story's most puerile details. Bishop did not conceal her distaste for poets who invited such readings by exploiting the simple shock value of sexual revelation. Speaking in 1967 of neoconfessional poets like Anne Sexton, Bishop had her own interpretive pleasure in mind when she complained, "You just wish they'd keep some of these things to themselves" (Cory and Lee 68).

Doubtless, Bishop had social as well as aesthetic reasons for choosing to base her poetics on the power of "dark speech" and secrecy. The era in which Bishop came of age as a poet and a lesbian offered her little incentive to invite carnal readings of her work (in any sense of the word). In midcentury America, the poet's love for other women would have been judged unnatural in most social circles and in most courts of law. There was as yet no vocal community to either encourage or demand such proclamations of the truth. Even had she received encouragement to speak, Bishop would have resisted such overtures on the grounds that a poet's voice should be allowed its full range and distinctive timbre and not be constrained to sing for one audience only and to one purpose alone. For this reason, she made it difficult for readers to enlist her into the ranks of any single constituency.

Still, Bishop's decision to keep her sexual disposition to herself did not prevent her from publishing narratives of love including relatively early poems like "O Breath," "Anaphora," and "Insomnia" that are at once sensuous and esoteric, playing with the reader's desire to divine all that must remain hidden. Certainly, the opacity of Bishop's early allegorical works has often been discussed, but the poet's manner of cloaking her personal experiences is too often dismissed as a sign of her own weakness and duplicity or excused as a symptom of the repressive times in which they were written. But Bishop herself sees obscurity as a powerful tool, a fact that is substantiated by her writing journals. Not only do these notebooks clarify the private history behind her cryptic parables, but they rehearse a theory about strategic darkness that Bishop carefully evolves over time.

More than once in her journal entries, Bishop speculates on the role that eroticism—particularly homoeroticism—plays in the formation of a writer's literary style. She turns her attention repeatedly to admired figures like Gertrude Stein who made a virtue of necessity by embracing the power of the verbal hieroglyph. In the opening pages of one Key West notebook, for instance, the question of Stein's hermeticism seems to be uppermost in her mind. Commenting on Gertrude Stein's *Autobiography of Alice B. Toklas*, Bishop stresses what she calls the "physiological causes for types of writing" (KW2 4). She subsequently crosses out or conceals the telling passage that follows: "G[ertrude] Stein's reason for 'concealment' of the 'automatic' nature of her writing = [equals] or, is another form of her 'concealment' of the 'homosexual' nature of her life—False Scents, we all give off. cf. [compare] Freud on 'misplaced accent' in dreams" (KW1 2). Bishop refers here, of course, to Freudian dream theory, which reads the "misplaced accent" as an abstruse code in which consciously unacknowledged desires can be manifested while maintaining their aura of mystery. Bishop's allusion to Freud's hermeneutics, with its distinction between the manifest and the latent content of dreams, shows that she was thinking along the same lines as Kermode and that we would not be misrepresenting her own efforts if we were to keep this distinction in mind when approaching her published verse. At the same time, her insight into Stein's reasons for subterfuge cannot help but reflect back upon Bishop's predicament as a homosexual (or by some accounts, bisexual) woman and its impact on her own writing style.

Bishop's comparison of Stein's deflection with Freud's "misplaced accent" actually anticipates the comments of later readers like Pamela Hadas who find in Stein's *Tender Buttons* a submerged eroticism

"at least as naturally 'overdetermined' as most dreams" (73 n. 15).
Studiously recorded in her journal, Bishop's notes on *Tender Buttons*
show just how impressed she was by Stein's passion for the carefully
observed object that quivers with some unexplained but palpable
meaning. Like Stein, Bishop describes her pleasure in the caressive
body covertly through her pleasure in the caressive word or image.
Both writers encrypt their bodily experiences and personal attach-
ments in what Catharine R. Stimpson calls "somagrams" (67)—or
what Bishop herself calls the "false scents we all give off" (KW1 2).
Ultimately, as Jeredith Merrin observes, Bishop "delivers poetic
pleasure—even as she both keeps and tells her 'secret' " by means
of certain figures or tropes that "are actually ingrained habits of
mind, powerful psychological gestalts producing many of Bishop's
patterns of imagery and other poetic structures" ("Elizabeth
Bishop" 164).[1]

In an effort to penetrate the poet's intended obscurity, this chapter
concentrates on manuscript material that makes explicit what re-
mains teasingly opaque in Bishop's more familiar explorations of
social, sexual, and artistic deviation from the norm. The discussion
looks to suppressed sources for help in identifying certain ingrained
figures or tropes for sexuality that recur throughout her published
oeuvre. Early in her career, for instance, Bishop deployed a number
of conventional terms to describe unconventionality, especially the
negatively charged "inversion" (Havelock Ellis's nineteenth-century
rubric for homosexuality, still in common use in the mid–twentieth
century). Yet when concepts like inversion or "reversal" do appear
either directly or implicitly in poems like "Love Lies Sleeping,"
'Sleeping on the Ceiling," "Sleeping Standing Up," or "Insomnia,"
she is careful to cloud and complicate their more apparent meanings.
In Bishop's journals, on the other hand, notions of sexual inversion
and "perversion" are addressed far more directly, as she tries to
settle on an image of erotic delight powerful enough to escape her
culture's strict code and symbolic order.[2]

While the invert, the vampire, and the hermaphrodite surface
more frequently in her working notebooks than in her acknowl-
edged writings, the factors that shape their transgressive lives (their
monstrosity, invisibility, and sterility) appear in Bishop's published

work as signs of strength. Living on the border between male and female, right and wrong, life and death, they stand for the outcast artist and her ability to avoid her culture's sexual, ethical, and ontological straitjackets. Bishop's notebook experiments serve as a training ground for her, where she can learn to hone her representation of quirkiness. In her published writings, Bishop replaced the conventionally drawn figures of perversity that populate her notebooks with a more inventive menagerie of hyphenated creatures (mothmen, mirror-men, dolphin-men) who seem always on the verge of crossing borders or shifting shape. "Wobbling and wavering, / undecided" like a compass needle that refuses to stand still long enough to reveal a single direction or bent ("Sonnet," *CP* 192), they enact the poet's refusal to be compassed round by material circumstance. The poems that house her elusive personae are themselves hybrid creations, juxtapositions of formal control and subversive tendency. Thus, the body of a Bishop poem, like the body of a Bishop protagonist, is defiantly protean.

"A Few Weird Pleasures"

During the era in which Bishop came of age sexually, medical textbooks promoted the theory that the "mannish lesbian" suffered from a congenital form of inversion. Most early twentieth-century sexologists encouraged the popular belief that lesbians constituted "an intermediate sex" whose "degeneracy" or "sickness" was, paradoxically, both beyond the victim's control ("congenital") and morally reprehensible ("sick" and "unnatural") (Faderman 59–60). Since the practice of "queer" sex produced no offspring, Sue-Ellen Case explains, it was thought to impel lovers out of the cycle that generates life and history and "ultimately out of the category of the living" (4). A freak of nature whose desire was "dry" or "sterile" (Case 8), the woman-loving woman was all too readily linked with other macabre literary creations (the vampire, the parasite, the carnivorous plant) who embraced a sexuality that was other than natural and transgressed the borders between life and death.

Condemned as a lesbian to stand outside "the category of the living" and outside the bounds of language itself, Bishop may be forgiven for remaining relatively mute on the subject of her homo-sexuality. The remarkable thing about the poet's unpublished writings on the subject, however, is that they actually attempt to transform negatively charged figures for transgression, like the invert, the "queer," or the vampire, into positively charged tropes for sexual and artistic freedom. Bishop's juvenile writing and later notebook entries frequently propose the possibility of a subversive terrain where an alternative approach to sexuality is celebrated. The inhabitants of this subterranean world are free to partake in "weird pleasure" (KWi 137), the poet's phrase for erotic delight that does not end in reproduction. Evading the cultural imperative to be fruitful, this vampiric pleasure is forced underground, where it dwells in the realm of the perverse, a realm Bishop privately calls "the queer land of kissing" (KWi 140). In the pages of her journals, she populated this land with beings who were either "neuter" (neither masculine nor feminine) or "complex" (an hermaphroditic combination of both), using these ingrained tropes and figures to reconceive the various strengths of her own taboo position.

From her earliest juvenile writings through to her final poems, Bishop remained fascinated with the hermetic being whose sexuality is either neuter, like the self-generating armadillo who replicates through cloning (often called "twinning"), or complex like the hermaphrodite. As a teenager in boarding school, Bishop first tackled the problem of gender confusion and conflation in "The Thumb," a short story that appeared in the Walnut Hill School's literary magazine and was recently reprinted in *The Gettysburg Review*. At the center of the tale is the narrator's perverse fascination with Sabrina, a beautiful woman disfigured by a disturbing flaw. The strange thumb in question, as large as a man's appendage, is attached incongruously to Sabrina's delicate hand: "Good God!— the woman had a man's thumb. . . . It was a horrible thumb, a prize fighter's thumb, the thumb of some beast, some obscene creature knowing only filth and brutality" ("The Thumb" 29).

The presumably male narrator dwells on "what it would be like to touch her—to take that hideous hand and hide it in my own" although he realizes "that all this was bound to lead me into something wrong" ("The Thumb" 30). The question of gender reversal looms large here, and one cannot help wondering whether Bishop is using the story to explore her own attraction to a forbidden object of love, the "mannish" woman with a "brutish thumb." The problem of unclean or unnatural love is underscored within the story when the narrator compares Sabrina's flawed beauty to Baudelairean "Flowers of Evil" ("The Thumb" 29), but the situation just as easily calls to mind the macabre dimensions of Poe's fiction—or, even more tellingly, Jean Genet's *Our Lady of the Flowers*. Genet's onanistic fantasy also revolves around a narrator's obsession with a beguiling "heroine," a man-woman whose "ravishing feet" are offset by "too massive a thumb" (86). There is no way of knowing how young Bishop was when she first encountered Genet's homoerotic dream book, but comments hidden among her unpublished papers show that she read *Notre Dame des Fleurs* with interest ("On Existentialism," VC).

After publishing this piece of juvenile prose, Bishop would never again use the dynamics of gender reversal or inversion so directly. This reluctance testifies not only to her growing fear of exposure but to her awareness of the genre's limitations as well. In an unpublished sketch for a prose piece on existentialism, Bishop explains that she found Genet's work, and much of what she calls "homosexual" literature, "monotonously shocking . . . purely mechanical and sentimental and obsessive, obsessive of course to the point of madness" ("On Existentialism," VC). She is both moved and repelled most by Genet's "will to find beauty" in the sordid world around him. But his obsessive attachment to the man-woman with the dainty feet and brutish thumb is a "kind of inverted U[nited] S[tates] love for Mary Pickford in 1918," a regrettable form of "wishful daydreaming" ("On Existentialism," VC). Bishop discovers that Genet, even at his most shockingly inverted, simply reinforces the fantasy of traditional romance, with its stereotypical representations of masculinity and femininity. Commenting that Genet's tone "reeks" of unreality, Bishop asks herself whether "it impossible to write about sex frankly without wishfulfillment seeming so obvious" ("On Existentialism," VC). It was a question that would shape the course of her relation to matters of identity, gender, and the poetry of love.

As a young writer, Bishop tried on and discarded a number of models for describing the kind of unlawful desire she was beginning to experience. During her college years, the figure of the hermaphrodite seemed to offer the best vehicle for expressing her sexual perplexity. Asked to write a paper on the noble savage, Bishop uses the assignment to probe private concerns about sexual identification and the theatrical nature of gender identity. She introduces her reader to Zubinko, a "natural man" transported to Europe as a curiosity ("The Noble Savage," box 70, folder 6, VC). Forcibly removed from his native element, he makes his living in the theater, challenging and subverting his audience's assumptions about gender, race, age, and beauty. Ironically, the so-called "natural man" turns out to be a natural poseur, transforming into a variety of characters from Dryden's Alamanzor to Oroonoko to Mrs. Inchbald's "Amos, a negro slave." His life as a professional chameleon changing characters as easily as he changes costumes calls into question the entire notion of an innate or natural identity. A sexually and racially indefinable figure, Zubinko lives in the polymorphous world of masquerade, and the young Bishop concludes that his magical transmogrifications can be explained in only one way:

I can reach only one conclusion: Zubinko was an hermaphrodite. He or she was capable of impersonating either sex upon the stage in a perfectly satisfactory manner, and his or her character, resting always on the bed rock of Freedom, could display either a manly or a womanly side. We must not blame or belittle so great an artist for what must after all be considered as merely incidental; rather we must pity him that his private life was thus made even more lonely, and he was denied the great loves he enacted on the stage. ("The Noble Savage," box 70, folder 6, VC)

As Lorrie Goldensohn notes, Bishop's portrait of Zubinko gives the poet an early opportunity to gauge "the links between the social and psychological repressions of race and gender" ("The Body's Roses" 86). At the same time, this college exercise conveys a sense of the young author's own identification with "so great an artist" as Zubinko, an artist who dares to disrupt social hierarchies but is able to do so only because he is "embarrassingly" different and subject to being either "blamed" (as willfully perverse) or "belittled" (as subhuman) ("The Noble Savage," box 70, folder 6, VC). Zubinko is painfully constrained as a human being and a representative figure by his position as a biological sport, and, ultimately, he can serve the young writer only as an emblem of deprivation. The hermaphrodite's sexual self-containment can breed only loneliness, since he-she can never know the pleasures of coupling. Ironically, Zubinko will spend his professional life going through the motions of heterosexual courtship, portraying a kind of erotic fulfillment he will never experience in his private life.

The double life of the hermaphrodite who posed as heterosexual on the world's stage must have seemed particularly poignant to a young woman forced to keep up appearances. In the years immediately following her graduation from Vassar, Bishop would experience a disturbing confusion in her personal relationships, an indecisiveness about her own sexuality that surfaces in her repeated references to hermaphroditism. While on her first trip to Europe in 1935, a twenty-four-year-old Bishop would have occasion to meditate again on the unique problems of the changeling-artist. She was admitted to the American hospital in Paris for a mastoid operation to remove inflamed cells from the temporal bone behind the ear. One side of her head was shaved, and for several weeks after surgery, she wore a turban. Writing to Frani Blough Muser, she describes her appearance as she wandered, turban-less, around the apartment on the rue de Vauragard that she was sharing with her friend Louise Crane: "I look like the half-man–half-woman in the circus" (14 February 1936, VC).

Both Zubinko and the image of a turban-less Bishop express the young writer's anxiety about social and artistic deviance.[3] Increasingly, the hermaphrodite, and other liminal beings, came to represent aspects of Bishop's own sense of sexual difference. Though scrupulously hermetic, or abstruse, in their effects, many of the poems that make up Bishop's first collection hint at her fascination with "thirdness" as an alternative to sexual conformity. These early parables are given over to beings who, like title character of her poem "The Gentleman of Shallot," struggle to balance their self-image with their reflection in the cultural mirror. They are denizens of the night ("daytime sleepers"), living in a world upside down (an "inverted world"), where "the shadows are really the body"

("Insomnia," *CP* 70).[4] While there is nothing intrinsically homosexual about sleeping all day and walking the world only by night, as Lorrie Goldensohn points out in her reading of "Insomnia" (*The Biography of a Poetry* 31), Bishop's evocations of an inverted and underground existence align themselves with the vampiric or hermaphroditic representations of lesbian love so popular in the twenties and thirties.[5]

Because it was thought to lead its victims out of the world of generation and into the realm of sterile obsession, the kiss of the lesbian, like that of the vampire, was said to puncture the boundary that separated the living from the dead. As early as she could remember, Bishop had been charmed by undeveloped, boyish, even skeletal girls and women who seemed to carry about them an attractive hint of mortality. In the diary she kept after graduation from Vassar, Bishop writes of her distaste for the "plump, solid sort" of girl favored by Russian filmmakers and German advertisers, a girl literally overflowing with fertility. Instead, she prefers abbreviated, somewhat ethereal women whose potential for procreation is doubtful at best: "Margaret [Miller] always likes to see the skeleton, and I myself prefer an equilibrium of life and death in the face—The Russian girls [in the movie, *House of Greed*] were too much 'mortals' for my taste" ("Recorded Observations," 1934–37: 9, VC). Bishop's desire for other women leads her to imagine a new notion of the feminine, one that confuses the girl with the boy, the fertile with the sterile, the living with the dead.

There would have been ample precedent for linking same-sex desire with the blood lust of the vampire. Perhaps to ease the pain of exclusion, Bishop confronts what Case has called "the recreational use of the lesbian" (2). In private musings, the poet identifies for a time with the insulting association linking the lesbian and the monster, both of whom flaunt their deviance before flying into invisibility. As "The Thumb" proves, Bishop had already experienced *Les Fleurs du Mal* as an adolescent when she probably had her first taste of the "recreational use" of decadence. Baudelaire's "Femmes Damnées Delphine et Hippolyte" could not have escaped her attention, with its vision of the predatory lesbian bestowing on her mistress a wounding kiss of love:

Reclining at her feet, elated yet calm,
Delphine stared up at her with shining eyes
the way a lioness watches her prey
once her fangs have marked it for her own.

(*Les Fleurs du Mal* 304)

The fanged kiss of Baudelaire's *femme fatale* may have had more than
a little to do with the venom at the heart of Bishop's "Scorpions," a
verse fragment Bishop toyed with in her Florida notebook.

With "Scorpions," Bishop describes an alternative topography
of love, an underworld invisible to the untrained eye but seething
with activity and danger. In a garden of embalmed darkness lit only
by the luminescence of her lover's mouth and tongue, the speaker
inflicts her lethal sting:

In the queer land of kissing
Creeping under over hanging boughs
In the dew-drenched total dark
Meeting a hollow wind like a coffin in the air
Searching for that rumoured pool—

There are stars in the roof of your mouth
And a glowworm at the root of your tongue.

(KWI 140)

In this tantalizing sketch for a never-to-be-completed poem, Bishop
conjures all the topoi of vampiric love: the stygian atmosphere, the
coffin, the musky perfume of decay, the search for "that rumoured
pool" of blood, and the deadly kiss. At the same time, she revitalizes
that moribund popular image of same-sex desire exploited by books
like Sheila Donisthorpe's *Loveliest of Friends* (1931), where lesbians
are seen as "crooked, twisted freaks of nature who stagnate in dark
and muddy waters . . . and crush the grape of evil till it is exquisite,
smooth and luscious to the taste . . . leaving their prey gibbering,
writhing, sex sodden shadows of their former selves, conscious
of only one desire in mind and body, which, ever festering, ever
destroying, slowly saps their health and sanity" (qtd. in Faderman
101).

The vulgarity of Donisthorpe's low-brow fantasies hardly made
them suitable for Bishop's purpose. She seems to be searching

throughout her working notebooks for a new type of erotic poetry, one that would enhance the reader's interpretive pleasure by achieving the proper balance of apparent and withheld meaning. By accomplishing such a mixture of the transparent and the opaque, she hoped to mirror that artful balance she was forced to maintain in her life as an unproclaimed lesbian. The image of the fanged kiss could hardly have made the transition from journal to print without destroying the balance between accessibility and concealment that would characterize both her art and her life. Other traits associated with the vampire or lamia, however, might yet be deployed and manipulated with relative safety, and Bishop does so in a series half-finished works about love, vulnerability, and shameful exposure.

Popular lore tells us, for instance, that the female victim is entranced and paralyzed, rendered comatose and pliable, by the look of the vampire. The woman's fascination with the monster, the special empathy that exists between them, could be read (as it was in Donisthorpe's overwrought novel) as a response to lesbian desire. We glimpse something of this and something of the coffined existence that the lesbian was forced to lead in drafts for a poem Bishop wrote in her late thirties for Marjorie Stevens, her lover at the time. Bishop awakens to a "grave dark morning" after a "bad dream" in which Marjorie "lay unconscious" and enshrouded in a long blanket (KW2 167). To "prevent [Marjorie] from slipping away," Bishop feels that she must take hold of her "wrapped" (or rapt) lover:

> even though a "host of guests"
> might come in from the garden
> at any minute
> and see us lying
> with my arms around you
> & my cheek on yours.

The threat of social censure obviously weighed heavily on Bishop's mind and is here transcribed into unmistakably funereal terms.

The matter of protection preoccupied Bishop, as can be seen in another candid fragment from her notebook. This untitled and admittedly slight bit of observation is nevertheless worthy of mention because it is so atypical. The poet is troubled by her own prurient interest as she watches the very public coupling of a naked

man and woman who mistakenly believe that the heavy leaves in a
public park will hide them from view (KWI 181). They "crouch
black hair facing each other," and around their necks they wear

> leather amulets
> God has given them
> to protect them from
> this very exigency.

The leather amulet is "packed with unmentionable items," as is the
poem itself. By placing Bishop in the uncomfortable role of voyeur,
witness to an act of seemingly "protected" copulation, this vignette
touches on the poet's own unease with sterile desire, the feature of
lesbian love most frequently condemned (Case 8). Here, in this
tentative draft, Bishop considers unpacking the unmentionable as-
pects of her own life, in which lovemaking must always be ungenera-
tive, furtive, and vulnerable in unanticipated ways. But, once again,
the cost of disclosure is judged to be too great.

Asking Bishop to publish a polished version of "Scorpions," with
its celebration of the fanged kiss—asking her, that is, to appear in
public as an unabashed lesbian—is like asking the vampire to appear
in the mirror. How can she appear, when the mirror world (the
commonly accepted referential order) still belongs to dominant
culture and its "terrible conventions"? But the vampire's peculiar
trait—her inability to see herself in a mirror—may have its own
special appeal for a poet who felt uncomfortable with what she saw
of herself in society's looking glass. Through the figure of the
vampire, Bishop is able to suggest the invisibility forced upon and
embraced by the sexual outcast. A few lines from one of Bishop's
Key West notebooks from the 1940s, for example, speak to her
painful estrangement from the "real" as it is represented and reflected
by the controlling culture. In this sketch for a never-completed
poem, she registers despair at the distance between "us" and "those
people" (KWI 96). It is "frightening" to her that there are "miles
of unknown things happening / Having no reference to us." In
their failure to correspond or sympathize with "us," the domestic
lives of others ("those people in their beds") and the ruling conven-
tions ("those stars") cannot help the poet and her lover define their

relationship. The representations of sexual desire abroad in the world clearly do not reflect her own experience, and miles seem to open up between the poet's sense of herself and her image in the mirror. As a consequence, she begins to question the verities of identity, orientation, and attachment to the world.

There may have been only one recourse open to Bishop, given the brutal economy of the era in which she came of age. She would have to strike a bargain with dull conformity. In yet another poetic fragment, "To the Stars," Bishop (like Blake before her) links the "terrible conventions" of her society with "the stars" that wheel mechanically through the heavens:

> Yes, we will come and dangle our feet in your canals
> And master all your terrible conventions,
> But you must give us in return a miraculous currency,
> A few weird pleasures, picnics in the coolest plush craters.
>
> (KWI 137)

For a few stolen moments of *jouissance*—for a few fanged kisses and delightful picnics in the "cool plush craters" of the loved one's body—the poet will learn discretion. What her friend James Merrill once called her "instinctive, modest, lifelong impersonations of an ordinary woman" (6) will buy her some measure of happiness, some soft hideaway, safe from prying eyes. In return for keeping up appearances, she hopes to be reimbursed now and again with the "miraculous currency" of "weird pleasures."

There is a certain sportiness and daring about this arrangement, since Bishop has chosen to hide this illicit "currency" in full view of her friends and reading public. Like Poe's purloined letter, Bishop's homosexuality would be something of an open secret: "Love [is] like money," she writes in her notebook: "The more carelessly [it is] concealed, the less apt to be discovered" (KWI 193). As Lloyd Schwartz suggests, those who would have been most offended by her sexual orientation would also have been the last to recognize it (90). But many of her published poems invite us to penetrate Bishop's modest impersonation of an ordinary woman, to recognize the extraordinary woman behind the measured exterior. This especially holds true for those works that feature a mirror and dwell on the problem of self-representation.

Through the Looking Glass

The frustration of having to remain invisible within her culture produced at least two works that the poet found worthy of publication, "To Be Written on the Mirror in Whitewash" (which materializes for the first time in a Key West notebook) and "Insomnia" (completed in 1950). In the first instance, her use of the mirror raises troubling questions about self-image:

> I live only here, between your eyes and you,
> But I live in your world. What do I do?
> —Collect no interest—otherwise what I can;
> Above all, I am not that staring man.

> (*CP* 205)

Where does the speaker live? Does she appear reflected in a lover's eyes? And who is the mysterious "you" of the poem—a lover, or the speaker's own reflection as she stands before a looking glass? Strangely, the glass contains the image of a "staring man" who cannot be a reflection of the speaker since she takes such great pains to disassociate herself from him. His perspective is not her own, and yet she lives in his world. It seems that the speaker cannot see herself, for each time she looks in her mirror, the face and shape of a man stares back at her.

In her own way, Bishop asks her readers to reconsider a metaphor made famous by Virginia Woolf: "Women have served all these centuries as looking-glasses possessing the magic and delicious power of reflecting the figure of man at twice his natural size" (*A Room of One's Own* 35). At the same time, the poem's gender reversal (a presumably female speaker gazes into a mirror only to see herself in the guise of a man) evokes the myth of the mannish lesbian (Faderman 58) to which Bishop was exposed in the 1930s. Aroused by the female form, the so-called mannish lesbian, or sexual invert, was thought to have a pathological tendency to envision herself and her desires as masculine.

But any reading of this kind is justifiable only so long as we presume that the speaker is a woman. In truth, the speaker's gender remains unknown, conspicuously ambiguous. There is a strong element of self-effacement operating in the poem. Not only is the speaker obscured, but the poem's very title instructs us that the poem itself must be used to obstruct the very process of imaging or representation. After all, the short verse is meant "to be written on the mirror in whitewash." Most lesbians in midcentury America were forced to keep their activities hidden from the gaze of the prevailing perspective (the "staring man"). This concealment involved a good deal of whitewashing as it is customarily defined: an attempt to gloss over faults or exonerate by concealing any evidence of criminality. But in this poem, whitewashing becomes one method of canceling out the mirror world and, in this way, combating the prevailing perspective. If anything is whitewashed or obliterated here, it is the power of the mirror to determine the inner reality, the self-image, of the speaker. No longer will the mirror (the dominant symbolic order) dictate the nature of things.

Ultimately, the speaker refuses to partake in an exchange based on staring—or, in the parlance of recent critical theory, refuses to participate in a specular economy. The voice in this poem will not allow itself to be formulated or to formulate others with an imperious gaze. But has the speaker, finally, any choice? Hoping to live as invisibly as possible, the voice of the poem realizes that all efforts to efface the world of "that staring man" must be futile. Living in the realm of social constructions where people put on a face to greet the faces that they meet, the poet can only express her disapproval by refusing to exploit the people and things to which she has loaned her attention—"Collect no interest," she advises (*CP* 205): neither profit from others discomfort nor attract too much attention to oneself.

As Jacqueline Brogan suggests, Bishop's unwillingness to take her place as an object within the symbolic and economic orders of her day redefines the entire idea of reticence. With "To Be Written on the Mirror in Whitewash," the poet embraces invisibility and silence (writing in white ink) to make a revolutionary point about perspective. The man's dominating stare effaces more than the body of the woman who is caught in his field of vision. In Brogan's words, the poem's " 'white' (or silent) text makes an even more ironic, if not perverse 'commentary' ": Women efface themselves "as they adopt the dominant phallic perspective and learn to see themselves precisely as objects of reflection" (41).

Learning how to see yourself apart from how others see you is a lonely occupation. And the loneliness of a young woman striving to live her life on her own terms is the single continuous thread that runs through all Bishop's published and unpublished poems of love from the thirties and forties. When the voice of Bishop's poem "Insomnia" decides to "wrap up care in a cobweb / and drop it down the well / into that world inverted" where "you love me" (*CP* 70), it would be a mistake not to hear Bishop's faint echo of *The Well of Loneliness*, the title of Radclyffe Hall's lesbian novel published in America in 1928. The reference to inversion in "Insomnia" combined with the three rhymes of the poem's middle stanza (hell, dwell, well) make this one of the few published works in which there is a suggestion of homosexual love coupled with the anger that accompanies suppression.

In her Key West notebook, just beneath her reference to the "queer land of kissing," Bishop scribbles a suggestive line: "The bureau trapped in the moonlight [looks] like a creature saying 'oh'—" (KW1 140). A version of this sentiment seems to have been the starting point for "Insomnia" in which a surprised moon finds itself "trapped" in a bureau mirror. Bishop pictures herself in this poem as the aloof and infuriated female moon (a moon whose gender is stressed in the poem's second stanza). She draws a distinction from the start between the moon as it is and the moon as it is figured within a social structure, a structure represented here by the domestic dressing table and its mirror. A prisoner of this mirror world, the moon's reflection "looks out a million miles / (and perhaps with pride, at herself, / but she never, never smiles)" (*CP* 70). The actual moon stands distant and alone, "a million miles away" and "by the Universe deserted." Evoking derogatory images of femininity (frigidity, chastity, pride, rage, even sullenness), the real moon is monstrous in its frightening size, power, and complexity.

But everywhere in this poem there is a sense that the moon's dynamic force has been reduced to living in the cramped space of a bureau mirror. The actual moon, like the complex female identity, is confined and constrained by the various cultural and literary associations that have come to define that heavenly body over time. Those who sleep by night and wake by day accept the common order of things, but the night-stalking moon, like the sleepless poet, tries to subvert that order through inversion. Yet, lingering over the poem is a sense that this form of rebellion can only prove self-defeating. After telling the universe to go to hell, "she'd find a body of water . . . on which to dwell" (*CP* 70). This immersion in narcissism is also a form of drowning, of fatal introversion. Cosmic loneliness and alienation are problems that the speaker of "Insomnia" cannot easily solve. As Bonnie Costello observes, the poem undermines the speaker's initial attempts to see in the moon's dilemma a mirror image of her own insomnia and a solution to her misery (*Elizabeth Bishop* 32). The anxieties that lead to sleeplessness will not go away simply because the speaker chooses to remain aloof from life ("a million miles away") and devote herself entirely to introspection (finding a "mirror on which to dwell"). The figure of the angry moon in "Insomnia" helped express Bishop's fear that alienation might lead her, disastrously, toward a more inward-looking and self-absorbed approach to poetry.

Well known for the planetary roundness of her own face, Bishop might conceivably be referring to herself in a fragment from a Key West notebook in which she describes the moon as "the medieval monster with the round-face" (KW1 140). Her identification with the moon is more explicit still in a dream that she recorded on the first night of July 1935. In keeping with the strange logic of dreams, she at first appears as a young boy, then the moon, and finally as herself, suggesting the many facets of her self-image at the time when she struck friends and acquaintances as alternately hoydenish and womanly:

Last night I had a very strange, pretty dream. I was seeing what I told myself was an "Allegory" taking place. A tiny little boy on a little yellow sled was sliding rapidly down through great cloudy-looking snow-hills. He was muffled up all in gray-blue, quite deep, and I kept saying "How pale he is. How pale he is." His hands were all inside his blue clothes; the sled went without being guided in and out and up and down over the snow-hills which were really clouds. Then I realized that the little boy was the moon, going through its various phases out in the sky. I said to myself, wrongly, (but the attempt towards the right vocabulary is rather interesting), "Oh, there is the *solstice*." As I watched, I became the person seated on the sled, wrapped up in blue; I became the moon. I bumped over one cloud and became a snow-ball, rolling larger and larger, and the moon was growing full; the cloud reeled off again, and the moon was waning. Then the common falling sensation of dreams began; I shut my eyes and fell, and when I opened them the sled had landed in front of the drive of the house in Great Village, and I was sitting on it, still the moon. My grandmother was standing near me, not paying any attention, not having even noticed that the moon had fallen from the sky. It was early, early morning. She was dressed in black silk, and was holding out in front of her with one hand a small gold watch, worn on a gold chain around her neck. ("Recorded Observations," 1934–37: 29, VC)

By the end of the dream, the sled seems linked imagistically with Ione's famous description of the moon's chariot in the apocalyptic finale of Shelley's *Prometheus Unbound*:

> I see a chariot like that thinnest boat
> In which the Mother of the Months is borne
> By ebbing light into her western cave
> When she upsprings from interlunar dreams
>
> . . . .
>
> Within it sits a winged Infant, white
> Its countenance, like the whiteness of bright snow
>
> (*Works* 200–201)

The chariot is a thin crescent-shape, like the new moon, carrying within it the old moon ("Mother of the Months") to the cave where she is reborn during that period when the moon is invisible (sleeping in "interlunar dreams"). In Ione's cosmic marriage song, the chariot bearing the moon is Ezekiel's chariot of divine glory, portending the arrival of a "new heaven and a new earth." This apocalyptic overthrow of the old world and birth of the new is celebrated in the jubilant dance of a love-intoxicated moon ("insatiate bride" and "enamoured maiden") around her brother, and lover, the revivified earth (*Works* 204).

In Bishop's dream, the dancing spheres, moon and earth, unceremoniously collide. When the poet imagines herself landing back in the world of her childhood, like a moon strangely stranded in the front drive of her grandmother's house in Great Village, her pratfall seems to play comically (and poignantly) off Shelley's apocalyptic vision. In the last moments of her dream, it is early morning, but her grandmother, too busy reading the face of her gold watch, fails to notice that her granddaughter has just fallen from the sky in pale lunar disguise. The grandmother's inability to see this cosmic event cannot help but suggest Bishop's sense of estrangement from even her closest relatives. The capacity of her black-clad mother and grandmother to make her feel invisible is well documented in "In the Village" where the child Elizabeth tends to vanish in an effort to escape the tensions in the household (*CProse* 253). Though her memories of childhood will become the cave where she gives birth to herself as a poet, they will also prove to be a space in which she feels herself to be most invisible, like the moon in its "interlunar dreams." Picturing herself as an exotic abruptly deposited once again on her grandmother's doorstep—a moon woman come back down to earth—the dreaming poet, like the moon of "Insomnia," appears trapped among bureaus, timepieces, and other domestic and diurnal exigencies.

Bishop's early preoccupation with the equation between lesbianism and vampirism seems to dissipate over time. References to moons and mirrors, the daytime sleepers, furtive nightwalkers, and inverted worlds grow rarer as her work matures. Increasingly she sets her sights on creating a new symbolic order of her own, to match a new poetic style. Significantly, Bishop turns once again to the metaphor of the mirror, when she declares her intention to flout the "terrible conventions" of her culture. The moment occurs in "The Riverman." No longer identifying with the compromised figure of the vampire, Bishop chooses a new, empowering self-representation. In "The Riverman," she is a shaman in touch with superhuman forces and able to plumb the depths of her own soul. In order to be reborn as an artist and a "woman," she writes:

> I need a virgin mirror
> no one's ever looked at,
> that's never looked back at anyone,
> to flash up the spirits' eyes
> and help me recognize them.

(*CP* 107)

She cannot find this magic glass in the common marketplace, however, where girls are taught to see themselves as others see them and trade on their appearance:

> The storekeeper offered me
> a box of little mirrors,
> but each time I picked one up
> a neighbor looked over my shoulder
> and then that one was spoiled—
> spoiled, that is, for anything
> but the girls to look at their mouths in,
> to examine their teeth and smiles.

> (*CP* 107)

Henceforth, Bishop's "need for a virgin mirror," for a language and an aesthetic uncorrupted by stereotypic notions of "life / death, right / wrong, male / female" ("Santarém," *CP* 185), will carry her toward a distinctive poetic—a poetic as heterodox and hermaphroditic as her imagination.

The Androgynous Poem

The mature Bishop poem is itself a hybrid or metamorph. It is a portrait of naked experience wearing the fantasia of rhyme and meter. More than a template for her early bifurcated characters, the hermaphrodite becomes the poet's chosen emblem for the poem itself. Like Zubinko, the natural man who poses as the man of culture and custom hiding his difference behind the mask of conformity, Bishop uses the theatricality of verse to simultaneously unveil and disguise her unorthodox identity. Her poetic personae—her masks—are necessary. Without them, she would stand exposed to the world's contempt. The plight of the "depilated" animal Bishop describes in "Pink Dog" (*CP* 190–91) suggests the degree of dread that Bishop felt at the prospect of parading her body before the world. Kept home from school as a young girl when her skin grew inflamed with eczema and still sequestered years later because of her body's "queer" desires, Bishop empathized with the eyesores of Rio de Janeiro, unlovely strays or beggars flung into rivers by the good citizens of the city and left there to bob "in the ebbing sewage" (*CP* 190–91). The poet advises the poor naked bitch trotting openly in the city's thoroughfares to be practical and learn to conceal her sad state behind a *fantasía* (*CP* 190–91). Bishop's own carefully crafted tercets, sestinas, and villanelles are her costumes, sensible fashions to clothe her unorthodoxy. Like the riverboats that skitter back and forth across the Amazon and Tapajós waterways in "Santarém" (*CP* 185), Bishop's poems are mongrels of a sort and all the more resilient because of their mixed pedigree.

Bishop clearly felt that exhibitionism and formal control must be delicately balanced in a work of art, as in life. The mad hatters of her "Exchanging Hats" testify to the frustrations of repressing the truth about oneself and the hysteria that results when that repressed truth inevitably erupts. Balance is not maintained in the lives of the mannish aunt and effeminate uncle who must keep their secrets to themselves. "Aunt" and "uncle," after all, were well-known code words throughout the first half of this century for men and women who remained maids and bachelors on the margins of the bourgeois family and always, for that reason, suspect. Under pressure of concealment, Bishop's "unfunny uncles" and "anandrous aunts" give way to clownishness, a symptom of their hysteria. "In spite of our embarrassment," says the poem's speaker, we can see that their capers expose "the slight transvestite twist" that we all share, despite our well-practiced normality (*CP* 201). But the dilemma of these figures, trapped as they are within the cultural roles assigned them, is finally "unfunny," and their madcap attempt to violate the rules is a "joke [that] falls flat." They have not been able to find in their lives a healthy balance between propriety and play, restraint and exhibitionism, masculinity and femininity.

Our lives are compassed round by social strictures difficult, if not impossible, to breach. But art provides a more effective holiday from regulation than the family picnic or yachting expedition. In "Exchanging Hats," Bishop implies that the only satisfying arena for ethical, verbal, and even sexual experimentation is the poem. "Exchanging Hats" ultimately places the various emblems of cultural power (the headdress, the crown, the miter) on a par with the poet's meter and asks, "what might a miter [meter] matter"?

(*CP* 200). Inside the playground of the poem, the "might" (and the "right") of any cultural form is always open to doubt. Playfulness inhabits even the most disciplined feature of a work of art, its formal structure. The outward appearance that each work happens to take is known to be nothing more than an expedient disguise, worn for one poem and discarded for the next, since a poet is never tied to any single means of expression. Thus, formality is constantly played off against a casual disregard for prescriptions and meter placed in the service of subversion.

Bishop often found a "slight transvestite twist" (*CP* 200) or androgynous quality in the poets she admired. George Herbert once appeared to her in a dream, with curled hair and in a "beautiful dark red satin coat" ("Recorded Observations," 1934–37: 30, VC). Herbert's crimson *fantasía* mingles ecclesiastical associations with a cross-dressing twist. Interestingly, Bishop imagines herself having a long conversation with Herbert on the subject of meter, anticipating the question on which "Exchanging Hats" will hinge: "What might a miter [meter] matter"? Commenting on this dream, Jeredith Merrin notes that Herbert's bishoplike appearance evokes "a visual pun on Bishop's surname" (*An Enabling Humility* 41). Bishop's Herbert is a fellow changeling, a writer who mingles femininity with masculinity in his person and in his poetry and a formalist who nevertheless questions the power and importance of human institutions (suggested by the bishop's miter) and artistic monuments (represented by the poet's meter). The quality that Bishop found most appealing in his verse was its capacity to perform the "double function" of parabolic narrative: Herbert composes beautiful cages of verse that simultaneously proclaim and conceal his private ardor and turmoil.

For many years, Bishop planned a poem in honor of two other devotional poets, Emily Dickinson and Gerard Manley Hopkins, each of whom seemed to possess a spirit as paradoxical as Bishop's own. Bishop apparently worked on the poem as early as 1956 when she spoke of "trying to write a double-sonnet about Hopkins and E. Dickinson, together" in a letter to Herbert scholar Joe Summers (10 December, VC). Drafts for the unfinished poem show that both Dickinson and Hopkins struck Bishop as androgynous in nature, reminding her of "peeled withies," slender, flexible twigs that are surprisingly tough (box 74, folder 14, VC). The central icon of the proposed "double-sonnet" would have been the deceptively fragile feather, or quill, which her notes observe "are really horn, horny outgrowths" (box 74, folder 14, VC). Though this eccentric pair outwardly conform to the decorums of "a village elegance," Dickinson and Hopkins both conceal iron wills. As obdurate as they are flexible, both writers embraced lives of celibacy and voluntary circumscription—Dickinson in her well-appointed bedroom and Hopkins in the priesthood: "They chose, themselves, their cages . . . sinister a bit of gilding—a purple cover at night." The cloistered life enables them to test their backbone, and they emerge as "peeled withies . . . sustained by the same god."

In her last enigmatic notations for the poem, Bishop seems to be on the verge of drawing a connection between the peculiar lives of Dickinson and Hopkins and the structural peculiarities of their verse. Written with quill pens, their poems convey the feather's fragile strength: "Respendents [resplendent] hues are produced by structural peculiarities of the colorless horny surface of the deathers [feathers]" (box 74, folder 14, VC). These two respected predecessors seem to be caged birds whose songs gather emotional force from the discipline and confinement they have accepted for themselves. In choosing to work within the constraints of meter and rhyme, Bishop follows in their footsteps. The cage of meter provides the most powerful foil for the peculiarity of Bishop's matter. Bishop played her linguistic and sexual deviation from the norm off against the world's restrictions, just as she set the stories of her perverse protagonists within the strict confines of traditional poetic forms. In this respect, as in so many others, the structure of a Bishop poem reflects the architecture of the poet's mind.

Ultimately, as an image both of a complex sexuality and a complex poetic, the figure of the hermaphrodite becomes a partial means of conveying Bishop's nonconformity. While the young Bishop stressed Zubinko's loneliness and estrangement, the hermaphrodite is reimagined as the poet grows older and the figure becomes less a freak of nature and more a paradigm for artistic shape shifting and flexibility. Hermaphroditus (the son of Hermes and Aphrodite) incarnates mixed essence and the prospect of radical change, since he was joined in one body with a nymph. His father was known to the Greeks as Hermes and to the Romans as Mercury, the god of lyric poets and travelers, the patron of all shape shifters, transients, alchemists, and tricksters. As a go-between, Hermes ferries between the realms of the living and the dead (conducting the souls of the dead to Hades), travels between the worlds of waking and dreaming (or of the manifest and the latent), and, with a sleight of hand, transmutes insignificant matter into precious metal.

Hermes the messenger communicates between two parted realms—a blurring of boundaries associated with thirdness. The possibility of a higher form of listening and connection seems to be offered by this liminal position. For this reason, Kermode invokes Hermes as the "god, one might say, of the third ear"—those with the most acute powers of interpretation all have this tertiary sense (5). Bishop is a poet who knows the value of indefiniteness, finding in vagary what Jeredith Merrin has called "the chance for an almost alchemical change into some other reality, some third thing or *tertium quid*" ("Elizabeth Bishop" 167). From her earliest fables to her final poem, Bishop displays a fondness for the "third thing." When she represents the self or the psyche, as she does in "The Imaginary Iceberg" and in "At the Fishhouses," it is envisioned as a vital combination of vulnerability and durability, like the "peeled withy." Bishop's iceberg, for instance, with its upward thrust and its power to "correct elliptics in the sky" (*CP* 4), at first reminds the reader of Emerson's virile, moralizing "I"—an erected or phallic intelligence—but this arctic mountain is also "fleshed, fair" and surprisingly feminine. Likewise, in "At the Fishhouses," the soft breast from which we imagine all knowledge to flow, is "rocky," stiff, and surprisingly implacable (*CP* 66). Even Bishop's most famous masculine figure, the title character of "The Fish," is actually mercurial. A battered warrior wearing old fish hooks like medals of honor, this trophy from the sea is also fleshed and fair, its swim-bladder "pink . . . like a peony" (*CP* 42).

Mercury becomes, at last, a pivotal presence in Bishop's posthumously published "Sonnet" (1979). There, a "broken / thermometer's mercury / running away" (*CP* 192) released from all physical constraint, becomes Bishop's image for the freedom to be mercurial—and pleasurably perverse, no longer imprisoned by conventional views of her woman's body and its proper desires. At the end of her life when she came to write her last "Sonnet," Bishop was still exploring the vexed question of how to both proclaim and conceal her "weird pleasures" (KWı 137). A reading list appended to one of the drafts for the poem hints at the dilemma she found herself in at the time. She jots down the titles of several works by Roland Barthes that she either had read or intended to read: "*Roland Barthes* by Roland Barthes, *A Lover's Discourse*, R[oland B[arthes], *On Racine*, Critical Essays; *Mythologies?*, *Tel Quel* magazine—ask Celia" (drafts of "Sonnet," box 60, folder 8, VC). The difficulty of discoursing on love is felt throughout "Sonnet," where the poet masks her body in mechanical conceits: it appears as a "spirit-level," a thermometer, and a beveled mirror. This is the body trapped by culture, its dimensions tailored to standard measurements.

Framed by the new context that Bishop's reading list supplies, "Sonnet" becomes, at least in part, the poet's response to Barthes's critical activity in the late seventies, when he seemed to be searching for a way of representing a transformative love—a love that escapes the confines of the social order. At this crucial time in his own career, Barthes manifests what Danielle Schwartz has called "the regret and the wish for a counter-language, for an emancipation from constraints" that would allow him access "to the linguistic *neutre*, and to sexual neutrality" (56). Jane Gallop has linked Barthes's desire for a language "outside the ideological war of the sexes" to his own homosexuality and refers specifically in this context to his *Inaugural Lesson at the College de France*, where Barthes shows his frustration with the French language and its gendering properties. The comments that Barthes makes in this 1977 lecture bear a certain resemblance to the argument of Bishop's "Sonnet," where the poet identifies with a caught and divided creature, wavering between two equally untenable positions: "I am forced always to choose between the masculine and the feminine; the neuter [neither masculine nor feminine] or the complex [presumably some combination of the two] are forbidden me" (Barthes, qtd. in Gallop 112). We may wonder whether Bishop, too, dreamt of a language freed from the claims of the mimetic, a language that might resemble the rainbow bird of "Sonnet" released from its now-empty mirror, "flying wherever / it feels like, gay" (CP 192).

"Sonnet's" "rainbow-bird" is the poet's figure for the soul in an ecstatic state of endless renewal, freed finally from the constraints of definite bodily form. If anything, Bishop seems to look forward to a genderless, even neutered, existence, a utopia quite apart from the world of breathing passion. Apparently, Bishop could not imagine a time in this life when she would be free to speak openly of her love for other women. She could no more divest herself of the social trappings and material conditions that helped shape her existence than she could untether the spirit of her poem from its verbal and metrical moorings. But she could turn her predicament to her poetic advantage—and this she most certainly did. While other writers reveled in self-disclosure, Bishop held fast to her own idea of poetry and taught succeeding generations the power and the pleasure of dark speech.

3 *The Rose and the Crystal*

Elizabeth Bishop offers only rare glimpses of love or sexuality in print and few moments that linger over the human face or take delight in the human touch. Her decision to suppress her more explicit poems speaks volumes about her understanding of what was expected of her as a poet and how much her audience would tolerate before taking offense. This self-censorship is one of Bishop's crucial artistic choices and a decision crucial to this book. Certain ethical problems inevitably attend a study of this kind, which approaches an author through her suppressed work. The job of deconsecrating a poet's carefully managed reputation is always a troubling one. And the usual questions of disclosure are compounded in Bishop's case because, far from encouraging inquiry into her life, she actively resisted all attempts to penetrate her studied reserve. But at the same time, Bishop took great pains to preserve many of her working notebooks and unfinished drafts, and she prepared her papers for sale before she died. These papers, now archived primarily at her alma mater, Vassar College, contain highly personal, even damaging, material, and yet she understood their scholarly value and tacitly approved of their use.

Many of her unfinished poems must have been abandoned, not solely because of their dangerous content but primarily because of their insurmountable shortcomings. A good many of Bishop's unfinished drafts simply did not attain the level of her best published writing. It could be argued, of course, that the effort to translate disturbing material into verse may have produced the very technical problems that condemned these works to oblivion. But it also may be said that Bishop made a greater impact as an artist by withholding her most explicit musings and by exploiting what Octavio Paz called "the enormous power of reticence" (16). Still, there are a handful of aborted works about love that seem to have been sacrificed primarily to the mores of Bishop's particular era and class. They offer tantalizing intimations of what might have been had the poet simply been born a generation later.

One abandoned poem, in particular, rivals the freshness and power of Bishop's more canonical work. Dating from the early forties, "Vague Poem (Vaguely Love Poem)" upsets all our preconceptions about Bishop's natural reserve. With open tenderness, the work speaks of the poet's desire for other women and the delight she takes in the female body. In the poem's startling central image, the beloved's breast is likened to a soft, pink rose with rocky, crystalline nipples. The adamantine, yet yielding, image of the rock rose helps the poet convey the androgynous quality of lesbian love. This element of joyous eroticism is conspicuously absent from the only published work in which the rock rose appears, "Faustina, or Rock Roses." There, Bishop alludes to a variety of flower that grew just beneath her window in the inhospitable soil of Key West, Florida. But in "Vague Poem," the speaker is evidently searching for another kind of "rock-rose"—a variety of barite crystal formations that mimics the petals of the unfolding flower and reminds her of the paradoxical nature of love. This geological oddity takes its place among the other hybrid forms that populate Bishop's familiar writings, where the borders between the mineral and the botanical, the inanimate and the animate, the masculine and the feminine, are so often transgressed:

An Army house?—No. "a *Navy* house." Yes,
        that far inland.
There was nothing by the back door but dirt
or that same dry, monochrome, sepia straw, I'd seen every-
    where.
Oh, she said, the dog has carried them off.
(A big black dog, female, was dancing around us.)

Later, as we drank tea from mugs, she found one,
"a sort of one." "This one is just beginning. See—
you can see here, it's beginning to look like a rose.
It's—well, a crystal, crystals form—

> I don't know any geology myself . . ."
> (Neither did I.)
> Faintly, I could make out—perhaps—in the dull,
> rose-red lump of apparently soil?
> a rose-like shape; faint glitters . . . Yes, perhaps
> there was a secret powerful crystal inside.
>
> I *almost* saw it: turning into a rose
> without any of the intervening
> roots, stem, buds, and so on; just
> earth to rose and back again.
> Crystallography and its laws:
> Something I once wanted badly to study,
> until I learned that it would
>   involve a lot of arithmetic, that is, mathematics.
>
> (Box 67, folder 23, VC)

Late in the poem, we discover that an image of a rose rock (an inversion of Faustina's rock roses) has been recalled from the past, or from the world of dreams, as a kind of gift—an offering of love:

> Just now, when I saw you naked again,
> I thought the same words: rose-rock; rock-rose . . .
> Rose, trying, working, to show itself,
> forming, folding over,
> unimaginable connections, unseen, shining edges,
> Rose-rock, unformed, flesh beginning, crystal by crystal,
> clear pink breasts and darker, crystalline nipples,
> rose-rock, rose-quartz, roses, roses, roses,
> exacting roses from the body,
> and the even darker, accurate, rose of sex.

In the last lines, the poem's central icon provides Bishop with a way of visualizing the transforming powers of sexual pleasure—the wavelike alternations between quiescence and arousal that overtake the female body during intimacy. In the privacy of this never-completed poem, Bishop celebrates the impenetrable female body and the unimpregnating pleasure of lesbian sexuality. In this way, she captures her own experience of an erotic relationship that lies outside of the conventional romance tradition. Perhaps because the poet's estrangement from that heterosexual tradition is so palpable, so unmistakable, in "Vague Poem (Vaguely Love Poem)," Bishop could not bring herself to publish the work.

In general, Bishop's polished poetry is far more vague on the subject of sexuality than this buried work. The Bishop we do see in print may remind us of a rose rock: accessible one minute and impenetrable the next. In the preceding chapter, the strengths of combining clarity with mystery were explored in the light of the poet's desire to enhance her reader's interpretive pleasure. The aim of the present discussion is to place Bishop's preference for dark speech within the larger context of literary tradition. The pivotal metaphor of the rock-rose (or rose rock) opens an unprecedented window onto Bishop's poetic principles in relation to that tradition. Each component of the image emblematizes a distinct aesthetic philosophy: the rose of romance or romanticism is juxtaposed against the crystal purity of modernism. Bishop's search for the rock-rose may be said to parallel her pursuit of a combinatory poetic she first described in her college essay on Gerard Manley Hopkins, a poetic based on what she then called "crystallized emotion" ("Notes on Timing").

Naming the Rose

Bishop's efforts to describe the "accurate rose of sex" led her initially into crucial encounters with medieval romance and nine-teenth-century romanticism. She came to recognize that the use of the rose as a literary symbol of the most secret and treasured recesses of the female body was hopelessly mired in an ancient misogynistic tradition. The quest romance, with its rapacious hero and its mutely yielding prize, provided the basis for the way literature traditionally viewed woman (an object to be won) and nature (a body to be mastered). Given the traditional constraints placed on female desire, Bishop's reluctance to embody her woman's experience in song is far from surprising. But despite the risk, she did manage to produce publishable verse that challenged the traditional placement of women. Her published poems for and about women tend to subvert the courtly love tradition, which so often describes the aroused female body as a welcoming rose.

Although Bishop's use of the rose offers a general suggestiveness that cannot be tied to any one source, a brief glance at the literary debate or *querelle* surrounding the fourteenth-century *Roman de la Rose* illuminates the larger dialogue Bishop is holding with the traditional representation of female sexuality. In the romance's sustained allegory, the female body is a medieval castle, with crenellated turrets of squared stone and walls 100 fathoms wide by 100 fathoms high. At the deepest recesses of the castle lies the rose, the woman's concealed treasure that must be taken by force. The quarrel of the rose was sparked by this brazen display of the woman's *secrez membres*. The medieval philosopher Christine de Pizan initiated one of the longest debates in literature by insisting that an idiom of indirection be substituted for the romance's ribald exhibitionism. De Pizan refused to allow male scholars sole proprietary rights over the representation of women.[1] She underscored, instead, the inaccessibility rather than the penetrability of the female secretum.

As an author and scholar herself, de Pizan could not find a place for herself in the dynamics of the courtly tradition: she occupied neither the position of the male romancer nor the place of the romanced female rose. Instead, she necessarily inhabited a no man's land and traveled freely between "the defined masculine and feminine precincts" (Sullivan 465). Karen Sullivan, for one, argues that de Pizan as a woman who dared to pick up the pen was "always necessarily situated in an oblique rapport to her femininity" (465). The same may be said of Bishop, who shared de Pizan's distaste for the public naming of the body's *pars privees*. Like de Pizan, Bishop knew what it meant to be attacked as a prude for refusing to adopt certain modes of speech. Reflecting back on her choice in 1975, Bishop admits that her disdain for the drab phrase "to have sex" may strike younger poets as "hopelessly old-fashioned" (qtd. in Schwartz 90). But to her mind, the word *sex* seems "like such an ugly, generalized sort of expression for something—love, lust, or what have you—always unique, and so much more complex than 'having sex' " (90). Bishop is consistent on this point throughout her career. From first to last, her poetry draws attention to singular people "dragging in the streets their unique loves" ("Love Lies Sleeping," *CP* 17). Far from suggesting a hysterical fear of sexuality, however, Bishop's disdain for a vulgar, generalized view of love points to her larger dissatisfaction with the fixed location of women in relation to men. In Barbara Page's words, the peripatetic Bishop insists on being "truant from the rules governing the lives of women" ("Off-Beat Claves, Oblique Realities" 210). Like de Pizan's, the rapport that Bishop maintains with her own femininity is always necessarily oblique.

Bishop's love poetry typically undercuts the terms of medieval romance by concentrating on the vagueness or unfixable nature of female sexuality. In "Vague Poem (Vaguely Love Poem)," for instance, the beloved's body is not a fortress of chastity that must be breached but an ever-changing landscape. At once erotic and maternal—by turns, aroused ("a-rosed") and impervious to touch— the body of the loved one is allowed its own integrity, its own complex mystery. The poet accepts the shifting shape of her lover's emotions and the changing course of love, without trying to arrest those movements. In another unpublished prose piece reminiscent of "Vague Poem (Vaguely Love Poem)," Bishop continues to revise the courtly tradition of the *Roman de la Rose*: "The small shell-pink roses have opened so far, after two days in their bottle of water, that they are tired. The pink is fleeing—it is more mauve this afternoon.—The centers stick up further and are faded, too, almost brown. Still delicate, but reaching out, out, thinner, vaguer, wearier—like those wide beautiful pale nipples I saw somewhere, on white, white and strong, but tired nevertheless, breasts.—Time smeared them, with a loving but heavy thumb" ("After Bonnard," 1, box 73, folder 7, VC). Here, as in "Vague Poem (Vaguely Love Poem)," Bishop redefines the rose's metaphoric relationship to the female body. Bishop's small shell-pink roses remind her, instead, of the vaguely maternal nipple, the focus of homoerotic desire, rather than the pudendum, that center of heterosexual longing. Where the masculine tradition of love and conquest centers around the girlish bud poised on the edge of flowering (and defloration), Bishop's erotic musings typically call attention to the beauty of fading roses "opened so far . . . that they are tired," but still strong.

Unacknowledged works such as these help us to pinpoint the issues at stake in Bishop's public declarations of sexual desire. In "The Shampoo," for instance, the poet tries to evade the romance tradition by offering an unidealized vision of the female body. As

Bonnie Costello points out, this tender vignette, in which the poet washes her lover's silver-streaked hair "challenges the courtly convention . . . which recognizes as lovable only what is youthful or immutable" (*Elizabeth Bishop* 75). Written for Lota de Macedo Soares, this poem speaks of the way our loved ones are inevitably touched by time. Each tender stroke leaves another strand of white in her hair, but Lota "pragmatically" welcomes the transformation. "Battered" and "shiny" as an old, tin washbasin, Lota ages beautifully, gracefully (*CP* 84).

Like Dickinson's coachman-death, Bishop's "Time" is a consummate courtier, attentive and "nothing if not amenable" (*CP* 84). Time proves to be the poet's only rival for her beloved's affections, but nowhere in the poem does Bishop imply that time may be vanquished through verse. Instead, the poet expresses her willingness to share Lota with time—and to share time with Lota. Unlike the rocks that age so imperceptibly that "within our memories they have not changed," the faces and forms of these two lovers will alter within their mutual memory. In their own softening limbs and graying hair, they will preserve a record of their years together—and the prospect is a happy one.

We can see the poet of "The Shampoo" searching for a vision of the female body that conforms more closely to her vision of the natural, and this places Bishop in direct confrontation with nineteenth-century romanticism as well as the medieval romance. The strands of white in Lota's hair, for example, remind the poet first of lichens that grow by "spreading, gray, concentric shocks" and then of "shooting stars." There is nothing reassuring about either of these natural images—no sense of Platonic perfection, timelessness, or transcendence. The first metaphor carries with it a sense of moldiness or decay, while the second underscores the element of sudden shock apparent in the first. This vision of the mutable female form, however, is consonant with Bishop's own experience and cognizant of the natural shocks that flesh is heir to.

Bishop's distrust of the romance's etherealizing impulse carries over into her approach toward landscape poetry, the special haunt of the romantic poet. As a specialist in descriptive verse, Bishop had to come to terms with the powerful legacy of Wordsworth and

Emerson—a legacy that deftly converted the medieval romance to its own purposes, defining the poet's relationship with nature largely in terms of certain courtly conventions: Nature was womanly and therefore pliant and pregnable; Emerson's visionary poet, a latter-day romancer, was capable of "penetrating" this feminized nature, who would then be "made to serve" and to "receive the dominion of man as meekly as the ass on which the Saviour rode" (Emerson, *Nature* 50). The object of man's quest, then, was to inseminate the landscape with a higher meaning, subduing it to his own expressive purposes. In the end, a vulgar, material world would be hallowed and purified and made to serve the mind of man.

In a famous passage from "Self-Reliance" with which Bishop must have been familiar, Emerson shows how this goal was to be accomplished when he contemplates—or manhandles—the common rose. The flower under his window, he tells us, "is simply the rose . . . perfect in every moment of its existence" and understood by the educated man to be an emblem of God (*Selections* 157). Thus, Emerson succeeds in "impress[ing] his being" and his intellect on the world around him. Bishop might have shared the transcendental poet's eye for those miracles of the common day, but she could never share his confidence in the purification process. For Bishop, nature may have been sacral, but it was also always untidy in its implications and effects: she saw an "awful but cheerful" vulgarity at work in every natural scene (*CP* 61). Ultimately, she would rather show nature "smeared" by time than purified out of all existence ("After Bonnard," 1, box 73, folder 7, VC).

With her "rust-perforated roses" ("Faustina, or Rock Roses," *CP* 74), Bishop attempts to salvage nature from the ontological claims of romantic vision. And the pages of her Florida notebooks make this abundantly clear. They are filled with "frayed and flattened" roses, her favorite emblems for the bruised and aging body (KW2 197). A sketch for one projected poem, "Faustina II," confronts the romantic tradition of quest and conquest through the image of the faded rose. In this poetic fragment, Bishop's reading is interrupted by the sound of june bugs thumping against her window screen. It was as if "all the opened roses on the '7 sisters' rose-bushes, the opened ones faded to mauve and white, and frayed and flattened,

had turned to moths and were trying to get through the screen"
(KW2 197).[2] Here, Bishop's endlessly metamorphic roses have
turned, not to rocks, but to moths—moths known for their ability
to eat through clothing and protective screens.

When the rose moths infiltrate Bishop's well-protected home,
they remind the poet that nature can never be fully understood or
domesticated. Significantly, she had been studying the account of
Amundsen's arctic expedition in Chancellor's *Great Adventures and
Explorations* before being distracted by the june bugs. There, as her
notes on the book indicate, she found an image of the explorer that
corresponded in disturbing ways with her notion of the romantic
poet: both adopted an aggressive stance toward the wilderness.
Commenting on the "discoveries" of Amundsen and Ericksson,
Bishop writes,

> a violent trespass
> most violent of trespasses
>   kisses
>   theses
>   breaking every law
> fills them with such diseases.
>
>   (KW2 191)

Bishop associates the material conquest with the unauthorized pene-
tration or rape of nature ("trespasses / kisses")—and the rape of
nature with man's assertion of intellectual mastery over raw material
("theses"). The chain of association she develops (trespasses, kisses,
theses, diseases) serves as an indictment of empire building as a
cultural and a poetic enterprise. Bishop's rose moths, then, may be
said to interrupt, or undermine, her reading of this masculine poetic
enterprise, which she can no longer passively accept.

Finally, the rose moths of the unfinished "Faustina II" provide
a suggestive context for reviewing "Faustina, Or Rock Roses," a
completed work from the early forties that found its way into *A
Cold Spring*, Bishop's second collection of poems. This published
poem may be read as a companion piece to "The Shampoo": both
works pivot on the question of the aging female body and how it
is to be approached both in life and in art. While the heroine of "The
Shampoo" makes peace with Time, the old invalid of "Faustina, Or

Rock Roses" wars against it, battling old age with talcum powder, pills, and cans of "cream." The bedridden woman is dressed like some transplanted Mrs. Havisham in what looks to be a moldering bridal gown. In reality, she is wrapped in winding sheets that remind her visitor of "wilted roses" (*CP* 73). A victim, it seems, of the romance tradition, this old woman passed her prime paying obeisance to Poe's nineteenth-century notion that the slow death of a beautiful (and youthful) woman was the "most poetic topic in the world" (*Essays and Reviews* 19). A Southern belle now visibly decaying, Bishop's protagonist can no longer play the "blessed damozel" and so has outlived her role in the romance of the rose.

If latter-day romancers like Poe were drawn to the macabre image of a lovely bride translated into a toothless hag by death, Bishop focuses, instead, on the embarrassing image of a hag who struggles vainly to remain as lovely as a fresh white rose. As such, Bishop's poem is an antiromance set in Florida, the land of beautiful flora. For Bishop, the old woman's efforts to conquer her body and arrest its decay recall all the ironies attached to the conquest of the New World. Europeans, after all, were first drawn to St. Augustine by the promise of eternal youth but found there instead the "corrupt" landscape Bishop describes in the poem "Florida"—swampland that reminds her of "a gray rag of rotted calico" strewn with skeletons and circled by buzzards (*CP* 32). Like her own disintegrating body, the sick woman's house is in the process of being reclaimed by nature: the home is moth-eaten and "the floorboards sag / this way and that," mirroring the owner's "crooked" shape (*CP* 72). The speaker of the poem visits the invalid, bringing her a bunch of "rust-perforated roses" that aptly suggest the old woman's declining state of health: like the unpetaling flowers, she is smeared by time's heavy thumb.

Much of Bishop's indictment of the idealizing impulse in poetry is conveyed through the figure of Faustina, the black servant who tends her decrepit white mistress. Like a wizened Belinda at her dressing table, the mistress is waited on by Faustina, a high priestess of the cosmetic powers who performs the daily rites of restoration. As her name implies, Faustina is seen by her white employer as something of a conjurer (or obeah woman), but her inner life is concealed from view. In the eyes of the visitor (presumably white herself), this black woman's feelings are a "conundrum" (*CP* 73). Her "sinister kind" face is a practiced mask, an inscrutable surface that registers, to the visitor's mind, the long corrupt history of relations between white and black, rich and poor, master and servant. Watching the powerful black woman tend her infantilized charge, the visitor's thoughts also travel back to primal moments of tenderness between mother and child. This disturbing overlay of images awakens the visitor's profound fears about the unidealized, the true, nature of intimacy: in this case, Bishop shows how women may be attached to one another both by their childhood "dream of protection and rest" (*CP* 73) and their worst nightmare of mutual dependency and enslavement.

Troubling questions about the triangular relationship between the old doyenne, her servant, and her visitor become "helplessly proliferative" by the poem's conclusion (*CP* 74). They are also questions of "acute" personal importance to the poet. The conundrum of Faustina is a case in point. Faustina's power to turn dreams into nightmares and to overturn the balance of power between servant and mistress casts doubt on the Wordsworthian dream of protection and rest in nature's cradling embrace. Traditionally, romanticism ascribes greater integrity of being to those with less power and privilege, associating these mute figures (mothers, maids, children, and idiots) with a sacral and silent nature. All that the romantic poet represses when constructing an image of a maternal nature returns with a vengeance in the shape of Bishop's Faustina, who embodies nature's darkness, opacity, and potential malice.

As a woman of privilege, the poem's visitor finds herself falling into romantic assumptions about her own relation to this household, despite her awareness that it is no longer possible to conceal the complex interdependence of these women's lives: "the eighty-watt bulb / betrays us all" (*CP* 72). The visitor's position parallels Bishop's own throughout much of her life, since the poet was herself tended by maidservants, particularly during her years in Brazil. Women from another class substituted for the absent mother since they served her material needs and made her writing possible. As Jane Gallop explains, "The desire for the maid, along with the writer's resemblance to and difference from her, must also be understood in terms of the mother" (174). The woman writer, Gallop argues, "transfers her relation to her mother (and her lover) onto her maid," who becomes the silent keeper of secret knowledge—a knowledge of the flesh from which the writer is estranged by virtue of the fact that she writes, and in writing, becomes abstracted from her own body. Almost in spite of herself, then, the visitor in "Faustina, Or Rock Roses" (a surrogate for the poet herself) begins to assume that the black servant possesses some secret knowledge that she willfully refuses to divulge.

Turning once again to Bishop's Florida notebooks from this period, we find that Bishop actually knew a local Key West character named Faustina, a fortune-teller who certainly claimed her share of secret knowledge. A formidable presence, Faustina became associated in the poet's mind with the "vulgarity" of the flesh; she embodied the "vulgar views of nature" that Emerson strove to purify and transcend (*Nature* 73). In Bishop's notes for "Faustina II," for instance, this large, black woman emerges as an emblem of the gauche (the sinister, the dark, the unwanted). The poet remembers the "old pirate scarf" Faustina would wear and "the blue flaming alcohol [that] ran down [her] throat and breast" (KW2 173). Addressing herself to Faustina, Bishop writes, "I love that darkened (blackened) gibberish you speak" (KW2 173), and the way "you lift up your black body to its future," while pulling "one eye down to show . . . its reddened tear" (KW2 180). In these descriptions, Faustina retains an unmediated connection with her body, which she lifts to the future; her body preserves her affective history ("its reddened tear"), and she comes to stand for all that is corporeal and indecipherable ("darkened gibberish").[3]

As a woman who writes, Bishop maintains an oblique rapport with her own corporeality. She is in touch with Faustina's secret knowledge of the body and abstracted from it at the same time. Like Christine de Pizan so many years before her, Bishop is estranged from the women she defines in her writings, and her observations raise acute questions about the woman writer as visitor or detached observer. In "Faustina, Or Rock Roses," visitation borders on trespass, but the poet fights her impulse to master what she sees. She may be tempted to romanticize Faustina, treating her as a vulgar and mute canvas on which to impress her own intellect and being. But she pulls back: her initial question instantly "blurs further, blunts, softens, separates" (*CP* 74) and refuses to crystallize. The same is true of her vision of Faustina. The poem's intimate view of the female body and female relationships retains a healthy vagueness reminiscent of the unpublished "Vague Poem (Vaguely Love Poem)." Battling the rigid prescriptions of the romance tradition, she brings a salutary sense of blurred boundaries as well to her descriptions of womanliness. Her published portrait of Faustina, like her suppressed love poetry, captures the paradoxical nature of love—the dream and the nightmare—through the central image of the "rose rock."

In order to arrive at her own approach to the role that her own feelings and experiences might come to play in her poetry, Bishop first would have to come to terms with modernism's disdain for sentiment and its call for a depersonalized poetry. If romanticism relied on the ancient avatar of the rose to convey its sense of timeless beauty and emotional accessibility, modernism chose the crystal and its variants (the bright star, the faceted jewel, the optic prism, the camera eye) to represent its ideal of intellectual disengagement from emotion. Baudelaire, for instance, (whom some might call the father of modernity) wrote of a "*rock-crystal* throne / of contemplation, once so aloof, so serene" where he longed to lodge his soul ("Les Bijoux," *Les Fleurs du Mal* 26; my emphasis). But women, and the emotional turmoil they had come to represent, threatened to undermine what little peace the poet had achieved. The poet regains his throne of detachment only by immobilizing the restless, feminized spirit of nature—punishing "in one *rose* / all Nature's insolence" ("A celle qui est trop gaie," *Les Fleurs du Mal* 49; my emphasis).

Signaling a profound fear of the feminine, modernism's banishment of unmanning desire became a serious obstacle to the kind of poetry Bishop envisioned. Her age, sex, and temperament made it impossible for her to fall in line with either the modernists who were her immediate poetic predecessors or the postromantic confessionalists who were her younger contemporaries. Negotiating her own path between these two extremes, Bishop worked toward a personal aesthetic of both sense and sensibility: a poetic of the crystal rose.

The Laws of Crystallography

Hoping to release the complex female body and the mutable body of nature from the terms of romance, Bishop was tempted to take refuge in the modernist aesthetic. Declaring the obsolescence of the rose, the modernist poets turned to the crystal for an emblem of the intellect suitably detached from the vagaries of time and sentiment and a poetic language purified of all emasculating emotion. The quartz mineral's geometric perfection made it a favorite reference point for the modern poet struggling to break free of the body and its passions. In 1923, William Carlos Williams set the tone for the modern trend when he wrote, "Poetry has to do with the *crystallization* of the imagination—the perfection of new forms as additions to nature" and not as imitations of nature (*Collected Poems* 1: 226; my emphasis). This was, after all, the age of Duchamp and the rotary precision optic machine, Alfred Stieglitz and "straight" photography that approached "the abstract and crystal purity of poetry" (Jolas 123).[4]

If new forms were to be crystallized, old forms needed to be discredited as imitations. Novelty, in the modern era, became an absolute good and redundancy an evil linked with inefficiency and, worse yet, emotional effusion. For this reason, Williams took pruning shears to Coleridge's garden of metaphors: "The one thing [romantic poets] have never seen about a leaf is that it is a little engine" and one of the things that "make a plant GO" ("Belly Music" 26). In his 1944 "Author's Introduction" to *The Wedge*, Williams makes what is probably his most famous pronouncement about poetry: "There's nothing sentimental about a machine, and: A poem is a small (or large) machine made of words. When I say there's nothing sentimental about a poem I mean that there can be no part, as in any other machine, that is redundant" (*Collected Poems* 2: 54).

When Bishop concedes, in the unfinished "Vague Poem (Vaguely

Love Poem)," that she once wanted to study "crystallography and
its laws," she echoes the advice of Williams, who in his 1925 essay on
Marianne Moore recommended that every poet learn the "geometric
principle of the intersection of loci" (*Selected Essays* 122) at work in
the crystal.[5] For Williams, Juan Gris was the artist who had most
thoroughly mastered the laws of crystallography. According to Wil-
liams, Gris's precisionist paintings make the romantic notion of
the rose "obsolete." The flower and the "weight of love" so long
associated with it can now be seen from a much "sharper, neater,
more cutting" point of view (*Collected Poems* 1: 195). Bishop clearly
had Williams's comments in mind when she wrote about Gris in
one of her Florida notebooks. She was impressed with the way
Gris caught things "looking the way they look when we aren't
looking at them." It was a quality he shared with her mentor,
Marianne Moore, who also had an eye for "oblique realities that
glance off a larger reality [mirror] illuminating like light caught in
a bevel" (KW2 189).

As a young writer, Bishop found the crystalline aesthetic seductive
and chilling in equal measures. During the year she spent in New
York following graduation from Vassar in 1934, she was intrigued
by the gem room of the Museum of Natural History, where she
was especially drawn to the sapphires from Ceylon that were cut
to resemble six-rayed stars of light ("Recorded Observations," 1934–
37: 11, VC). Her earlier work shows the influence of the star sapphire:
the Etoile in "Paris, 7 A.M.," for example, or the glowing rock that
illuminates the Nativity scene in "Over 2000 Illustrations and a
Complete Concordance." In each case, the images of a rock "break-
ing with light" suggest the lost star at the center of personal and
cosmic history, the prophesied source of a divinely willed universe.
Beckoning from across a great expanse of time, however, the star
crystal is always evoked elegiacally like some distant and irrecover-
able home.

As often as not, Bishop invokes the crystal as a sign of her own
isolation. In the year of her mother's death, 1934, she makes a
glancing allusion in her journal to her sense of homelessness and
the ache of feeling small, isolated, and set apart from the world
around her like a "little object . . . sadly flawed" inside a "crystal

ball" ("Recorded Observations," 1934–37: 31, VC). The poems that fill her first collection tend to place us inside that "crystal ball," a perfect setting of the poet's devising, one that may help her to control and contain her loneliness. In "Love Lies Sleeping," for instance, the "immense city" of New York is reduced to the size of a bell jar or a glass terrarium "made delicate by over-workmanship" and introversion (*CP* 16). Miniaturized, the metropolis takes on all the fragility and pathos that the poet once associated with her own position as a child living among strangers.[6] As the urban skyline "grows in skies of water-glass from fused beads of iron and copper crystals," it wavers and trembles with Bishop's subjectivity. In works such as this one, the poet concedes that any control she obtains over the stresses of life is only a Coleridgean "miracle of rare device" ("Kubla Khan" l. 35). Like a skyline wrought from beads of glass, her verse is crafted from brittle and breakable words.

In "Love Lies Sleeping," the poet ultimately reminds us of a withdrawn child trading life in a real but dangerous world, for the comforts of a glass menagerie. But even in this phase of her career, when she was most tempted to introspection and retreat, Bishop had her doubts about the purely aesthetic solution to life's difficulties. She worried that her poetry from this period sounded a bit too precious, or jejune—too captivated, one might say—by the ideal of the elegant, rationalized poem. As her maturing work will show, modernism's attempt to divorce poetry from all organic and bodily experience became increasingly troubling to her. Her growing dissatisfaction with the aesthetic of emotional detachment is apparent in what could be called her "crystal trilogy": "The Unbeliever," "The Imaginary Iceberg," and "Paris, 7 A.M." With each poem, Bishop comes closer to dislodging her soul from what Baudelaire called "the rock-crystal throne of contemplation, so aloof, so serene" (*Les Fleurs du Mal* 27). Each of these works stages an encounter between the poet and the poet's own autonomous human soul, then moves toward a destabilizing moment of choice when the pleasures of detachment are weighed against the merits of full participation in life's cruel conundrums.

Sailing toward eternity, Bishop's "Unbeliever" (as the name implies) remains unsupported by religious faith but relies on the vessel of art (or dreams) to carry him forward. His eyes firmly shut to the world, he sleeps on the top of a mast with the sails falling away below him "like the sheets of his bed" (*CP* 22). By comparing his position to that of a "gilded bird" in a cage, Bishop associates her "unbeliever" with Yeats's bird of hammered gold. Like the modern aesthete, Bishop's mast-sitting dreamer longs to escape from his own vulnerable body, from the tatters in his mortal dress. He chooses to model himself after Yeats's sailor searching for Byzantium, a realm of art divorced from nature, where he may sing of life's sorrows from a serene vantage point, removed from the fray.

Recoiling from the touch of time, he conjures a dreamworld where clouds and gulls turn to marble, seas to diamonds, and tears to pendant jewels. But there is nothing reassuring about this attempt to mineralize nature, as though Bishop were having her doubts about the efficacy of the modern aesthetic. It is as though she were reading Baudelaire's "Parisian Dream" through a glass darkly. In that poem, the French master escapes the unrelenting strokes of his clock (and the sordid reality of his life) by entering the crystal palace of art, where every growing thing is beautifully immobilized: heavy cataracts of water turn crystal, trees become marble colonnades, women are transformed into statuary, the seas into "jewelled conduits" now "submissive" before the poet's "erected" will (*Les Fleurs du Mal* 107). For Bishop, however, Baudelaire's fantasy of a world detached from time and feeling seems more threatening than pleasant. With her image of the "spangled sea . . . hard as diamonds" and beckoning the "unbeliever" toward his own destruction, she takes the delight out of Baudelaire's vision of the ocean as a "diamond gulf." Instead, Bishop's cold and unnerving sea suggests the dangers of a crystalline aesthetic. Living in his precarious position, her mast sitter must be ever on guard, vigilant against the powerful pull of that aesthetic (it "wants me to fall," the unbeliever fears). The poem reveals Bishop's growing disenchantment with the modern view of art as a replacement for religion, an intellectual haven, and a sanctuary from nature, time, and the body.

In "The Imaginary Iceberg," another winter's tale, Bishop paints a scene that "a sailor'd give his eyes for" (*CP* 4). The scene was suggested to her by R. H. Dana's *Two Years Before the Mast*. Dana's sighting of an iceberg during his polar expedition becomes one of the highlights of his mariner's tale, and Bishop copies a few choice passages in the pages of her journal: "And there lay, *floating in the ocean*, several miles off, an immense, irregular mass, its top and points covered with snow, and its center of a deep indigo color . . . its cavities and valleys thrown into deep shade, and its points and *pinnacles glittering in the sun* . . . Its great size;—for it must have been from two to three miles in circumference, and several hundred feet in height;—its slow motion, as *its base rose and sank in the water*, and *its high pts. [points] nodded against the clouds* . . . all combined to give it the character of true sublimity" and in the "steady breeze" the ship's sails look "like *marble*" quietly doing their work (qtd. in KW1 213–14; my emphasis).

Dana's language is the scaffolding on which Bishop builds her vision of the iceberg as the sublimated soul or psyche. The first stanza of her poem explains the appeal of the iceberg as an image of the indissoluble, imperturbable soul: it stands "stock-still like a cloudy rock" while the surrounding sea resembles "moving marble" and the ship's sails that are laid upon that sea are themselves as undissolved and marbleized as the water (*CP* 4). The second stanza focuses on the iceberg's relation to the sky and the stars: Its "glassy pinnacles" have the power to make apparent what the universe obscures by "correcting elliptics in the sky." "Elliptics," with its verbal play on the geometric "ellipse" and the grammatical "ellipsis," suggests that the human soul, here symbolized by the iceberg, imagines itself capable of "correcting" the cosmos in a dual sense: first, it believes itself powerful enough to "correct" the shape of the universe, which has deviated from the perfectly spherical; second, it is confident in its own ability to close the gaps or aporias in human knowledge.

The relation between the iceberg and the sky in Bishop's poem is adversarial, but the antagonism is slightly comical. It is this touch of enmity between the ice mountain and the heavens that struck the poet as she transcribed the following passage from Dana's description of the iceberg: "It was a clear night and we could plainly mark the long and regular heaving of the stupendous mass, as *its edges moved slowly against the stars*" (qtd. in KW1 214; my emphasis).

Beside this sentence, Bishop jots down a parenthetical exclamation point. Dana's "points and pinnacles glittering in the sun" are transformed by Bishop into emblems of the mind's rapierlike wit able to "correct elliptics in the sky" and "spar with the sun" (*CP* 4). But there is something faintly ludicrous about this quixotic sword play, this tilting with the heavens, when all the world's a "shifting stage" (*CP* 4). The human mind emerges from the poem as a kind of *milos gloriosos* attempting to "stand and stare" down the enemy and maintain his balance at the same time. There is something self-adoring about the iceberg's perpetual self-adorning, something of the braggadocio ("fleshed, fair, erected indivisible" [*CP* 4]) in its performance.

Dana's voyage provides Bishop with the rudiments of her poem, principally because his emphasis on the iceberg's "sublimity" links the self-perpetuating, unfathered mountain of ice with the poetic imagination that Wordsworth celebrates—a soul conscious of its own "glory" and "strength of usurpation" (*The Prelude* 6, ll. 595–601). The last word of the poem (and the final name for the iceberg) is "indivisible," a mnemonic for the ancient Greek notion of the monad, that elementary individual spiritual substance from which material properties were thought to be derived. Bishop's ship steers clear of the monastic and monolithic soul, defending herself against its siren call. Turning her back on this vision, Bishop proclaims her intention to abdicate this crystal palace for warmer climes, "where waves give in to one another's waves," where arms embrace like waves, icebergs melt, and poets are "uncrystallized" by thoughts of love.

Still, Bishop's imaginary iceberg is more than an image of phallic self-sufficiency, "fleshed, fair" and "erected" (*CP* 4). It is also a crystalline form, and "like jewelry from a grave," it "cuts its facets from within" reflecting the abstract purity that characterized the modernist poetic (*CP* 4). Once again Bishop finds precedent in Dana for her description of the iceberg as jewel. Dana thought that the smaller icebergs looked "like little floating fairy isles of *sapphire*" (qtd. in KW1 214; my emphasis). After noting this lovely image in her journal, Bishop immediately turns her attention from *Two Years Before the Mast* to the qualities that distinguish Moore's poetry.

Speculating on what she would write if she were to review Miss Moore's *What Are Years*, Bishop comes up with a possible title for the piece, calling it "The Price of Originality" (KW1 215). Moore's singularity resides, Bishop argues, in "the general effect of extreme *purity* & independence" to be found her carefully crafted poems (KW1 215; Bishop's italics). For this reason, Bishop is surprised by the carelessness she sees in "What Are Years?" the title poem of Moore's 1941 collection, complaining that "in places [Moore] has not used the 'light' rhyme carefully enough, so that in reading it casually, one is apt to run the lines over and give them quite an ordinary iambic or trochaic meter with end-rhymes" (KW1 215).

For Moore, the meticulous attention to stanzaic and accentual patterns is one way to show that "he who strongly feels, / behaves," and this decorum is a sign of moral character ("What Are Years?" *Complete Poems* 95). As her notes on Moore reveal, Bishop recognized in Moore's sharply fashioned verse a certain sadness: "(The independence of Miss M[oore]—commanding natural respect without effort, & yet a little sad)—It sometimes [is] the dangerous purity that leaves one more vulnerable to disease, and the independence of the child that refuses to come to meals" (KW1 215). Further down the page, Bishop tries to pinpoint the "dangerous" quality of Moore's "purity": "Coldness? what is it—a slight rippling *chill*—a sense of draught . . . like bird songs—like the bird-songs here [in 'What are the Years?' perhaps]—the tonality & rhythm eludes us—shades away obliquely" (KW1 215; Bishop's emphasis). It is difficult to tell for certain whether Bishop's journal entries on Moore were written slightly before or after the well-documented disagreement between the two poets over what Moore considered to be the indelicacy of Bishop's reference to a "water-closet" in "Roosters," a poem completed in 1940. In a letter to Moore concerning the poem, Bishop explains that "Roosters" speaks to her impressions of wartime Key West "and also of those aerial views of dismal little towns in Finland & Norway, when the Germans took over, and their atmosphere of poverty" (17 October 1940, RM). The roosters, fighting brutally until they lie face up on dung heaps with "open, bloody eyes, / while those metallic feathers oxidize" (*CP* 37) were intended to portray what Bishop refers to in the same letter to Moore as "the essential baseness of militarism." Writing the poem entirely in triplets, Bishop forces deliberately "awful" rhymes to emerge, compounding the brute vulgarity of the images:

> Cries galore
> come from the water-closet door,
> from the dropping-plastered henhouse floor,
>
> where in the blue blur
> their rustling wives admire,
> the roosters brace their cruel feet and glare
>
> with stupid eyes
> while from their beaks there rise
> the uncontrolled, traditional cries.
>
> (*CP* 35)

The poem met with an "immediate flurry of criticism" (*CProse* 146) from both Moore and her mother, first conveyed over the telephone and later in writing. Particularly offensive, it seems, was Bishop's use of the word, "water-closet," which Moore feared would leave too visual an impression of a reader "not *depersonalized*" enough to accept the picture rather than the thought (letter to Bishop, 16 October 1940, VC; my emphasis). In other words, its use did not conform to a modernist creed that prized what Moore called "heroisms of abstinence" above the "important violence of tone" that Bishop refused to sacrifice (letter to Bishop, 16 October 1940, VC). When Moore rewrote "The Roosters" in an effort to cleanse it of crudeness, eliminating the rooster's "cruel feet," "stupid eyes," and "torn-out, bloodied feathers," Bishop's response is respectful but firm: "I cherish my 'water-closet' and the other sordidities because I want to emphasize the essential baseness of militarism" (letter to Moore, 17 October 1940, RM).

Turning to her private notebooks for release, Bishop underscores her awareness of crucial differences between herself and Moore—differences that are most apparent in their attitudes toward the body. Moore startles her readers by disturbing the conventional body of the poem, twisting its syntax in unsettling ways. But the shock value of scatology or sexual explicitness held little appeal for Moore, who instead translates her meticulous observations of the

material world into surprising, ingenious abstractions that preserve
what Kalstone calls "a purity of possession" (93). The forces of
natural decomposition are unveiled in Moore's verse, but there is
nothing tentative about her descriptions, nothing to suggest their
own vulnerability to decomposition. As Kalstone reminds us, Bish-
op's poetry by contrast makes a method of tentativeness, and "the
benisons of morning, the signs of fresh natural creation, are en-
twined with the residue of dreams and with bafflement about human
motive and pain" (93).

During the 1940s, Bishop grew increasingly independent of
Moore's guidance, while the older poet's life became taken up with
nursing herself and her mother through a succession of illnesses.
In her notebooks, Bishop's concern for Moore and for the shape
her own personal and professional life is poured into her plans for
a projected play to be based on the Book of Job. "Job's Comforters"
would focus on Job's physical disintegration and on his refusal to
relinquish his vision when advised to do so by those who claim to
have his best interests at heart. For Bishop, Job's suffering is the
inevitable consequence of "implacable views in a superior person"
(KWI 91–93). Bishop's Job ("Why did he get boils?") resembles
Bishop's portrait of Moore, an original artist whose "dangerous
purity" leaves her "more vulnerable to disease" (KWI 215). Bishop,
whose own body was so susceptible to morbid inflammations, also
sees in the figure of Job and his battle to preserve his independence,
a template for the drama unfolding in her own career: " 'Lilies that
fester smell far worse than weeds.' The impossibility of reaching
anyone in that frame of mind—(Miss M[oore])—how you find
yourself making up things—being *profound*, etc.—Like when you
criticize a poem—and the writer says 'But I like it that way'—
balked. Bildad [Job's comforter] felt balked" (KWI 91; Bishop's
emphasis). When Bishop uses the word *balked*, she echoes Moore's
comment on the vulgarity of most modern poets who feel duty-
bound never to "balk at anything like unprudishness" (letter to
Bishop, 16 October 1940, VC). In retaining her "cherished sordidi-
ties" (letter to Moore, 17 October 1940, RM) Bishop joins those
who are not checked in their course by the fear that they may appear
vulgar. At this juncture in their relationship, it is Moore who is

"balked" by Bishop's insistence that poetry describe the festering lilies of the field. To Moore's criticism of "Roosters," Bishop replies, "But I like it that way."

The chill that Bishop feels while reading Moore's poetry certainly suggests the nature of the gap that would open up between mentor and protégée as Bishop began to assert her artistic independence. Bishop was disconcerted each time she felt Moore's disapproval, and she felt that disapproval most immediately whenever she presented Moore with a poem that steered away from abstract purity to "run in a warmer sky" ("The Imaginary Iceberg," *CP* 4). After sending Moore "Insomnia" and "The Shampoo," Bishop heard nothing but silence and felt the "slight rippling chill" of Moore's reproof. Bishop confides in a letter to May Swenson that Moore's coldness made her "think there was something indecent about ['The Shampoo'] I'd overlooked." Continuing on the same topic, Bishop writes, "Marianne also thought that 'Insomnia' was like a 'blues' song— which I wish it were, but I think she meant something rather different and not a bit complimentary! I'm afraid *she never can face the tender passion*" (6 September 1955, WU; my emphasis).

"Crystallized Emotion"

Breaking free of Moore's influence, Bishop is at last prepared to encounter the sensual world on her own terms. From this time forward, she will no longer adopt the perspective of the distant star, so aloof from "earth's human shore" (*CProse* 172) nor will she approach nature the way Baudelaire and his descendants approached the female body—as something to be mastered or crystallized in verse. In the words of George Lensing, "Bishop's poems would never possess the disinterested coolness of Moore's unique examples" (53). She swerves away from the tone of moral certainty or "purity of possession" so characteristic of Moore's generation of poets. The poems Bishop would come to write as she traveled southward toward warmer climes were less influenced by the modernist insistence upon precision at the expense of flexibility. Her early allegories, with their icy landscapes, seem to melt into longer narratives; her poetic line becomes as "flexible" and "attenuated" as the waterspouts she first saw in Florida and would memorialize years later in "Crusoe in England" (*CP* 163).

The emblematic "rose-rock" with which this chapter began captures the dual nature of Bishop's mature poetry, where questions become keener, more acute, just at the point when the poet's personal presence begins to blur in the minds of her readers. The rose that Bishop cultivates in her poetry becomes an emblem, then, of the poet's own blurred, softened, and blunted emotional presence in her poems. These complex, shifting emotions are crystallized during the process of poetic composition. As a student, Bishop had already begun to gravitate toward this hybrid aesthetic. Studying the "sustained emotional height" of Hopkins's poetry, Bishop began to formulate her own metaphor for the translation, or displacement, of pent-up emotion into art. In her college essay on Hopkins, subtitled "Notes on Timing in His Poetry," Bishop praises his way of capturing the changeability, the vacillation, in his own thoughts and feelings: Hopkins is able to "catch and preserve the movement of an idea—the point being to *crystallize* it early enough so that it still has movement" ("Notes on Timing"; my emphasis).

The moving, melting, or liquefying crystal becomes a favorite Bishop metaphor for the poetic structure she would pursue.[7] It was just this quality of liquidity that drew her to Hopkins's poetry, with its "fluid, detailed surface, made hesitant, lightened, slurred, weighed or feathered" as the poet chooses ("Notes on Timing"). Liquidity would play a principal role in her earliest attempts to describe the process of poetic composition.[8] For the *Vassar Review* she wrote in 1934, "A poem is begun with a certain volume of emotion, intellectualized or not according to the poet," a volume that is depleted and refilled during the activity of writing: "The whole process is a continual flowing fullness kept moving by its own weight, the combination of original emotion with the created, *crystallized emotion*,—described by Mr. T. S. Eliot as 'that intense and transitory relief which comes at the moment of completion and is the chief reward of creative work' " ("Notes on Timing").

Commenting on this passage, George Lensing discovers in it "a physics of emotional displacement by which subtraction and reduction lead to a new 'filling up' " (59). Generating a kind of hydroelectric energy, the poet's powerful emotions are pumped through the comparatively small conduit of the poem. The original, or mutable, emotion is continually being played off against the formalized, or crystallized, emotion. Each part of the poem simultaneously "arouses" new feelings and "serves as a check, a guide, and in a way a model, for each following part" ("Notes on Timing"). This judicious balancing of mobile and crystallized emotion becomes Bishop's new definition of poetry. The image of the melting crystal serves to suggest the flexible structure of her more mature work—a structure that reflects the poet's willingness to take greater artistic and emotional risks.

In the poems of her second collection, *A Cold Spring*, Bishop leaves behind Baudelaire's "rock-crystal throne" and immerses herself in life. In doing so, she faces the relativity of knowledge and the uncertainty of all personal attachments. Bishop's orphanhood and rootlessness had given her a heightened awareness of the elusiveness of true affection and the instability of our knowledge, which is always "historical, flowing, and flown" (*CP* 66). The poet could not be true to her understanding of life's vagaries and still embrace Moore's crystalline aesthetic with its strong strain of intransigence. She had to discover a poetic form capable of accommodating pent-up passion and suffering without brooking self-pity. The rhetorical structure she adopts in her second volume is heavily dependent on enjambment and anaphora, two poetic devices that help to channel the flow of her emotions without arresting their movement. Where Moore's concision projects a glacial control over her material, Bishop relies on deliberate hesitations and indecisiveness to establish what George Lensing calls "a companionable familiarity between her and her reader" through "the groping repetition of single words and phrases" (53).

Repetition, or anaphora, became Bishop's "natural medium" (Kalstone 97). In this, she seems to have taken to heart a lesson learned from one of the shortest and best-known lyrics of the twentieth century: "A rose is a rose is a rose." Like Stein before her, Bishop is interested in finding a form of writing that preserves the sense of vagueness and mutability she recognizes in the natural world.[9] Without naming the body in either graphic or conventionally erotic terms, she conveys her sensual experience through her tender reiteration of certain talismanic words—words and phrases that gain their power through insistence, through playful echoing and reversal ("rose-rock, rose-quartz, roses, roses, roses" ["Vague Poem," box 67, folder 23, VC]). Through reiteration, Bishop communicates the progressive excitement of trying to see a thing clearly, grasp the significance of an experience, or name the object of her affection.

Perhaps the pivotal moment in the development of Bishop's more conversational, and more accessible, style comes with the appearance of "At the Fishhouses." Significantly, the poem marks a break both imagistically and stylistically from what I have called the "crystal trilogy" of "The Unbeliever," "The Imaginary Iceberg," and "Paris, 7 A.M." The isolated psyche—portrayed in these early works as an iceberg, or an indivisible jewel that "cuts its facets from within" (*CP* 4)—is reconnected with the world in this later work. In her first collection of poems, far more rigid in their construction than later works, the poet's tears tend to congeal into crystals or floating fields of ice. But in "At the Fishhouses," the landscape is marked instead by fog and mist, as though memory and feeling had been given freer reign and allowed to permeate the atmosphere, lending a certain iridescence to the world. No longer a crystal palace or artificial paradise, art strikes the poet of "At the Fishhouses" as a means of conveying the "drift of bodies," minds, and hearts in a world given over to transience ("Anaphora," *CP* 52).

This remarkable poem's taut free verse depends on enjambment and anaphora to create momentum; each repeated word, each run-on line is loaded with barely disguised emotional energy, reminding us of the poem's description of the sea: "swelling slowly as if considering spilling over" (*CP* 64). Witness, for example, the repeated refrain of the poem's last half:

> I have seen it over and over, the same sea, the same,
> slightly, indifferently swinging above the stones,
> icily free above the stones,
> above the stones and then the world.

> (*CP* 65)

Like this icy sea, the poet's private loves and sorrows remain opaque. But they are always on the verge of becoming translucent, of swelling up and spilling over into speech. The conversational structure of "At the Fishhouses" creates a fluid ribbon of sound—sound that moves in "rhythmic waves" like a "slowly melting floe" (*CP* 141).

Bishop plays with our desire to know her deepest secrets by introducing the figure of the old fisherman who seems to stand at the center of the poem like some fisher of souls or Wordsworthian oracle. Tellingly, he is also a personal touchstone for the poet—a friend of her maternal grandfather, the patient mentor of her childhood. But just as she keeps herself relatively hidden from view, she leaves her fish gatherer weaving his nets, lost in the gloaming. Determinedly, she keeps his mythic significance at bay, held off by the calculated use of deflation. As the poem moves away from the old solitary man and toward the sea, we are teased with the sense that a revelation is at hand; after all, the waters that were introduced as opaque have become suddenly "cold dark deep and absolutely clear." But that does not make them accessible to us. Bishop's sea of knowledge is an "element bearable to no mortal" (*CP* 65), recalling T. S. Eliot's warning that humankind cannot bear too much reality.

Finally, Bishop musters her new repertoire of retarding devices (particularly the repetition and reversal of verbs like "drawn" and "derived") to indicate how far we inevitably are from the source of knowledge. Our understanding of life will always be derivative rather than primal. If we are honest with ourselves, then, we must acknowledge that the laws of nature must remain beyond our ken. Looking out at the sea, Bishop refuses to offer a romanticized portrait of this womb of life, and the truths it harbors, nor will she make its activities accord with any human standard of benevolence. The ocean mother of "At the Fishhouses" is coolly indifferent to our sufferings. Intimate knowledge of life can be gained only through bitter experience and offers no assurance of salvation. The "cold hard mouth" and "rocky breasts" this implacable world offers will not fulfill our lifelong "dream . . . of protection and rest" (*CP* 66, 73), and unconditional, maternal love.

The knowledge of life that the poet displays in "At the Fishhouses" is based on the experience of an unbeliever who casts a skeptical eye on the traditional articles of literary, as well as religious, faith. Because she has felt the joys and "cruel conundrums" of maternal love, the poet knows better than to believe in the uncomplicated vision of women and nature promoted by the romantic tradition. Given the biases of our Western literary legacy, Bishop had difficulty addressing herself to the traditional feminine topics of verse, especially the complexities of intimacy. In the face of modernism's dismissal of sentiment, and her era's social taboos, Bishop was forced to suppress her more overt sexual statements and rethink the place of the rose in her lexicon of love. Learning to combine the accuracy of Moore's jewel-like artifacts with Hopkins's fluid poetic line, Bishop found her own way of marrying the crystal to the rose. In the process, she salvaged her own woman's experience from the grip of tradition, returning female sentiment and desire to the realm of the complex and the unfixable.

Without the guidance of Bishop's unpolished manuscript material, we might never be able to see the role that her woman's experience played in the formation of her poetic. Certainly, the poet's unfinished drafts cannot be compared with a fully realized work like "At the Fishhouses." But the poet's abandoned drafts help us to trace the relationship between her vision of the female body and her disaffection from the Western literary tradition—a tradition that had long undervalued the potency of women and of nature. One such work is tentatively titled "The Waterfall," a fitting close to this story of the rose and the crystal, since Bishop's poetic of "crystallized emotion" is the very essence of this orphaned work. We will never know how she would have (or could have) readied this poem for publication, but we see in it a poet who approaches both the body of a poem and the body of a woman with the same tender regard. In it, Bishop channels her fear of intimacy and betrayal through the cool, long arteries of verse. While this is a characteristic feature of her greatest work, it becomes the very subject of this unfinished poem. In "The Waterfall," a woman, a cataract, and a poem form a single "water-body" filled with "a muffled cry of loss" (KWI 219):

> She comes down her dark stair
>   threading the stone
>   threading the air
> doomed in her distantness,
>   doomed again
>   in deafness;

colorless fact on fact
    colorless limb
    on limb, on rock
where a dark veining appears
    suitably delicate,
    but not her
whose cool long arteries
    conduct to crystal
    capillaries
to flesh, fabric, an unfounded
    water-body
    water-bounded.
Oh fear her fearful thoughts
    that falling follows,
    where you can not;
itself and selves again

a muffled cry of loss
    in cold mist

Was she self-willed, or wronged?
    The inhuman instant
    is prolonged;
the human traveller creeps
    clumsily down
    her broken steps.

(KW1 219)

4 "Abnormal Thirst"
Addiction and the
Poète Maudit

Late in life, Elizabeth Bishop admitted to her student Wesley Wehr that her poetry often gave readers the wrong impression about her personality. She was not, in fact, as coolly detached, as ironic, as sane as the confident surface of her poetry implied. "I am not a calm person at all, I can understand how they might think that I am," she confides, "but if they really knew me at all, they'd see that there are times . . . when I really start to wonder what holds me together—awful times" (Wehr 324–25). Still, she felt it was her responsibility at least to appear collected so that young people in particular would not get the idea that "*all* poets are erratic" (Wehr 325). And so when she returned to the United States from Brazil to teach, first in Seattle and then at Harvard, Bishop set about enlisting the complicity of her friends in fabricating an innocuous public persona. The fact that her colleagues at the University of Washington had no inkling about her true character seemed to astonish and amuse her. Writing to a Brazilian intimate, Lilli Correia de Araujo, Bishop describes the effect she produced at a New Year's Eve party given in her honor: "It's so funny—I go around so sedate and neat and *sober* (yes—absolutely), all in black last night, my new Esmerelda dress—everyone treats me with such respect and calls me Miss B—and every once in a while I feel a terrible laugh starting down in my chest—also a feeling of great pride because nobody knows.—And how different I am from what they think" (1 January 1966, qtd. in Millier, *Elizabeth Bishop* 375–76). At times the poet chafed under the limitations of her image as a "schoolmarm" (Wehr

325), but for the most part, she considered it a great advantage to be mistaken for a sober and sexless older woman.

This rigorously enforced dichotomy between her life and art forms a central theme in Bishop's career. Although she became well known for the powerful current of pathos that ran beneath the unperturbed surface of her work, Bishop did not consider her daily agitations and compulsions fit subjects for published verse. And yet, like so many of her notoriously tormented colleagues, she often seemed incapable of controlling her actions. Given her own impulsive behavior, the poet found herself drawn toward literary forebears who laid claim to a skewed, even maddened, approach to experience. As a young woman visiting Paris in the 1930s, for instance, she fell under the spell of the French decadents, symbolists, and surrealists who celebrated the harrowed body and soul and made an art of self-torture. Still, a strong sense of shame coupled with a distaste for morbid self-indulgence led her to adopt a different strategy toward what Keats called the "disagreeables" of life.

Certainly, nothing in Bishop's experience could have been more "disagreeable"—more downright destructive—than her lifelong addiction to alcohol. Ultimately, as with so many other ailments and inconveniences in her life, Bishop refused to romanticize her condition. Whatever pain her personal demons inflicted, she was determined to translate that injury into a poetic based on power and not disability. While self-confessed alcoholics like John Berryman made much of their unhinging drunkenness, Bishop clung to sanity, insisting that physical and psychological disintegration were not essential to her art. At first, she drank excessively to overcome her shyness in social situations and later simply to stave off a habitual feeling of loneliness and depression. The long fallow periods between creative bursts were caused in large measure by her troubles with liquor, since she could write only when sober. Unlike so many other of her contemporaries, she never claimed to find any inspiration in a reality that had been induced, altered, or heightened by alcohol. Nevertheless, her unpublished notebooks and unfinished poems testify to the power that her addictive personality had over her view of the world and the crucial role that it played in the evolution of her artistic principles.

This chapter begins by tracing the history of Bishop's "abnormal thirst" ("A Drunkard," box 64, folder 19, VC), which she believed to be rooted in a primal fear of emotional and metaphysical abandonment. After considering the arc of her disease over an entire lifetime, the discussion focuses its attention on the pivotal years between 1936 and 1947 when her drinking was most disruptive and her poetic most unsettled. Working notebooks from this period place Bishop's drinking habit within the context of a larger tradition readily available to both herself and her poetic generation, the tradition of the *poète maudit* whose art is born out of private depravity. Early published works like "The Man-Moth" (1936) introduce the figure of the *poète maudit* as an alter ego, a distanced version of the poet's unrevealed self, but more commonly, the idea of the morbid artist remains closeted, emerging only in unpublished poems and sketches from her Key West years, a particularly unstable time in the poet's life.

Essentially, the *poète maudit*, characterized by a furious appetite for death and willingness to suffer all manner of degradations in the service of art, served Bishop as a foil against which she could come to define her temperamental and stylistic difference as a poet. Bishop's struggle to avoid the blandishments of liquor coincided with her attempts to evade the godlike posture of the *poète maudit* and the modernist heirs to that tradition. Metaphor would not function for her as it functioned for the great lyric poets of the nineteenth century and their descendants. She would not use similes to dissolve, unify, and simplify all that remained incongruous, jarring, and unassimilable in lived experience. Bishop was determined that her writing would enact a sober view of the world—a world, as she saw it, populated by people and things whose ties to one another were tenuous at best and at worst nonexistent.

But as every poet knows, there is something inherent in poetic form that continually works to undermine sobriety: namely, the poem's addictive rhythm. Writer and reader alike are tempted to lose themselves in the narcotic lull, the incantation, of verse. Certainly, the Baudelairean *poète maudit*, in keeping with Edgar Allan Poe's principles of composition, readily exploits poetry's "intoxicating monotone" ("Parisian Dream," *Flowers of Evil* 53) to achieve his artificial paradise. Studying the poetics of Poe and his followers early in her career, Bishop began to eye poetry's habit-forming rhythms with deep suspicion.[1] In an aborted poem from the Florida years, "Edgar Allan Poe & the Jukebox," in her reaction to Robert Lowell's "The Drinker," and in a series of charged encounters with both Poe and Baudelaire (whose portrait hung over her writing desk), we can glimpse the workings of Bishop's mind as she begins to settle on a clear-eyed response to the intoxications of lyric music.[2]

While confronting the *poète maudit* tradition, Bishop eventually seized upon a new poetic style that she could call her own. To school friend Frani Blough Muser she explains that her new experiments in composition—including her most Poe-like stories, "The Sea and Its Shore" (1937) and "In Prison" (1938)—were inspired as soon as she abandoned Poe's metronomic verse and turned instead to his fiction: "I did work on our original 'operetta' for a couple of days, but lately I've been doing nothing much but re-read Poe, and evolve from Poe plus something of Sir Thomas Browne, etc., a new theory of the story, All My Own—its the 'proliferal' style, I believe—and you will shortly see some of the results" (2 May 1938, VC). Strictly Bishop's own coinage, the word *proliferal* seems to yoke the two defining qualities of Bishop's new poetic—its "peripheral" perspective and its eye for "proliferating" detail. At the same time, Bishop's neologism comments on her own "littoral" existence in Florida where she lived on the geographical and emotional fringes of society. Her new poetry casts a fugitive glance on the literal world around her and on the telltale litter that builds up in our lives day after day. This "proliferal" style makes itself felt not only in her prose pieces from the time, but in her Florida landscape poems as well, particularly in "The Bight" where she fondly but firmly distances herself from Baudelaire.

Bishop would never find a workable cure for her own alcoholism, springing as it did from what may have been irresolvable difficulties: her early dislocation from family and experience of emotional severance. But she does find in her study of Poe's fiction and in the very formlessness, dilapidation, and vagrancy of her life in Florida a vital model for de-composition. From the early 1940s forward, her poetics will reflect a real world of contingency, not an artificial paradise (that last refuge of the deserted child, the sentimental poet, and the drunkard). Bishop sacrifices the finality of formal closure for her own "proliferal" style, and produces a new kind of poem: a postcard from the edge, full of unforeseen syncopation and a healthy dose of off-beat humor.

The Drinker

This chapter takes its title, "Abnormal Thirst," from "A Drunkard," a poem Bishop began as early as 1960, worked on as late as 1972, but left unfinished at the time of her death. Centering on one of Bishop's earliest memories of abandonment, this late work tries to describe the psychogenesis of the poet's alcoholism. As the poem unfolds, we enter the imagination of a three-year-old child trapped in her crib during the Salem fire of June 1914. Though she is in no physical danger herself, the light from the fire across the bay in Marblehead, Massachusetts, is frightening, bathing the enameled crib, the sky, the sea, and the distant shape of her mother in a lurid red. The child's throat feels parched from the heat. That night she cries in vain for her mother, who is busy giving coffee to the homeless people arriving on the beach by boats. She will awaken the following morning with an "abnormal thirst" for maternal solace, a yearning for reassurance, a need to be told that loss and severance is only temporary and remediable (box 64, folder 19, VC).

Walking the beach with her mother the morning after the fire, the three-year-old Elizabeth stops to pick up a woman's black cotton stocking from among the other remnants of furniture and clothing washed ashore by the tide. When her mother scolds her, *"Put that down!"* the child takes this reprimand as a sign of a more general rejection: the "woman's black cotton stocking," evoking perhaps a world of secret delights and intimacy, must be put down or suppressed; the child's curiosity about herself in relation to that world is summarily dismissed. The only words exchanged in the poem are sharp ones, and the distance between the child in her crib and the mother "out on the lawn" speaks to the emptiness Bishop will find at the center of her life from that moment onward. The poem's speaker takes comfort in the bottle because she could find none in *amor matris*. In the end, the poet advises us to remain skeptical about the authenticity of this tale, reminding us that it was written "under the influence," but this only reinforces the poem's concern with originative moments whose influence cannot be evaded.

Four years before her death in 1979, Bishop confided to Anny Baumann that she considered alcoholism to be her "saddest problem" (5 December 1975, VC). Clearly, she had inherited a susceptibility to hard liquor as she had to asthma, since her father, grandfather, and three uncles all were forced to give up drinking. That her asthma and her alcoholism were somehow connected in her own imagination is apparent from a lengthy letter to Baumann written during the forties. While assuring her doctor that she was trying to "stay on the wagon," Bishop makes an offhand remark: "My record is still perfect—do you suppose my system is wheezing away for alcohol? Horrors" (letter to Baumann, Stonington, Maine, 5 August 1948, VC). Both genetic legacies were aligned in her mind with the "fierce odor" of family mortality, compulsion, and shame and a heightened fear of closeness, on the one hand, and desertion, on the other. While the poet's wheezing lungs registered her efforts to expel intrusive and intolerant relatives, Bishop's parched throat expressed an unsatisfied desire for contact or emotional, physical, and metaphysical connection.

From her days at Vassar (where she drank bad wine out of tea cups with her smart set of literary friends) to the end of her life, with only a brief respite in Brazil, Bishop drank heavily and destructively. Her drinking took its toll on her body, on her productivity as a poet, and on her relationships with those she loved. Believing that sobriety required only an exertion of will, Bishop never gave herself the chance to indulge in self-pity long enough to mourn her losses and sort out the reasons for her drinking. Instead, she chided herself for what she considered to be failures of nerve and lapses in discipline. Throughout her life, Bishop brought enormous pressure to bear on herself in order to prevent embarrassment—and yet her drinking bouts, like her asthmatic attacks, signaled the failure of that attempt at insulation and repression.

By the time she was thirty, Bishop had begun to have recurring blackouts. She started making long-distance telephone calls in the middle of the night to friends and casual acquaintances alike who listened as the poet confessed things that could only have been said under the cover of drunkenness. The telephone wire may have seemed her only means of connection during the years she spent in Florida leading an untethered existence. Until her arrival at Santos in 1951, when she was nearly forty-one, Bishop led a life essentially without moorings: there had been the year in New York after graduation from college in 1934; almost three years traveling in Europe and North Africa, then nearly a decade of living in Key West, Florida, interrupted by an extended stay in Mexico and by summers spent in Maine, North Carolina, and the writer's colony at Yaddo. She spent the disastrous summer of 1949 at Yaddo, visiting the colony again in the autumn and winter of the following year. Across the cover of her diary for 1950 Bishop wrote "just about my worst year so far" (box 77, folder 4, VC). Though these years of waywardness and improvisation were crucial, providing the shifting ground for her emerging poetic style, they were marked by a series of failed romantic relationships that exaggerated the poet's sense of loneliness and self-doubt and threw her into periods of heavy drinking.

In the winter of 1949, Bishop was overwhelmed by serious depression. She was facing a move to unfamiliar Washington, D.C., in the fall to take up her duties as consultant in poetry to the Library of Congress, where she would be called upon to make public appearances and give readings; at the same time, she was anxious about spending that August at Yaddo, where the atmosphere of creative competition would remind her of all she dreaded about the New York literary scene. Faced with these twin terrors, she seems to have fallen apart, and Pauline Hemingway's sister, Virginia Pfeiffer, drove Bishop to Blythewood, an expensive psychiatric hospital and rest home. There she stayed for the next two months, getting constant care and writing nothing. Blythewood did her very little good. She arrived at Yaddo on 23 July and almost immediately fell into a bout of drinking brought on by trouble in love and her own overpowering shyness and insecurity in the company of the other artists at the colony.

The poet's chief worry was that Dr. Baumann and her closest

friends at the time, including Margaret Miller, Marjorie Stevens, and Cal Lowell, would all "come to dislike her" and "give her up" (letter to Loren MacIver, 31 July 1949, VC). To her dear friend Loren MacIver she wrote, "The only thing to do now is to stay on the wagon and try not to worry—but if the first is hard the second is impossible. I have never felt so nervous and like a fish out of water—and dizzy all the time—although I have had nothing to drink since last Wednesday and won't either" (31 July 1949, VC). In this same letter, she goes on to admit that her "heart [had been] smashed to bits" by unnamed romantic difficulties, and she "wanted to die quite quickly." She closes by saying, "I wildly overestimated my own strength, I guess. . . . I don't want to be this kind of person at all but I'm afraid I'm really disintegrating just like Hart Crane only without his gifts to make it all plausible." When she returned to Yaddo in the fall of 1950, she found herself identifying with a stray cat that the writers all fed on the sly: "[The cat's] caught on to the fact that at Yaddo one must PRODUCE—and brings these poor wretched mice up to the door to show me or the unappreciative cooks" (1950 diary, 14 November, VC). Obviously unsure of her own meager output among such prolific producers, trying to embrace for the first (and last) time the unaccustomed and antipathetic role of self-promoting poet, and ashamed of her uncontrolled drinking, Bishop suffered from what she called the "embarrassment that always comes from some falsity—the situation, the manners, or a work of art" (1950 diary, 23 July, VC).

Wintering at Yaddo in 1950, Bishop became surprisingly productive, writing poems that took up, albeit indirectly, her personal problems with asthma ("O Breath"), sexuality ("Insomnia"), and alcohol ("The Prodigal"). But despite the gratifying intensity of this first writing "binge" at the colony, Bishop's many lapses into drunkenness led her to question whether or not to go on living and, at least on one occasion, brought her close to death. She took pains during the 1940s to find a succession of caring intimates who would bring stability to her life—friends that included Marjorie Stevens, with whom she lived for some time in Key West, and her doctor, Anny Baumann, who time after time saved the poet from the threat of total immersion.

On 10 November 1951, Bishop left the United States for an ambitious South American journey that turned into a long expatriation. Bishop's first years in Brazil came as a welcome respite from embarrassment and loneliness. There she fell in love with the dynamic Lota de Macedo Soares, an intellectually gifted and pragmatic woman who approached the problem of Bishop's alcoholism with sensitivity and uncommon strength. In July 1953, Bishop set down on paper in a letter to Robert Lowell the sense of release she felt in her new home in Petrópolis, so far removed from North American literary circles:

I was always too shy to have much "intercommunication" in New York, anyway, and I was miserably lonely there most of the time—here I am extremely happy, for the first time in my life. I live in a spectacularly beautiful place; we have between us about 3,000 books now; I know, through Lota, most of the Brazilian "intellectuals" already and I find the people frank,—startlingly so, until you get used to Portuguese vocabularies—extremely affectionate—an atmosphere that I just lap up—no I guess I mean loll in. . . . I arrived to visit Lota just at the point where she really wanted someone to stay with her in the new house she was building. We'd known each other well in New York but I hadn't seen her for five or six years—picture enclosed—I certainly didn't want to wander around the world in a drunken daze for the rest of my life—so it's all fine & dandy. (28 July 1953, VC)

Under Lota's watchful eye, Bishop's drinking finally began to subside, tapering off to one or two evenings a month. In the Rio apartment and the Petrópolis home she shared with Lota, the poet was released from the weight of addiction—the recurring cycles of intoxication and guilty recovery—but at the same time she came to feel the heavy burden of staying sober. The first years in Brazil were productive ones for Bishop, justifying her initial feeling on arrival that she "must have died and gone to heaven without deserving to" (letter to Baumann, 16 September 1952, VC). Still, the revealing afterthought—"without deserving to"—puts a damper on all the happiness that precedes it. Even at the height of her early enthusiasm for this new world, Bishop surrendered to puritanical guilt over her failings and concern about whether she was worthy of salvation.

From her late twenties well into her sixties, Bishop played the naughty child for a series of maternal, monitory figures who could be relied upon to dole out the proper doses of chastisement and consolation, chief among them Lota and Dr. Baumann. Bishop's correspondence makes it clear that she continued to think of herself in the role of wayward daughter even when she was old enough to have grandchildren of her own. In her late fifties, Bishop still took a certain degree of pleasure in aggravating figures of authority, reporting rather proudly in a letter to a close friend that she had given Dr. Baumann (now "Anny") reason to complain about her lack of "self-discipline" and "practicality" (letter to Dorothee Bowie, 3 January 1968, VC).

During Bishop's most prolific years as a writer, Lota took on the policing role, forcing Antibuse down her throat to stop her from drinking. But this regimen was halted in the final years of their relationship when it became Lota's turn to disintegrate both emotionally and physically, her nerves frayed by the pressure of transforming an urban landfill in Rio into a public park. When Lota's obsession with the park became too much for her, Bishop escaped from the strain by taking a temporary teaching job at the University of Washington in Seattle where she found herself freed from supervision for the first time in years. On 1 September 1966, Bishop wrote a lengthy letter to Dr. Baumann (VC) revealing her doubts about leaving Lota alone for even a short period, her guilt over the tension that her drinking had introduced into the relationship, and her belief that the cure for alcoholism would necessarily take the form of a punishment:

While I was in Seattle there appeared an article about antibuse, etc. in the Sunday Supplement . . . well, the gist of it was that antibuse is regarded as a "punishment" remedy (heaven knows why—since anything of the sort would seem to be)—but the important point was it said that it produces "despondency" in the patient . . . I thought it was worth finding out about. You see, poor dear L has such an obsession about my drinking (which is of course entirely my fault and which I can't forgive myself for) that during some stretches she has even been almost physically forcing me . . . to take one of the pills, a whole one, every day. I was already pretty "despondent"— if this piece of journalism is true, no wonder I was getting more so. I ran out of antibuse about 6 weeks before I left for Seattle . . . and I went without—and I had no trouble at all. As I think I told you—only three people there, that I know of, knew anything about my problems and they can all testify to this, if necessary. In fact I did not miss a single class because of drinking—and that's better than anyone can say of any of the other poets who have had that job before me! [Bishop's immediate predecessor in the position had been Theodore Roethke.]

Describing the procedure in a letter to Baumann, Bishop writes as though she were an adolescent squirming at having to be spoon-fed like an infant; she addresses her complaints about Lota's "bossiness" and "bullying," ironically enough, to Dr. Baumann, Lota's North American counterpart: "But I really do not LIE—I think the only times I lie about drinking are when I have already started.— She wouldn't believe I really had "flu" etc. either. . . . She doesn't seem to realize that I have perhaps grown up a lot (!—about time) in the past 15 years, and can really manage pretty well on my own, and stay sober about 98 percent of the time—I know I can, because I DID (1 September 1966, VC).

Bishop's confidential letters to Anny Baumann confirm a central truth that David Kalstone intuited from Bishop's response to Robert Lowell's poem, "The Drinker": Bishop had internalized the alcoholic's deep need for punishment. Kalstone points out that Bishop "obviously understood the vicarious pleasure one might take" in Lowell's introduction of the mounted policemen at the end of his poem, a "final glimpse of fanciful guilt and punishment" (Kalstone 210). Bishop explains the power of the poem's closing image with her customary wryness: "The cops at the end are beautiful, of course, with the sense of release that only the poem, or another fifth of Bourbon, could produce" (letter to Robert Lowell, 27 July 1960, HL).

When Lota's suicide in 1967 made the thought of remaining permanently in Brazil impossible, Bishop returned to the rootless, emotionally unanchored existence of earlier years, and she began to drink heavily once again. In her final decade, Bishop's close friends no longer policed her habit. They acquiesced to it instead. While she was alive, no one outside Bishop's small circle was to know the truth: she was a woman who drank almost every day, injuring herself and those who loved her.

The *Poète Maudit*

Bishop's battle with alcoholism had no small influence on the shape her poetic would eventually take. As we have seen, Bishop's struggle to tame her body's allergic swellings became aligned in her own imagination with her effort to introduce leanness and economy into poetry. In a similar fashion, she associated her struggle to quit drinking with her fight to rid poetry of various intellectual crutches that she identified primarily with the *poète maudit* tradition. At first, drinking offered Bishop a seductive and habit-forming sense of security and well-being. Gradually, she began to equate the attractiveness of alcohol with the allure of poetry that aimed for transcendence and promised to gratify her primal longing for a world of sublimity and sanctity. As she grew contemptuous of the one, she grew suspicious of the other.

For Bishop, inebriation seemed to lighten harsh realities, particularly the prospect of a transient life and the thought of a universe similarly devoid of purpose or volition. Under alcohol's influence, the world appeared whole and intelligible. However, as a heavily crossed-out entry from Bishop's Key West notebook attests, the drug's hallmark was its insincerity:

> The Need for Flattery
> Alcohol the flatterer
> Mounts by the ear and whispers to the Brain
> "That you can be The Perfect Interpreter"
>
> (KWi 95)

"Alcohol the flatterer" seemed to gratify some of the human demands once satisfied primarily by religion—and, from the nineteenth century forward, by lyric poetry. As Bishop was well aware, both Poe and his disciple Baudelaire underscored the connection between poetic vision and delirium, calling for a poetry of passion, "which is the drunkenness of the heart" (qtd. in Raymond 9). For the *poète maudit*, drunk with interpretive powers, the natural world became a "forest of symbols"—a forest of magical, and decipherable, correspondences (qtd. in Raymond 10).

Bishop would contemplate the French symbolist theory of "correspondences" with increasing distrust as she set about establishing her own approach toward art and nature. Ultimately, she could never bring herself to accept an aesthetic that despised the observable world and celebrated the triumph of the expanded mind over incoherent nature. Such an aesthetic, like alcohol, was simply too flattering to an artist's ego for Bishop's taste. Incapable of acknowledging the world as it was (an "awful but cheerful" mess), the "delirious writer" sought in poetry and in liquor the feeling of coherence was so elusive in life. Offering his peculiar experience as a window into universal truth, the Baudelairean poet hoped to impose his own pattern of thought on other minds. Under the influence of liquor and lyric sublimity, he placed himself too firmly at the center and circumference of his vision, accepting his own perspective as an infallible measure of what could and could not be seen.

Bishop's own potential for delirium and self-deception would be a continuing source of anxiety throughout her life. Well into her fifties and reeling from the shock of being told that she would have to leave Lota because her presence was harmful to Lota's mental health, Bishop sat in her hotel room and read, looking to books for comfort as she had always done. Her reading notes display her preoccupation at the time with her own uncontrolled drinking and how she might appear to others. In this frame of mind, she copies out a pertinent passage from Auden, "DO NOT FORGET this FIRST QUOTE . . . *MOST IMPORTANT OF ALL*: 'The drunk is unlovely to look at, intolerable to listen to, [and] his self-pity is contemptible. Nevertheless, as not merely a worldly failure, but also a [willful] failure, he is a disturbing image for the sober [citizen]. His refusal to accept the realities of this world, babyish as it may be, compels us to take another look at this world and reflect upon our motives for accepting it' " (qtd. in notes, 6 January 1967, HL). Following Auden's advice, Bishop tended to regard her own drunken behavior from a stoical distance, having the "tact and decency" to look the other way when her suffering self was acting shamefully. But as a young writer, she seems to have felt more vulnerable before the "disturbing image" of the drunken poet, and this frailty comes across in "The Man-Moth" (first published in

1936). The work may be read as a seriocomic homage to the "delirious poet" and to the cruel condition that haunts art of the *poète maudit*. In refusing to accept the realities of this world, the poem's protagonist is forced to pit his "lofty will" against intransigent nature in a futile attempt at transcendence.

"The Man-Moth"

When a misprint in the *New York Times* (*manmoth* for *mammoth*) caught her eye, Bishop was intrigued by the pictogram it suggested—a man-moth, a hybrid monster, stranded between identities, perhaps poised on the verge of extinction like the Pleistocene mammoth, yet representative somehow of the spirit at work in the great metropolis itself, a romantic spirit immense in its dreams and its appetites. The man-moth evinces "the finest spiritual oversensibility," a phrase that Bishop would later use to describe Poe's monomaniacal narrators ("True Confessions," box 55, folder 5, VC). Excessively conscious of his mixed essence, this insect man is drawn involuntarily in opposite directions. From time to time, he is driven by his desire to break the law of gravity and soar heavenward, enacting Poe's famous image of man's thirst for transcendence: "the desire of the moth for the star" (*Essays and Reviews* 77). But no sooner does he fail in this attempt than he plummets to earth, retreating to the cocoon of the subway, where he follows a path of brute impulse. Conceiving a strong aversion for the body to which he nevertheless is almost lovingly attached, the man-moth feels this cruel ambivalence as surely as any Baudelairean protagonist and finally surrenders to his involuntary drives with ecstatic horror.

But for all his outsize longings, Bishop's man-moth is a mixture of Poe and Pierrot, Baudelaire and Emmet Kelly, Hart Crane and Buster Keaton. An existential clown with possible links to Beckett, the man-moth is ruled by what psychologists might call repetition-compulsion. He is drawn toward two equally unpromising avenues of escape from the tedium of existence: transcendence and death. Frustrated in his quest for sublimity, he lives each day underground, riding the subway, flirting with self-pity and suicide. Thus, while the man-moth's climb rehearses the *poète maudit*'s quest for divine

joy and union, his fall into subterranean depths and endless recur-
rence (repeating dreams), nostalgia (traveling backwards), and self-
destruction (the lure of the dangerous, electrified "third rail") sug-
gests the ineluctable pull of the flesh:

> Each night he must
> be carried through artificial tunnels and dream recurrent
>   dreams,
> Just as the ties recur beneath his train, these underlie
> his rushing brain. He does not dare look out the window,
> for the third rail, the unbroken draught of poison,
> runs there beside him. He regards it as a disease
> he has inherited the susceptibility to. He has to keep
> his hands in his pockets, as others must wear mufflers.
>
> (*CP* 15)

For good reason, Bishop's *poète maudit* "has to keep his hands in
his pockets." He has "inherited a susceptibility to" addiction, an
overwhelming desire to touch the "third rail" and to imbibe its
"unbroken draught of poison."

Bishop's fascination with the "third rail" stems from a set of
private associations the poet refuses to develop within the poem.
These associations are preserved, instead, in her working notebooks,
where a direct relationship is forged between the fatal third rail and
the dangers of alcoholism. In the journal she kept following her
graduation from Vassar, Bishop plays with certain ideas that would
eventually find their way into "The Man-Moth," including the ob-
servation that "the third rail is almost worth some sort of prose
poem. Running along silently, as insincere as poison" ("Recorded
Observations," 1934–37: 6, VC). As we have already seen, she would
come to think of alcohol as a poison with "flattering" effects, thus
establishing a connection between ingratiating liquor and the "in-
sincere" third rail that runs beside the subway track like an "unbro-
ken draught of poison" (*CP* 15). Alternating between a tone of
elevation and deflation (to match the ascending and descending
fortunes of her protagonist), Bishop creates in her hyphenated
creature a veiled portrait of the artist as addict.

Underscoring this theme of consumption and addiction is the
man-moth's resemblance to the Baudelairean vampire, imbiber of

forbidden fluids. Each night the man-moth enters the coffined world of the subway car and calls this place "his home" (*CP* 14). On those rare occasions when he emerges from his subterranean home in quest of the moon, he "begins to scale the faces of the buildings . . . his shadow dragging like a photographer's cloth behind him" (*CP* 14). Like the vampire, the man-moth seeks to penetrate the physical boundaries of his universe and be born into a new existence, one that escapes the laws of mortality and gravity that weigh down the natural man. Thinking of the moon "as a small hole at the top of the sky," his aim is to "push his small head through that round clean opening" (*CP* 14). But instead of escaping those laws, he is trapped in an existence ruled by bodily drives and marked by reiteration (he "must be carried through artificial tunnels and dream recurrent dreams").

Along with the inference of sexual deviance or unnaturalness that vampirism inevitably suggests, Bishop's allusions to the undead reinforce the impression that she is grappling in this poem with the compulsive artist, a slave to the body's mechanisms and to the machinery of art. This enslavement becomes more evident in the poem as the man-moth returns to his subterranean world. There, "the pale subways of cement he calls home" become an extension of the protagonist's own body. Bishop likens the subway train to the man-moth's own "rushing brain" (*CP* 15). And the recurring ties beneath the subway train are said to underlie his brain as well. These ties resemble the cerebral nerve cells, each tie or cell stimulated by electricity to activate the next cell, which then produces an electrical wave of its own as the nerve impulse travels its course. Moreover, the "rushing brain" that Bishop describes in "The Man-Moth" is one whose nerve cells are firing in response to a single stimulus, the "juice" from the electrified third rail. The man-moth's nervous system is dependent on that draught of poison and trapped in a cycle of consumption.

Bishop stresses the connection between urban machinery and the mechanisms of the human body in the same notebook in which she sketches "The Man-Moth's" early features.[3] Within a few pages of her remark about the "third rail" and its metaphoric possibilities, Bishop's notebook shows that she had been reading Hart Crane's

"Essay on Modern Poetry" with sympathy. Beneath her transcription of its title she adds in parenthesis, "What I tried to say at college—rather less." She carefully transcribes the following passage from Crane's essay: "I mean to say that mere romantic speculation on the power and beauty of machinery keeps it at a continual remove; it cannot act creatively in our lives until, like the unconscious nervous responses of our bodies, its connotations emanate from within—forming a spontaneous terminology of poetic reference" (qtd. in "Recorded Observations," 1934–37: 12, VC). More than simply providing the poet with a lexicon of poetic reference, the city's underground railway system offers Bishop an actual analogy for the "unconscious nervous responses of our bodies" in a state of drug dependency.

By the poem's close, Bishop has done more than simply stress the similarities between the city's machinery and the man-moth's autonomic system, however. The onrushing subway train also is meant to represent the poem itself, which is, to borrow a phrase from William Carlos Williams, a "machine made of words" (*Collected Poems* 2: 54). The poem's message travels across recurring verbal ties—repeated phrases, aural cues, enjambments, and similes ("train"/"brain," "tie"/"underlie"). But, according to Poe, such musical repetitions inevitably frustrate the poet and reader alike. The poem machine awakens but never allays what Poe calls our "thirst" for true ties or connections in the universe because a poem's harmony is artificial and can never entirely or permanently take the place of the cosmic harmony for which we yearn. As readers, we weep at our inability to grasp the joys briefly glimpsed through the poem. Aroused but unsatisfied, we return again and again to drink from Poe's "sacred fount" of verse (*Essays and Reviews* 77).

Bishop is especially disturbed by Poe's assumption that verse must produce tears to be effective. In the final moments of "The Man-Moth," she raises the question of whether poetic pathos can be trusted. Bishop appears to recoil from the cycle of yearning, defeat, and self-pity built into Poe's rationale of verse, where the poem endlessly generates and feeds upon its own melancholia. Such a cycle can be broken, she seems to imply, only if the artist learns the lesson of the man-moth, who is offered the chance to turn his back on futile introspection, and part once and for all with the hoarded tear that is "his only possession, like a bee sting" (*CP* 15). The poem ends with a ritual of divestiture, a potential relinquishing of bee stings and bitter secrets, and a sluicing away of the body's poisons. Once it is handed over to the safekeeping of others, the proffered tear is no longer a corrupting draught. Instead, it tastes "cool as underground springs and pure enough to drink" (*CP* 15).

Although Bishop's alcoholism, the source of her pain, was meant to remain a secret to her readers, we can still sense in the poem's closing image the poet's private struggle to translate bitter waters into healing—albeit underground—springs. Bishop would eventually create a style of poetry that questioned the naturalness of poetic tears, while challenging the compulsory and compulsive properties of poetic form. When she composed "The Man-Moth" just two years out of college, Bishop was just beginning to forge her own distinctive poetic structure—one that actively worked against predictable rhythms and facile emotions. In subsequent years, she would develop a style "all [her] own"—a style far more comfortable with detours and derailments—and she would do so by turning to an unexpected source, the compositional theories and fiction of Poe.

"Edgar Allan Poe & the Jukebox"

Key West would be the scene of some of Bishop's most difficult battles with alcohol, but it would also be the crucible out of which a new poetic would emerge. When Bishop chose to live an outdoors existence à la Hemingway in the rough and tumble world of the Florida Keys, she shed many of the inhibitions associated with ladylike behavior, including the prescription against hard drinking. Once settled in this outpost, she began to feel even more acutely her disconnection from the mainstream and her marginality as a woman artist. With greater personal freedom came a greater urgency to rethink the entire question of living on the frontier. However truant themselves from the mores of refined society, Bishop's predecessors in Florida (from Wallace Stevens to Hemingway) were, after all, men—and, as men, they rarely looked at life completely from the sidelines. It was with this understanding that Bishop decided to make a virtue of her peripheral status as a single woman and a professional fugitive. If others were to occupy the center and dictate what was "universally" true, she would cast a fugitive glance at their authorized accounts, including the privileged position that drunkenness held in their aesthetic of exile.

Left "high and dry" in a "Key of Bones," the poet, already in her thirties, contemplated the unhappy prospect of a wasted, directionless existence where days slip by in endless succession, "accretions to no purpose" (*CP* 78). Like her preoccupied sandpiper, Bishop was "looking for something, something, something" (*CP* 131) at this point in her life—looking for a principle of poetic order capable of embodying the values of vagrancy, while at the same time escaping the tedium and sense of purposeless that may come to haunt the steps of the "solitary walker." With no organizing principle in sight, she found herself drawn into the *poète maudit*'s life of extremity. During the crucial decade she passed primarily in Florida, Bishop fought two temptations simultaneously, a fact confirmed by her private notebooks. On the one hand, she longed to lose herself in drinking, and, on the other, she felt the narcotic pull of poetry itself, the lure of incantatory verse. To lose oneself in one was to succumb to the other, and she could afford to give in to neither artificial refuge.

Throughout her private working papers, Bishop struggled to come to terms with her fall into alcoholic degradation. This struggle is most apparent in her working and reworking of "Edgar Allan Poe & the Jukebox," a poem she never could complete to her satisfaction. An unfinished short story disingenuously titled "True Confessions" provides a telling gloss on this enigmatic experiment. Both works describe Bishop's downward spiral into alcohol abuse largely as a confrontation with Poe, the man, the poet, and the theorist. As artifacts of her imagination, the stillborn poem and the unfinished story provide a valuable focus for the double lens of my interest in physical addiction, on the one hand, and in poetic form, on the other.

Bishop's manuscript writings ponder the intense human appetite for humiliation. Poe called this urge for self-abasement the "Imp of the Perverse" that lives in each of us, in the tedium of our daily existence, and in the telltale heartbeat of our poetry (*Collected Works* 3: 1221–22). Although the lives of Dylan Thomas and Hart Crane interested her to a certain degree, it was Poe's disintegration that seemed to have been on her mind the longest. Sometime during her last year in college, she slipped within the covers of her notebook a newspaper clipping that features Poe's mysterious final days, the delirious visits to friends, the last stupor before death. Poe figures prominently in "True Confessions" (ca. 1940), where Bishop offers a surrealistic account of her journey southward to Florida and the accompanying descent into alcoholism. Anticipating the revelations of "A Drunkard," these "confessions" link Bishop's drinking with early displacement, but the story acknowledges that dwelling in the past can itself become a compulsion, or, as Bishop cautions herself in the pages of her Key West notebook, "The mother-beaters-'society' is like drinking—it's too hard to stop at any particular point" (KW1 110).

Lying behind "True Confessions" is Bishop's fascination with the narrators of Poe's short fiction whose madness is brought on by their "monomaniacal grasping after the infinite." Bishop's story opens *in medias res* with a protagonist who has already succumbed to obsession and has landed in a "strange sort of institution"—an asylum for people who are "in the same fix": "It was extremely mournful . . . there were plenty of graves there, and a cat with one white eye. It was not a story by Poe. The people in the graves had not been people of the finest spiritual oversensibility. They had been owners of the stock exchange. They had had railroads and wheat and many heavy burdens. They lay heaped under pine needles as under the weight of their sins and the wind soughed [coughed] half-heartedly, not really giving a damn one way or the other. On the grave of the chief of the clan stood a beer can" (1, box 55, folder 5, VC).

From here, the narrator gives us an off-kilter version of Bishop's geographical drift southwards: "I dropped down to another place, dropped, dropped, as far as I could go . . . lowered down [like a spider on a thread] through the lowest clouds I ever saw through the most fantastic waters" ("True Confessions" 2, box 55, folder 5, VC). As she recalls it, she immersed herself the "careless, corrupt state" of Florida (*CP* 33) and in its combustible waters. In a world of inversion and immersion, she lived, "delighted, believe me, for some time and constantly taking photographs of banana trees in blossom—upside down like myself" ("True Confessions" 2).

According to "True Confessions," Bishop had lowered herself into the "Rum Latitudes" (2, box 55, folder 5, VC). From there, she descended still further into the subterranean, lantern-lit cabarets and honky-tonks of Key West: "This Down There was almost too bright. The juke box songs were fearful beyond belief. You made me love you didn't want to do it I didn't want to do it" ("True Confessions" 2). In her notebooks from that time, she describes "the ungoverned flow" of alcohol and the touch of "(groping) hands" that mark a night's casual encounter (KW1 198): "Glowing in the dark—the awful music falls so easily in the dark and the love that falls as easily as the hands fall under the table, everything descending (descent of love from the eye = our idea of it, anyway), everything descends, falls, falls, the drinks down the throat, one down beat. . . . .What are you going to do about it?" (KW1 194). Beneath this prose poem, she leaves a cryptic gloss: "In my resentment I fight / with love all night / in a dream that I arranged myself . . . we fall and find degradation."

These words form the overture for "Edgar Allan Poe & the Jukebox." In the notebook pages that follow she struggles through draft after draft before abandoning this poetic project entirely. In the final version of the work, its opening lines appear without any of the parenthetical second thoughts or alternative phrasings that usually indicate unfinished work:

> The juke-box turns; blue as gas,
> blue as the pupil of a blind man's eye;
> the music falls easily through the darkened room.—
> *Starlight, La Conga,* all the dance-halls
> in the block of honky-tonks,—
> cavities in our waning moon
> strung with bottles and blue lights
> and silvered coconuts and conchs.
>
> As easily as the music falls,
> the nickels fall into the slots,
> the drinks like lonely water-falls

in night descend the separate throats,
and the hands fall on one another
darker darkness under
tables, clothes & all—descends,
descends, falls,—much as we envision
the helpless earthward fall of love
descending from the head and eye
down to the hands, and heart, and down.
The music pretends to laugh and weep
while it descends to drink and murder [?].
The turning box can keep the measure
strict, always, and the down-beat.

(KWI 239)

The accent is on falling—the record that falls easily, automatically, onto the waiting turntable, the already drunken patron who falls down the stairs and through the doors into the darkened cave of the dance hall and once inside falls victim to the bottle or the powerful pull of gravity on the flesh.

In this darkened room, we face the fact that our bodies are machines—machines that can be calculated to exact pleasure from the same set of stimuli over and over again, ad nauseam. The predictable fall of a record onto the turntable of the motorized jukebox sets Bishop to thinking about the predictable effect that liquor will have on the human nervous system. After several glasses of whiskey, the body will produce tears—tears that come too easily, self-pity that is mechanical, embarrassing: the drunkard only "pretends to laugh and weep." Could this pretense, this insincerity, also infect a poem through its very form? Bishop begins to wonder what type of influence a poem can have on its reader. If a poem is merely a music box, the poet need only set the works in motion and simply wait for the lachrymose response.

The moral and aesthetic dilemmas that Bishop confronts in this meditation are clearly dependent on her reading of Poe. In the final lines of "Edgar Allan Poe & the Jukebox," Bishop picks up on the figure of addiction latent in Poe's definition of rationalized poetry, which relies so heavily on the notion of predictability, or repetition-compulsion:

Poe said that poetry was *exact*.
But pleasures are mechanical

And know beforehand what they want
And know exactly what they want.
& they obtain that single effect
That can be calculated like alcohol
or like the response to the nickels.
—just how long does the music turn?
like poetry, is all your horror
half as exact as horror here?

(KW1 239)

"Edgar Allan Poe & the Jukebox," with its suspicious view of the pathos so easily generated by poetry, may go a long way to explain Bishop's characteristically skeptical deployment of the tear in well-known works like "The Weed," "The Man-Moth," and "Sestina." In her published writing, she evokes the traditional emblem of compassion only to question its exploitation within the poem. That Bishop was deeply concerned about the potential falsity of poetic tears is evident as well in her dairy entries. She took notes, for instance, on the mechanics of crying and grew fascinated with Grave's disease in which the series of kinetic reactions involved in producing tears from any psychological stimulus breaks down: "The flood-gates of tears are open much of the time . . . [but] both tears and pain [are] facile" and do not find their source any longer in natural emotion ("Miscellaneous Notes, Vassar College" 12, box 70, folder 3, VC). And later, in the barrooms of Key West, she would again be struck by the difference between natural and artificial tears. In a dream, for instance, she and a companion are drawn by Baudelairean marimba music into a cabaret afloat in a sea of liquor:

But when we get there it is silent.
Around us the impettalled fish
swim seriously;
it is not a cabaret at all.
It is an endless wax-works, dimly lit,
where rows of lonely figures sit
whose fresher tears naturally cannot fall

(KW2 33)

Entering the world of the *poète maudit*, expecting an atmosphere of lively invention and exotic correspondences, she finds instead a climate of stale tears and a moribund poetic.

Poe, we remember, compared the poem's undercurrent of rhythm with the sound of water dropping on a rock. Ultimately, in Bishop's "Edgar Allan Poe & the Jukebox," poetry's moving downbeat becomes a kind of aural torture, signaling the dread duration that marks a certain kind of existence. Bishop admired how effectively Lowell's poem "The Drinker" exploited the rhythmic downbeat as it simulated the drunkard's distorted sense of time—torturously retarded in a way that she finds "terrifying—have hours gone by, or one awful moment?" (letter to Lowell, 27 July 1960, HL). It is an effect she can appreciate in the verse of others but one that she refuses to experiment with in her own published work, and so her murky meditations on Poe and degradation are at last disowned and discarded.

Struggling to stay sober day after day, Bishop knew just how difficult it was to keep things light and cheerful and resist the laws of gravity—both the downward trend of love and the confessional turn that contemporary poetry had taken in America. As she was quick to admit, poets have a difficult time getting their songs to soar beyond their material constraints, simply because "it is hard to get heavy objects up into the air" (KW1 36). Punning in "Edgar Allan Poe & the Jukebox" on the psychological implications of the downbeat, Bishop tentatively probes the pathology creeping into postromantic verse.

A Style "All My Own"

Bishop's mature poetry achieves a formal radiance while avoiding commitment to the kind of predetermined form Poe calls for in his rationale of verse. Her distinctive use of shifting rhythms and shifting viewpoints became one way of undermining the narcotic, monotonal, and morbid qualities she associated with the verse of the *poète maudit*. But how did her unique style evolve? Remarkably, we find that the very condition underlying Bishop's alcoholism— a radical sense of disconnection—became the foundation for her mature art. As we have seen already, fresh manuscript evidence like "True Confessions" and "Edgar Allan Poe & the Jukebox" suggests that a conflict arose in Bishop's mind between the forces of disconnection at work in the world and the mystical power of art (and alcohol) to make things cohere. Bishop's task as she saw it was to come up with a form that broke the spell of lyric poetry's "artificial paradise," giving shape instead to life's energetic discord, its "untidy activity."

If Bishop cast a somewhat jaundiced eye on Poe's celebration of the downbeat, this is not to say that she did not admire his attention to craft. Like Poe, Baudelaire, and their modernist descendants, she valued poetic form as a means of overcoming the eroding forces of time and nature. But Bishop retained a steadfast skepticism about poetry's ability to forge true connections, just as she looked with suspicion on the drunkard's "flattering" impressions of the world. This skepticism is evident in her notebook, where she hints at the insincerity of poetic order: *"Rhyme* is *mystical*—asserting, or pretending to assert, powerful connections between" things (KW1 140; Bishop's emphasis). In Bishop's Florida landscapes, such manufactured correspondences are transient, soluble: objects held together by the centripetal force of rhyme or repetition or simile are destined to spring apart in the end.

Bishop's entire experience as orphan, woman, and traveler confirmed the world's natural unruliness, the recalcitrance that keeps paradise at arm's length, a dream deferred. A lifelong onlooker by virtue of her auslander status, she was repeatedly struck, as she says in a notebook, by the "inconsequence of maps" in the face of life's stubborn incongruities (KW1 13). For this reason, though Bishop shared with all poets the urge to chart powerful connections through sound and simile, she found herself underscoring the perversity of that enterprise. In the early days of her career, she would approach her literary elders with a measure of diffidence, but even as a neophyte her comments reflect a striking confidence and disdain for the generally sanctioned notion of a well-wrought poem. The work of Wallace Stevens and members of the Auden circle, for example, struck her as oddly prim, hinting at a kind of overcompensation. In an entry from her Key West notebook, she suggests that their poetry is fastidious to a fault: "They . . . still seem to be *holding onto* their poetry. It's still in their own grasp. . . . It's that deliberately unfinished—can't let-go—monkey with his hand in the bottle—

feeling that I don't like. They the poems aren't 'on their own' " (KW1 74). In another notebook aside, she complains that Stevens has polished away all spontaneity while serving his idea of order: "all the unconscious spots" have been rubbed out (KW2 89).

As she tackled the question of form amid the inchoate landscape of Key West, she found comfort not in modernist ideas of order but in seventeenth-century prose, and Pascal's *Pensées* in particular. Admiring Pascal's "French *clarity*" (letter to Marianne Moore, 5 January 1937, RM), Bishop strove for a similar style of clearheadedness and sobriety. Drawn to Pascal's view of nature as well as his loose sentence structure, Bishop saw in the *Pensées* a perfect conjoining of form and content that matched her own experience of Key West's disjointed scenery. Full of "magnet-sentences that accumulate strayed objects around them," the *Pensées* "fit in so well with the few, repeated natural objects and the wonderful transparent sea" (letter to Marianne Moore, 5 January 1937, RM). Later, a notebook entry will clarify just what Bishop finds so compatible in Pascal's view of art: "Nature has made all her truths independent of one another. Our art makes one dependent on the other. But this is not natural. Each keeps its own place" (KW1 13). This *pensée* recalls Pascal's definition of the universe, a universe where relativity is the rule—"a sphere . . . of which the center is everywhere, the circumference nowhere." However terrifying she may have found the decentered quality of her life in Florida, it accorded with her previous intuitions about reality.

These intuitions had first led her to Pascal and other baroque writers while she was still a college student. As she learned from Morris Croll's essay on the subject, the baroque sentence imitated the lack of connection in nature by juxtaposing disjoined statements linked merely "by *and*, *or*, or *nor*," conjunctions having "no logical *plus* force whatever" (437). We feel the power of this style in Bishop's poem "Over 2000 Illustrations and a Complete Concordance" where coupling verbs are so conspicuously downplayed and a traveler must come to terms with a wealth of sites and sights without the aid of any warrantable source of meaning, whether personal, literary, or religious. The poet traveler arrives finally at the realization that no copula or linking verb is possible in this world of miscellany: "Everything only connected by 'and' and 'and' " (*CP* 58).

Under the influence not of alcohol but of Pascal, Bishop became an artist of "found objects" unconnected by any stabilizing syntax: "I have that continuous uncomfortable feeling of 'things' in the head, like icebergs or rocks or awkwardly-shaped pieces of furniture," she once admitted to Marianne Moore (11 September 1940, RM). These objects seemed to accrete, or proliferate, in her mind, "as if all the nouns were there but the verbs were lacking." Obviously, Bishop's problem with poetry lay in the way its rhymes and rhythms too easily declared a foundation or base for its assertions. As Barbara Page first observed, the poet had difficulty with the predicate—the part of the sentence or clause that consists of a verb (at least) and affirms something about the relationship between subjects and objects, people and things ("Off-Beat Claves, Oblique Realities" 204). One might also say that she had difficulty with the predicatory, the quality of sermonizing or preaching implicit in the word *predication*.

At first, Bishop's enthusiasm for Pascal and the baroque prose writer seems to imply a rejection of Poe and rationalized verse with its predictability and its predication. A comment found in a Key West notebook juxtaposes "Poe's 'each law of nature depends at all points on all the other laws'—Versus Pascal's 'Nature has made all her truths independent of one another' " (KW1 34). Though the reference is enigmatic, Bishop seems to be referring here to Poe's argument that poetry should reflect the predestination extant in the universe; each word of a poem, like each particle of dust, must tend toward a final ingathering, a common embrace. But, as Bishop well knew, Poe celebrated the sonic bonds forged magically through rhythm and rhyme only in his verse. His prose fiction accomplished something very different indeed, parodying at times his own pursuit of a rationalized verse and a rational universe.

Poe's short stories, with their drunken, obsessive protagonists and perverse couplings of the living and the dead, actually mocked the *poète maudit*'s rage for order, for beauty, for closure, and the lengths the poet would go to in order to pursue the unattainable. At the same time, these stories were couched in a style remarkable not for its single-mindedness but for its surprising prolixity. Poe underscores the peculiar monomania of his typical protagonist by presenting us with an alternative: his prose style resists the monotone and the monochromatic, aiming instead for the qualities of dispersion, irradiation, proliferation evident in the natural world. Though his characters do not escape the fatal addictions and compulsions born of their desire to know the ineffable, Poe does by virtue of what Bishop termed his "proliferal" style.

In the early days of her Florida experiment, Bishop wrote Frani Blough Muser to tell her of her renewed interest in Poe's short stories and their relation to the prose of Sir Thomas Browne and other baroque writers. Out of their combined influence, she promised to extract "a new theory of the story, All My Own" to be called the "proliferal" style (2 May 1938, VC). When she hints to Frani that she has written several new stories with Poe and Browne in mind, she is almost certainly referring to "The Sea & Its Shore" (completed in December 1936 and first published in 1937) and "In Prison" (1938). In a letter to Marianne Moore, she describes the latter as "another one of those horrible 'fable' ideas that seem to obsess me" (31 January 1938, RM). To underscore the influence of Poe on this new phase in her development, Bishop turns to Poe's "Silence—a Sonnet" for both the title and principle theme of the first of these prose fables, "The Sea & Its Shore": "There is a twofold Silence—sea and shore—Body and soul" (*Collected Works* I: 322).

Bishop had already begun working on this parable of the "drunken writer" by the time "The Man-Moth" saw publication in the March 1936 issue of *Life and Letters Today*. The main character of Bishop's fable resembles the typical narrator of a Poe story in his drunkenness and excessive sensitivity. An inebriate, a beachcomber, and a recluse, Edwin Boomer, is identified with the author: he bears Bishop's own initials and his last name echoes "Bulmer," the family name shared by Bishop's mother Gertrude and her alcoholic brother "uncle Artie" whom Bishop would one day immortalize in the short story, "Memories of Uncle Neddy." Boomer/Bulmer becomes a wry caricature of the young Bishop foraging among the stacks of the New York Public Library, looking for some means of ordering her literary inheritance. The fragments Bishop finds from

Ignatius Loyola's *Spiritual Exercises*, Coleridge's *Biographia Literaria*, and Henry James's *The Golden Bowl*, along with the instructions for "JOKE SPECS WITH SHIFTING EYES" (*CProse* 175–77), all appear in her notebook, "Recorded Observations" (1934–37: 17–18, VC).

Boomer is a forerunner of Bishop's scavenging sandpiper and the title character of "Crusoe in England" who dreads having to register the flora and fauna of every island in creation. Boomer spends his days along the public beach, cleaning up the printed garbage that accumulates there. Quixotically tilting with scraps of paper, he finally skewers them with his sharpened stick. Boomer's littered beach resembles the writer's cluttered desk, with unopened letters and unfinished drafts impaled like invoices on a spindle. Each evening he returns to his house, or, his "idea of a house," four by six feet (*CProse* 171), and throughout the night he sorts the day's refuse, usually doing his work while tipsy. His sandpiper existence, "rushing distractedly this way and that" in search of "something" will linger in Bishop's mind (*CProse* 178), as will the image of Boomer's workshop, until it reappears in the late poem, "The End of March," as Bishop's "proto-dream-house, / my crypto-dream-house (*CP* 179).

Edwin Boomer is absorbed in a single task: he must impose on all the scraps of paper he collects some kind of order that will help him grasp the meaning of his existence. In this, Boomer is said to lead "the most literary life possible" (*CProse* 172). Pretty soon, he can no longer distinguish between the "printed" or literary world and "reality," so strong is his urge to see the shore as a single text whose message has been finally and truly revealed. Hoping that all the objects he salvages might conspire together to form a single revelation (and that this revelatory Word will have special meaning for him alone), Boomer borders on paranoia. His is a mind dominated by what Poe called in *Eureka* a "propensity to analogy"—or a "monomaniacal grasping after the infinite" (*Collected Works* 3: 129). Looking back on "The Sea & Its Shore" from a later vantage point, Bishop links the story explicitly with the kinds of concerns over artistic form that she raised in the unpublished poem, "Edgar Allan Poe & the Jukebox." In a passage from a Key West notebook, Bishop notes that the story "partly but poorly expressed" (KW1 95) the sentiments of a recent dream—a dream that focuses, like "A Drunkard," on her "abnormal thirst" for security and order. In the dream, she is walking along a road with a man who was wearing patent-leather shoes; it is very hot and they are thirsty. She remembers images of waterfalls and water tubs. The man dusts off one shoe with a large white handkerchief, which he then puts away, very quickly, like a magician, having used the handkerchief to gather up all the highlights from the patent leather: "Presto—the highlights are re-arranged to make a small glass goblet which he presents to me, smiling" (KW1 95). For Bishop, the magician's white handkerchief represents a "the artificiality we lay over the world on purpose to grasp it," just as we take "a cloth to unscrew a bottle-cap" (KW1 95). She goes on to write that this "artificiality" reminds her of a "form of art," implying that a poem's formal ordering of experience allows us to both grasp something of the world and slake our thirst for beauty and closure. The dream's emphasis is on the artificiality of the magic tricks that poetry performs. The artist works in good faith only so long as she remembers that her poetic structures and similes are sleights of hand.

In "The Sea & Its Shore," "the most literary life possible" (*CProse* 172) is a life spent trying to grasp the world. Like her character, Edwin Boomer, Bishop often longed for the refuges of art and alcohol, both of which helped to distance her from life's traumatizing disarray. But she knew that immersion in the waters of wine and of song could be hazardous. There is at first something sacramental about Boomer's task, which is compared initially to the "priest-like task" performed by the sea as it washes and purifies the shore (*CProse* 172). If art is introduced in the story as a ritual of purification, however, by the end of the parable, the artistic tidying up of reality is seen as destructive. Boomer is no longer likened to a laving sea but to a sea "of gasoline, terribly dangerous . . . brilliant, oily, and explosive" (*CProse* 174). There is, after all, something incendiary or apocalyptic about his unifying vision; under his gaze, nature's untidy activity is sacrificed, consumed in a conflagration, to be replaced by revealed text. Suggesting Bishop's anxiety about art and alcohol in lethal combination, the image of flammable seas would haunt her for some time, returning most strikingly in both "The Bight" and "At the Fishhouses."

While Edwin Boomer weaves his web of meaning from unrelated scraps of paper, Bishop continually unravels that web—and her manner of doing so becomes the true innovation of the story. Her storytelling is actually a proliferation of details, a series of observations with "no discernible goal" (*CProse* 174). Her sentences, like the papers that Boomer tries to catch on his sharpened nail, "soared up, fell down, could not decide, hesitated, subsided, flew straight to their doom in the sea, or turned over in mid-air to collapse on the sand without another motion" (*CProse* 174). She seems to be describing her new "proliferal" style as she pictures their flight: "If any manner was their favorite, it seemed to be an oblique one, slipping sidewise . . . [and] they made more subtle use of air currents and yielded to them more whimsically than the often pigheaded birds" [who flew in a line]. . . . they were not proud of their tricks, either, but seemed unconscious of the bravery, the ignorance they displayed." The idea of the unwinding sentence will serve her well not only in her prose work but in her verse as well where she will loosen her approach to the poetic line, making it a more flexible setting capable of capturing the slipperiness of life in all its accumulating detail.

The story she would complete in late January 1938 is often read as Bishop's most vivid rendering of her lifelong dream of leading a monastic life devoted to art. But "In Prison" is more than a parable about choosing a life of voluntary confinement or finding a pleasant niche in her vocation. Bishop uses "In Prison" as a forum for presenting her emerging philosophy of composition, since the male speaker's goal is to discover in prison a distinctive style. Bishop's experience of "hotel existence" in New York (*CProse* 182) forms the background for her depiction of the prisoner's cell, itself an emblem for the writer's circumscribed and disciplined existence. The narrow cell, of course, suggests as well the writer's dedication to the confines of literary form, a well-established metaphor dating back at least as far as Wordsworth's "Nuns Fret Not at Their Convent's Narrow Room" where the poet finds relief from "too much liberty" (too

many epic ambitions) by framing his thoughts within the circum-
scribed bounds of the sonnet (*Poetical Works* 3: 1).

"In Prison" concludes by making explicit the idea upon which
the entire story is founded: "Freedom is knowledge of necessity"
(*CProse* 191). One is free as a writer only when one accepts and
learns to thrive within the boundaries of form. But the fetters of
form, like the "large silver bird cage" of lines that dominate the
hotel wallpaper Bishop describes at the start of her story (*CProse*
182), must make sufficient room for those twists and turns of thought
that resemble the wallpaper's submerged pattern, its "magnificent
arabesques" of flowers and vines (*CProse* 183). Bishop discovers this
due balance of improvisation and precision not in Poe's metronomic
poetry but in his "proliferal" fiction, particularly his *Tales of the
Grotesque and Arabesque*, where the master of horror conveys a
sense of strange and subversive possibilities within the confines of
a scientifically exact narrative and descriptive apparatus.

The gist of Bishop's letter to Frani Blough Muser, in which she
first speaks of her new Poe-inspired "proliferal" style, is repeated
almost verbatim toward the end of "In Prison" when the would-
be inmate explains precisely what would be gained from incarcera-
tion: "In a place where all dress alike I have the gift of being able
to develop a 'style' of my own, something that is even admired and
imitated by others. The longer my sentence, although I constantly
find myself thinking of it as a life sentence, the more slowly shall
I go about establishing myself, and the more certain are my chances
of success" (*CProse* 190). This is the "proliferal" style in action. We
cannot help but recognize that Bishop is speaking here of her new
compositional style dependent on her new elongated sentence—a
sentence expanded to make room for qualifications, revisions, and
digressions.

Many readers have already noted how Bishop's mature composi-
tions strive to imitate the baroque sentence or "loose period" de-
scribed by Morris Croll—a sentence whose first member is "fol-
lowed by other members, each with a new tone or emphasis, each
expressing a new apprehension of the truth expressed in the first"
(433). Thomas Travisano was the first to observe that Bishop's

avoidance of symbolic overtones owes as much to Poe's "subtle, delayed effects" as it does to the baroque "loose period" (69). But the influence of Poe on Bishop's proliferating or "loose" approach to form is still insufficiently explored. A staple of Poe's own prose style is his use of the dash, which as he notes in his *Marginalia*, "gives the reader a choice between two, or among three or more expressions, one of which may be more forcible than another, but all of which help out the idea (*Essays and Reviews* 1425–26). Bishop's private letters are riddled with dashes to convey what Poe calls "a second thought—an emendation," and this acknowledgment of the uncertainty, the untidiness, the prolixity of life becomes a distinctive feature of her mature poetry. Although the instances of its employment are numerous in Bishop's collected work, perhaps the most representative of its uses occurs in "Poem" while the poet is considering her view of Nova Scotia and setting it side by side with her Uncle's George's painted perspective: "Our visions coincided— 'visions' is / too serious a word—our looks, two looks" (*CP* 177).

Nearly a decade after publishing "The Sea & Its Shore" and "In Prison," Bishop was able to write a poem in which the seductions of lyric music and the temptations of the *poète maudit* tradition are overcome in favor of her new "proliferal" approach to life and art. "The Bight" concentrates on the excavations underway at Garrison Bight, which Bishop could see from the front window of her Key West home. The harbor is littered with junky little boats run ashore by a recent hurricane and lying perilously close to water "the color of gas flame" (*CP* 60). In an early draft, she connects the splintered boats to the letters that lie unanswered on her desk, undoubtedly evoking in her mind the affairs and personal relationships she has neglected in the past decade. Depressed, she imagines the combustible air and water of Key West igniting the desk of letters: "Maybe it will burn everything up sooner or later, this afternoon,/ a conflagration/ awful but cheerful" (box 56, folder 12, VC). In the final version, however, Bishop resists the catastrophic ending, the closure achieved through apocalyptic immolation. The poem, instead, is filled with playfulness, an "off-beat" sense of rhythm and approach to simile. Her analogies, piled one on top of the other like shipwrecked boats, are as messy and comically off kilter as the scene outside her window: pelicans become pickaxes, bird tails turn into scissors, and everywhere there are "palpable drafts" (*CP* 60).

Where Baudelaire probably would have imposed his own system of symbols on the harbor, hearing exotic marimba music in its all-too-ordinary workaday rhythms (*CP* 60), Bishop shrewdly compares the disordered vitality of the scene to nothing more grandiose or profound than her own desk. She underscores the limitations of simile and analogy by showing how no artist can claim to be the "perfect interpreter." Neither alcohol nor inspiration of any other sort can help the artist to grasp once and for all the permanent nature of things or marry people and objects that must remain separate. Still, she need not embrace Baudelaire's "forest of symbols" or rest easy with the tradition of the "drunken visionary poet" to escape her fear of rupture through poetic form. Without too much fanfare, she uses her own window of consciousness to provide a perspective and momentary meaning. Her point of view structures the poem.

For both personal and professional reasons, Bishop was terrified of working entirely without structure; she did not like the sense of "the mind being 'broken down' " that formlessness conveyed (KW1 193). As she expresses it in her notebook, a "form of art" is neither a sign of universal order nor an artificial paradise but instead a "posing [of] an *imaginary* question" (KW1 95; Bishop's emphasis). When she watched the little ocher dredge excavating the marl at Garrison Bight, she posed an imaginary question about her own untidy activity as a poet: "How can I create a poetic structure that will mirror the 'awful but cheerful' flux around me?" In answer, she composed a poem of ever-accreting detail, one that avoids the unifying language of metaphor and instead relies on a metonymic naming and renaming of things in succession.[4] Nothing is beautified, nothing explained away—not the dredges, the bulldozers, the pelicans like pickaxes, the "man-of-war" birds, or any of the other images of latent violence and predation.

Subtitling the poem, "On my birthday," Bishop celebrates a turning point in her life and in her poetic. "Thirty-seven / and far from heaven" was her comment on this particular anniversary. Years of alcohol abuse and unsuccessful "cures" lay behind her—and still more lay before her. But at this pivotal moment in her career, she had discovered a crucial component of her poetic: "Far from heaven" she might be, but the artificial paradise of the *poète maudit* would no longer call to her as it had done in the past.

5 "Travelling Through the Flesh"

A Poetics of Translation

During her years in Florida, Bishop tried to define herself in relation to her friend "Cal" Lowell, who saw in the *poète maudit* tradition a way of expressing the grim vision of his generation. Once she found a home in Brazil, however, the difficulties of acclimatizing to an alien world became far more pressing than the dangers of indulging in the maudlin. For years Bishop had concerned herself with how to express isolation and ennui without self-pity, but now new concerns came to the fore: how to make contact with others; how to view her own experience and her own poetry in relation to the lives and the literature of her Brazilian neighbors. The Brazilian landscape possessed for Bishop all the mystery, the energy, and the frailty of a woman's body. She greeted it with a mixture of excitement and trepidation, all the while aware of how vulnerable Brazil had been and still could be. Her own hunger for physical contact with this new world reminded her, uncomfortably, of the many ways in which Brazil had been consumed and feasted upon in the past. She would not participate, if she could help it, in the violation of this body of land, its people, and their culture.

Bishop was forty years old when she first arrived in Brazil in 1951; she would remain there permanently until Lota's death in 1967 and then sporadically until 1971. As a privileged white tourist, she bore a certain resemblance to the sixteenth-century explorer, the nineteenth-century naturalist, and the contemporary anthropologist, figures who had always excited Bishop's imagination. Like those who had come before her, Bishop became a chronicler and a promoter of exotic sights and stories, but these were roles she accepted with a good deal of discomfort. In the letters she wrote to the friends she had left behind in New York and Florida, Bishop worried about the temptations of this picturesque world. Would she become a poet of exoticism, tailoring Brazilian exotica to the tastes of a North American audience? Would her poetry be populated, like the fairgrounds of eighteenth-century Europe, with movable wonders from the colonies, pygmy women and trained monkeys, albinos and aborigines? The prospect was a discouraging one. Yet, whatever her intention, Bishop's own discovery of the Brazilian sensibility would be shaped by the questionable appetites and values of the merchandisers who preceded her.

Brazil was a country decisively shaped by European dreams of conquest, and after Bishop settled there, she began to eye her own poetic mission with a greater degree of suspicion. Once in Brazil, she found it difficult to shake ancient notions about poetic power. After all, she was well aware of the Emersonian tradition in which the poet so often appears as an imperialist laying claim to the colonial subject he calls "Nature." Nature, Emerson wrote, "offers all its kingdoms to man as the raw material which he may mould into what is useful" (*Nature* 50–51). After centuries of being "mould[ed] into what is useful," Brazil had become a body pockmarked with mines and stripped of its natural resources. The poems and stories of her Bishop's Brazilian friends were themselves fragile bodies, raw material to be used to further her own creative ends. The prospect did not sit well with her.

After Bishop decided to undertake translations from the Portuguese, the moral difficulties of her position as a literary expatriate became clear in ways that they might not have otherwise. But the very task of translation helped her to clarify the qualities she valued most as a poet and person: forbearance, humility, and practical wisdom. Bishop's South American experience reinforced her belief that, in literary interactions, as in personal relationships, the poet must exhibit the proper degree of courtesy and deference toward all that she encounters in her travels. Bishop's translations from the Portuguese also help her readers to recognize the extent to which her own poetry focuses on the hazards of literary commerce and the ethics of observation. Keeping these translations in mind, it is easier to see how often the poems from her third collection, *Questions of Travel*, define the boundaries of literary authority, property, and propriety.

As a translator, Bishop resisted the urge to drain Brazilian culture of its unique force in order to feed her own creative vitality. She tackled only those foreign works that she felt she could translate faithfully. Bishop first took up translation in college, beginning with Aristophanes' *The Birds*. She went on to adapt poems by Max Jacob, Octavio Paz, Joaquin Cardozo, and Vinícius de Moraes, among many others and finally coedited *An Anthology of Twentieth-Century Brazilian Poetry* (1972), which contained a number of her own adaptations from the Portuguese. Bishop's task as she saw it was to convert those works that could make the passage from the foreign language into English with a minimum of bloodletting or seepage: "I only do poems that seem to go into English without too much loss—very limiting, naturally" (letter to Anne Stevenson, 20 March 1963, WU). She took pains to silence her own voice in an effort to be true to her source.

The act of translation, however, compelled or seduced Bishop into expanding her emotional repertoire as she toyed with the Brazilian voice, projecting a confidant sensuality and emotional bravado alien to her own recognizable genre and style.[1] The Brazilian poet's nonchalance about personal disclosure, the casual way of saying, "Carlos, go on! Be *gauche* in life" ("Seven-Sided Poem," *CP* 243) may have been partially responsible for the poems of *Geography III* where Bishop unveils a new emotional freedom, an ability to name herself ("you are an I, / you are an *Elizabeth*") in a way that seemed foreclosed to her in the past. If there is any one quality that defines Bishop as a translator, it is her refusal to pacify the landscape of Brazilian literature. Carried beyond herself, the translator was translated. She acquired a degree of imaginative support from the alien talents of the Brazilian writers.

Bishop acknowledges in "Questions of Travel" that the wayfarer selects one destination over another, following a private compass: "Continent, city, country, society: / the choice is never wide and never free" (*CP* 94). Perhaps the same might be said of the translator. It is safe to assume that Bishop's range of choice was narrowed first by taste and interest. Her selections, from Clarice Lispector's "The Smallest Woman in the World" and "Marmosets" to Carlos Drummond de Andrade's "Travelling in the Family," "The Table," and "Family Portrait," all speak to those concerns that Bishop handles with such understatement in her own poetry: childhood and kinship, memory and mortality. At the same time, her personal predilections frequently steered Bishop toward Brazilian narratives that mirrored the pleasures and perils of her own activity as an avid consumer of texts and connoisseur of the strange.

Many of the other Brazilian poems and short stories that Bishop chose to translate stage pivotal encounters between people alienated from one another, separated by the borders of language, culture, or generation. The effort to break down barriers and assimilate the substance of others is typically figured in the protagonist's hunger for love and often expressed through eucharistic imagery. The homeliness, the familiarity of this hunger for other people, for other lives, is apparent in Bishop's faithful rendering of Carlos Drummond de Andrade's bittersweet poem, "The Table":

> "Due to the disagreements
> of our blood in the bodies
> it runs divided in,
> there are always many lives
> left to be *consumed*."

(*CP* 253; my emphasis)

Like the other Brazilian narratives that Bishop selected for translation, "The Table" is a work darkened by the threat of predation but illuminated at the same time by the possibility of communion through a kind of *casamento genético*, or "cross-breeding" (*Brazilian Poetry* 72–73). In these poems and stories, the borders of the individual body and the frontiers of kinship are defined through appetite and abstinence, feasting, and forbearance. As such, the narratives are charged with meaning for the translator, whose ambiguous encounters with Brazilian literature blur the borders between languages and peoples through an ongoing exchange of substance and circulation of meaning.

Translation, finally, meant more to Bishop than the mere transmission of a text from one language to another. She was so conscious of transmuting the natural world into script that she often encoded the process in her poems (the scribbled black birds that hang "in *n*'s" in the painted skies of a "Large Bad Picture" [*CP* 11], the roads and burnt forests of "Cape Breton" that appear runic to the poet's eye, like "admirable scriptures on stones by stones" [*CP* 68], and the wooden songbirds' cages in "Questions of Travel" that remind the poet of cramped handwriting on a page or "weak calligraphy" [*CP* 94]). In 1978, an interviewer for the *Christian Science Monitor* asked Bishop whether "Crusoe in England," her portrait of a man forced to record every flora and fauna, was intended "to suggest the poet's duty or his burden" (Johnson 25). In her response, she defines poetic creation as an act of translation: "It's true that many poets don't like the fact that they have to translate everything into words."

Bishop admitted that "there is a certain self-mockery" in the poet's Sisyphean—or Darwinian—labors, but there is also something admirable about such devotion to duty. For Bishop, the task of translating "everything into words" is ethical before it is ludic. Her translations from the Portuguese provide us with a new vantage point from which to study her unique brand of devotional poetry.

The Translator as Cannibal

Although Bishop decided to leave North America and take up permanent residence in Brazil, she continued to define her own poetic practice against the example of her friend and professional adviser, Robert Lowell. In facing the challenge of translation, Bishop measured her approach against Lowell's self-dramatizing *Imitations*. As David Kalstone points out, their disagreement over "the autonomy of the original texts, is almost a parody of their temperamental differences about poetry." "What disquiets Bishop over and over," Kalstone argues, "is the force and scale of Lowell's language, and the word she keeps coming back to is 'over-riding' " (206–7). His reckless, freewheeling "adaptations" from the original Greek or French or Russian set the tone for Lowell's own poetry in the years to come. Increasingly, his work would prey on the identities and experiences of his closest friends and relations, adapting them to his own purposes in a way Bishop considered cruel and ungentlemanly. Critical to Bishop's own evolving poetics, the process of translation brought into sharp relief her difference as a poet and the qualities she most treasured in art, including modesty, care, and diffidence toward the world that exists beyond the self.

For Bishop, the peculiarly Portuguese rhyme schemes, meters, and stresses that surround a Brazilian poem and the sensibility or tone that accompanies a Brazilian story must be treated as a fragile tissue of sense and sound. She demanded that the translator preserve as faithfully as possible the body of the original verse, the outer sheath, the physical character of the poem on the page; to do otherwise is to betray and insult its material integrity. As Lowell freely admitted, he had few qualms about playing fast and loose with the lives and stories of other great talents—from Homer and Sappho to Baudelaire and Rimbaud—cannibalizing them to feed his depleted resources during periods when his own creative energies had lapsed. The body of the original verse became a host plant to which he attached himself in order to gratify his "voracious determination to survive" (Belitt 55–56). However much she loved and admired Lowell, Bishop could never bring herself to be an apologist for self-gratification of this magnitude.

Lowell's "over-riding" appetite for the stories and lives that might "amplify or explain" his own life (Kalstone 207) provided Bishop with a monitory example of literary predation. The body's basic instinct to feed itself, often at the expense of the environment, supplied Bishop with her chosen trope for the translator's motivations as he or she sets about assimilating or appropriating the literature, the landscape, and the culture of other peoples. What is so remarkable about much of the Brazilian literature Bishop chose to translate into English is how often these poems and short stories describe Brazil as a threatened body of land consumed or cannibalized over time by a succession of foreign invaders. Significantly, Bishop decided to work with material that mirrored the ethical dilemmas of her own position as a cultural go-between packaging Brazilian landscape and culture for foreign consumption. This is clearly the case in her rendering of Clarice Lispector's "The Smallest Woman in the World," one of five Lispector stories that Bishop translated in the winter of 1962/1963.

"In the depths of Equatorial Africa the French explorer, Marcel Pretre, hunter and man of the world, came across a tribe of surprisingly small pygmies" (Lispector 501). This is the opening line of Lispector's short story "The Smallest Woman in the World," as translated from the original Portuguese. In Lispector's fable of discovery, an ethnologist finds a woman of the Likouala tribe who is just 17¾ inches high—and pregnant. He names her "Little Flower," and she promptly "scratches herself where no one scratches" while the explorer looks the other way (502). The fastidious Frenchman assembles certain "facts" in an ongoing effort to "classify" his rare find. "Little Flower," he learns, belongs to a tiny race that will "soon be exterminated" (501). "For strategic defense, they live in the highest trees" (502) and are "retreating, always retreating" deeper into the dense foliage (501). They make "animal noises" alerting one another to potential dangers (502), just as the "little" Indian women in Bishop's own "Brazil, January 1, 1502" keep "calling, calling to each other" as they flee the marauding conquistadors (*CP* 92).

In Lispector's tale, the reason for the Likoualas' retreat is spelled out plainly enough: "Besides disease, the deadly effluvium of the water, insufficient food, and ranging beasts, the great threat to the Likoualas is the savage Bahundes, a threat that surrounds them in the silent air, like the dawn of battle. The Bahundes hunt them with nets, like monkeys. And eat them. Like that: they catch them in nets and *eat* them" (501; Bishop's emphasis). As the story unfolds, we find that the Bahundes are not the only gourmands who covet "Little Flower's" tiny body. Once a photograph of Little Flower is published "in the colored supplements of the Sunday papers, life-size," it stirs the "perverse tenderness" (or acquisitiveness) of the city dwellers who see it (502). They are reminded of their "ferocious" hunger for something to "love": "In the heart of each member of the family was born, nostalgic, the desire to have that tiny and indomitable thing for itself, that thing spared having been eaten, that permanent source of charity . . . [and, after all] who hasn't wanted to own a human being just for himself?" (504).

Lispector's fable calls to mind the subtle irony at the heart of Montaigne's essay "Of the Caniballes," which opens on a cautionary note: "Men call that barbarisme [*barbarie*] which is not common to them" (162). Montaigne applauds the civility of Brazil's native cannibals while chastising the Christian world for its barbarous eating habits. For Montaigne, the communal body is a notion that lies at the heart of Indian tribal culture. According to Montaigne, undisguised acts of human sacrifice reinforce a sense of community and constancy. By contrast, Europeans dine on the substance of others without giving back anything in return:

I am not sorie we note the barbarous horror of such an action [the eating of the enemy dead by South American Indians], but grieved, that prying so narrowly into their faults we are so blinded in ours. I think there is more barbarisme in eating men alive, than to feed upon them, being dead; to mangle by tortures and torments a body full of lively sense, to roast him in peeces, to make dogges and sweine to gnaw and teare him in mammockes (as wee have not only read, but seene very lately, yea and our own memorie, not amongst ancient enemies, but our neighbors and fellow-citizens; and which is worse, under pretence of pietie and religion) than to roast and eat him after he is dead. (Montaigne 166–67)

While Montaigne accepts the reports of cannibalism carried back from South America by European adventurers, he uses this fact to perform what Lévi-Strauss would one day call the duty of the anthropologist. In *Tristes Tropiques*, a book Bishop read while in Brazil, Lévi-Strauss argues that we are only able to detach ourselves from our own society by getting to know other cultures: "Not that our own society is peculiarly or absolutely bad. But it is the only one from which we have a duty to free ourselves: we are, by definition, free in relation to others. We thus put ourselves in the position to embark on the second stage, which consists in *using* all societies—without adopting features from any one of them—to elucidate principles of social life that we can apply in reforming our own customs and *not those of foreign societies*" (92). But Lévi-Strauss remembers that the history of anthropology cannot be disentangled from the West's longer history of colonization and therefore, even the most innocuous translation of the foreign into the familiar involves an element of use.

In choosing to translate Lispector's "The Smallest Woman in the World" into English, Bishop shows her willingness to accept cannibalism as an appropriate metaphor for her own activity as translator. In the story, Brazil appears in the guise of a pregnant pygmy as swollen and delectable as a jungle-grown fruit (Lispector 502). The "most perfect feeling" and the "secret goal of life" for this tiny human morsel is "not to be devoured" (505). Then along comes a French explorer who immediately claims her as his possession and places her "among the recognizable realities" of his own mental and verbal tapestry. She is now, quite simply, a marketable commodity, coveted by all who lay eyes on her. Here, in miniature, is the story of colonialism. But, for Bishop, it is the story as well of the poet's own love affair with her new homeland.

Translation as Violation

The word *translation* carries with it an aura of traducement from the Italian *traditore* for violation or betrayal. For a poet deeply committed to the moral value of patient, unassuming observation, the worst betrayal that an artist was capable of would be a betrayal of literal reality. Bishop always insisted that her translations were grounded in the solid truth of the original work of art. Given her fidelity to the literal, it is not surprising that Bishop would have been drawn to Carlos Drummond de Andrade's "In the Middle of the Road," which simply recounts the sighting of a stone:

> Never should I forget this event
> in the life of my fatigued retinas.
> Never should I forget that in the middle of the road
> there was a stone
> there was a stone in the middle of the road
> in the middle of the road there was a stone.
>
> (CP 259)

Like Bishop's "The Sandpiper," this poem speaks to the great burden of the poet who studies eternity in a grain of sand and bases her poetic on the principles of accurate observation and remembrance. Bishop's literalness, as Lee Edelman observes, became "a central gesture" of her verse (179). Bishop often claimed in interviews that the events recorded in her poems actually happened just the way she described them. These attempts to ground her poetry on some bedrock of reality "leads her, invariably," as Edelman puts it, "to the question of poetic positioning—a question that converges, in turn, with the quest for, and the questioning of, poetic authority" (179).

When Bishop tried to express her attitude toward the process of translation, she seemed troubled by similar questions of authority. The translator's position with regard to the original artifact is fraught with potential difficulties that Bishop would have just as soon avoided. When Anne Stevenson was preparing her 1966 study of the poet's work for publication in the Twayne series, Bishop wrote from Brazil: "I wish you'd skip the translations. They amount to next to nothing, no real work, and no real interest. Or just say I have translated some prose and poetry, from the Portuguese." The reason for Bishop's demurral becomes clearer in the remarks that follow: "I can't be considered a cultural go-between, nor do I want to be. The fact that I live in Brazil seems almost entirely a matter of chance . . . perhaps not, but that's the way it seems to me" (8 January 1964, WU). Bishop's attempt to deny that her expatriation was in any way willed (a denial that is immediately rescinded) is consistent in its own way with Bishop's refusal to allow her poetry to appear in exclusive all-women anthologies. She does not want to be confined in any one niche and so shrugs off the role of literary ambassador to Latin America. At the same time, she suggests something unsavory about the idea of brokering a relationship between the two Americas, North and South.

As it turned out, however, Bishop could not easily elude the role of cultural go-between, or interloper. Though she ultimately regretted her decision, she did accept Henry Luce's invitation to write a book about Brazil for the North American readership of Time/Life. Bishop eventually organized her study around a single theme: Brazil was a "miscellany of paradoxes." The nation's poverty and corruption clashes with its physical beauty, the warmth and tolerance of its people. The easy attitude toward miscegenation that makes Brazil, in Bishop's view, a paragon in the matter of race relations cannot be severed easily from the violent history of European aggrandizement. This historical fact led to the one central paradox that came to define Brazil in Bishop's mind: while Europe feasted on what Brazil had to offer, the country's natives starved.

Bishop traveled a long path, both literally and figuratively, before arriving at this dark conclusion about her adopted country. From the age of four or five, Bishop had cherished a dream of life below the Southern Cross. As a child, she learned to view the tropics romantically through the mediation of maps, nineteenth-century wood engravings, and books of discovery. Perhaps more than any other book, W. H. Hudson's *Green Mansions* fed her adolescent fantasies about the Brazilian rain forest and its inhabitants. Enchanted with Hudson's elusive bird-girl, Rima, the seventeen-year-old Bishop wrote an enthusiastic review of the book that closes on a personal note: "I wished that the book had been twice as long when I put it down, and I was filled with longing to leave for South America immediately and search for those forgotten bird-people. It seemed still unfinished, even more than that delightful region in my mind I told about, and I felt sure that if I could only find the right spot, the right sun-lighted arches of the trees, and wait patiently, I would see a bright-haired figure slipping away among the moving shadows, and hear the sweet, light music of Rima's voice" (qtd. in Goldensohn, *The Biography of a Poetry* 204).

In her imagination, the teenage Elizabeth populated Brazil with sweet-voiced Rimas and saw herself as the one outsider who might penetrate this hidden world. She adopted the vantage point of Hudson's male protagonist who pursues the sweetly singing Rima to her forest sanctuary. She identified, that is, with the knight errant, or gentleman traveler, of romantic myth. In this she bears a striking resemblance to Wordsworth as he encounters the solitary reaper. Like Rima, Wordsworth's Highland lass sings in a language the listener cannot fathom. But the romantic poet does not need to understand her ancient lay; it is enough that he is sensitive to its strains (Ross 404). He establishes his worth as a poet (and a sensitive soul) by uncovering nobility where others see only crudity. The reaper's song, "purified indeed from what appears to be its real defects, from all lasting and rational causes of dislike and disgust," is translated into higher terms by the poet's civilizing mind, "the still, sad music of humanity" (Wordsworth, *Poetical Works* 2: 387, 261).

Significantly, Rima and the Highland lass are effectively muted once their songs have been interpreted. Wordsworth so enchants us with his vision that he almost makes us forget about the material circumstances of the solitary reaper. She continues her backbreaking labor, while he, the consummate tourist, moves on to other sounds and other sights. Her reality as a woman and laborer is borne away, translated in the most fundamental sense of the word: from the Latin *translatio*, derived from the Greek *metaphora*, to remove something from its natural or proper place and conveyed to an alien context. Once her song has been consumed by his verse, Wordsworth is rejuvenated, nourished, and restored, while the Highland lass remains tethered to a single place, a single task, and a single meaning. Seen from this perspective, Wordsworth's poem, like Hudson's novel, illustrate the hazards of translation.

It would take years of travel and experience, however, for the young Bishop to recognize the ways in which *Green Mansions* had violated or betrayed its subject. Although her position as a woman poet (a reaper and a singer in her own right) might encourage a different identification, she could not at first empathize solely (or even primarily) with the "forgotten bird-people" or the Indian girl who worships her mother earth in the language of song. As Lorrie Goldensohn observes, Bishop's "projected identity is not with the female speaker, but with the male" seeker (*The Biography of a Poetry* 204). Goldensohn argues persuasively that Bishop comes to South America "not *as* Rima but as a *seeker* of Rima" (204). During those first, often disorienting, years in Brazil, Bishop needed a familiar pattern for approaching Brazil and its people—and she found that pattern in *Green Mansions*, where a male interpreter finds himself lost in Rima's distinctly feminine world.

Bishop never quite shook off her initial feeling that Brazilians were feminine in their behavior and sensibility. The entire country seemed to speak to Bishop in the female vocal register: "I wish some

Brazilian genius would come along and write like [Isaac Babel]," she confides to Anne Stevenson, "except that Brazil is closer to Chekov [Chekhov], a decidedly 'feminine' country and Babel is a masculine writer. If one should make these distinctions—but compared to England, or Germany—Brazil is 'feminine' " (16 February 1964, WU). Clearly, comments such as these remind us that Bishop had a native New Englander's phobic attraction to the sensual. She was alternately enthralled and repelled by the physical freedom of the Brazilians, their uninhibited movements, their excess, their perceived hysteria—and their vulnerability. Above all, the rain forest itself struck her as a sinuous female body subject to ravishment, plundered for its natural resources.

Bishop would have had ample reason for identifying with the long line of seekers, interlopers, and profiteers who mined the richness of Brazil. The poet's ancestors, after all, had made their living mining souls. She liked to think that she had inherited her taste for wandering from her mother's family, which included two great-uncles who were Baptist missionaries in India. From family legend coupled with extensive reading, the poet remembers "learning a great geographic jumble of things" as a child. She tended to "confuse" her relatives' missionary expeditions with tales of Indian famines, and Indian famines with yellow fever epidemics. The implicit linking of foreign contact with contamination is not an entirely naive one, of course. It would eventually form the cruel context for Bishop's poem "Brazil, January 1, 1502" (first published on 2 January 1960), which recounts the story of conquest from the point of view of the Portuguese.

The conquistadors in Bishop's poem take it upon themselves to translate a heathen land into their own familiar tapestry of associations. They are taunted by a forest filled with forgotten bird people—"maddening little" Indian women whose mystery eludes them. Out of avarice, homesickness, and exasperation, they rip through the jungle, intent on violating the women and their land. The terrible sequel is visible in the faces of modern Brazilians, where the country's long history of miscegenation is written. In "Brazil, January 1, 1502," the efforts of these Christian soldiers to convert or "translate" the heathen ends in brutal ravishment and betrayal, as Barbara Page observes: "The result of this aggressive sexual colonization was the destruction of Indian culture ("Nature, History, and Art" 43). Charles Wagley, one of Bishop's sources for her Time/Life book about Brazil, remarked, "There are few Indians left in modern Brazil. . . . The aboriginal population has been decimated by disease, slavery, and force of arms—or assimilated into the total population" (qtd. in Page, "Nature, History, and Art" 43).

Like the native Brazilian literature she translates, the Brazilian rain forest suggests to her mind a certain feminine vulnerability that lays itself open to attack. The conquering imagination of the translator has supreme power over the inert, obedient body of the original poem, just as the conquistador imposes his own values on the landscape that greets his eyes. Given her violent vision of translation, it is not surprising that Bishop's "questions of travel" so often return to the issue of sympathy and the extent to which she can empathize, both as a poet and as a translator, with the world she now inhabits as a stranger. By identifying Brazil's land and its literature with the ravished body of a woman, Bishop raises the stakes considerably. Sympathy is not simply the mark of a good guest in someone else's home, it is the only protective barrier between the poet and the poet's worst instincts.

While Bishop commiserated with Lispector's smallest woman in the world, Hudson's Rima, or her own "maddening" little Indian women who elude the Portuguese soldiers at the end of "Brazil, January 1, 1502," her poems do not offer themselves as protection against history, nor do they exempt the poet from participation in history. While her sympathies are reserved for things threatened with extinction, things that "can be seen, touched and loved by— and only by—individual persons" (Page, "Nature, History, and Art" 40), this seeing, touching, and loving of objects is not without its difficulties, since there is a fine line between seeing and overseeing, touching and appropriating, loving and possessing. For this reason, there is a vigilance in Bishop's writing, an alertness to the troubling reality that her own poetic transcriptions are enmeshed in older, more aggressive acts of conversion.

The Marketable Wonders of Brazil

The dark vision of Brazilian history in "Brazil, January 1, 1502" was not born in a vacuum. Instead, it was the culmination of many years of study, during which the poet learned to interrogate and challenge her own dreams of a South American garden of delights, comparing those personal longings with the motives of European missionaries, explorers, and naturalists. A sheaf of notes for a book of prose Bishop tentatively titled "Brazil; Brasil" contains an account of how she prepared herself for her first sight of South America:

> Then I began to read books about South America. There were sets of old magazines in the house, bound in cracked black leather, *Harpers* I remember among the other names I've forgotten—with the bad and usually bad and smeary wood-engravings of the 1850's—80's—and out of them a [I] learned a great geographic jumble of things, confusing arctic exploration with the 49'ers, the works of African missionaries Stanely [Stanley] & Livingston with horseback journeies [journeys] in the Ozarks, Tibet and the Taj Mahal with the Pao de Asucar [Pão de Açúcar] in the bay of Rio de Janeiro, and Indian famines with it's [its] fearsome yellow fever. (Box 73, folder 8, VC)

Listing the books that had inspired her own voyage of discovery, Bishop reveals how strongly she identified with the nineteenth century naturalists who came to Brazil to collect samples of the flora:

> Then came "The Voyage of the Beagle" with Darwin's fond recollections of his stay in Brazil as the pleasantest part of that long trip; then Humboldt, and Scott, and William Beebe, and then in 1949 E. Lucas Bridge's "The Uttermost Parts of the Earth," surely a book that although it is factual, and not a feat of the imagination, should be classed with "Robinson Crusoe" for a suspense of strangeness and ingenuity and courage and loneliness. I had to go to South America, somehow, and so finally, in November 1951, I got on a freighter and went. (Box 73, folder 8, VC)

We can see in this passage Bishop's characteristic admiration for the practical wisdom and ingenuity of self-made men like Darwin and the fictional Crusoe. But rereading Defoe's novel later in life, she found its sanctimonious tone tedious and its view of the cannibal, Friday, limited and patronizing. As she grew older, she recognized an uncomfortable kinship between the poet, the naturalist, and the imperialist marauder. Once she actually settled in Brazil, she found vestiges of the country's earliest invaders in the landscape of her beloved Ouro Prêto, the beautifully preserved capital of what had once been a thriving "constellation of mining towns." As she noted in her book for Time/Life, the town had been overrun first by sixteenth-century Jesuit missionaries who collected souls and then by the *bandieras*, eighteenth-century outlaws who drove themselves deep into the country's interior looking for slaves, gold, and diamonds (*Brazil* 30–31).

Bishop's brief sojourns in North Africa and Mexico had already prepared her for the moral ambiguities she would face once she began to question the tales of adventure she had loved as a child. In a Florida notebook, for instance, she recorded a particularly vexing passage from one of the most famous travel diaries, Henry Morton Stanley's *In Darkest Africa, or The Quest, Rescue, and Retreat of Emin, Governor of Equatoria*. The particular passage that captured Bishop's attention focuses on the problem of translation and describes the collision of two competing languages (KW1 71). Stanley, the journalist-explorer, comes upon a tribe of "mischievous pigmies . . . skilled in the invention of expedients" (qtd. in KW1 71). Like Wordsworth faced with the "blank confusion" of London's Bartholomew Fair, Stanley resorts to the machinery of the Augustan satirists and the classical canon in order to transcend "the press and danger" of these "out-o'-th' way, far-fetched, perverted things" and their incomprehensible language (*Poetical Works* 6: 256). Having voyaged from a world of comfortably understandable languages to a place of farfetched speech that nevertheless had to be acknowledged as language, Stanley and his fellow adventurers were forced to question their notions of "what a language was, and hence what a human was" (Cheyfitz 110).

The "gibberish" that greeted their ears in darkest Africa and the Amazonian jungle often came to represent all that these European explorers conceived of as obscene and bestial. In the passage that caught Bishop's eye, Stanley pictures himself as the champion of rationality, wit, and judgment confronting the language of the gutter: "For 10 minutes we remained perfectly still, waiting until the person, who proved to be a woman, deigned to answer. Then, for the first time in Africa, I heard as gross and obscene abuse as the traditional fishwoman of Billingsgate is supposed to be capable of uttering. We were obliged to desist from the task of conciliating such an unwomanly virago" (qtd. in KWI 71). Perhaps what is most striking about the passage is the way it sets out to demonize the pygmy woman (whom Stanley at first mistakes for a man and at last takes for a disengendered, or "unsexed," female). In the Victorian literature Bishop read as a child and young adult, the aborigine was depicted either as an impossible innocent or an "unwomanly virago." Either way, the native woman became a screen for the repressed fantasies and projected crimes of the Western mind.

The story of colonialism had come down to Bishop largely as a story of gender relations, with the "educated" Europeans imposing their will on the yielding land. Significantly, of the three translated Lispector stories that Bishop published in the *Kenyon Review*, two ("The Smallest Woman in the World" and "Marmosets") recount this story of colonial subjugation with a freshness worthy of Bishop herself. Both works link the literary marketplace in which the writer and the translator must peddle their wares with the European fair. From the sixteenth century, the fairground included all the "marketable wonders of the colonized world" (Stallybrass and White 40). "The Smallest Woman in the World" alludes in its very title to the freakshow atmosphere surrounding the fair. And the story's French explorer, like Stanley in Africa, reacts to his first sight of the pygmy woman much as Shakespeare's Trincolo does to his first view of Caliban: "Not a holiday fool there but would give a piece of silver. . . . When they will not give a doit to relieve a lame beggar, they will lay out ten to see a dead Indian" (*The Tempest* 2.2.29–33).

From Jonson, Dryden, Pope, and Wordsworth to the Baudelairean *flaneur*, poets have been driven to seek out strange sights. As sightseers, they plunge into the urban crowd (while trying to keep their heads well above it), conceiving of the world as a fairground, a great boulevard of shops, a sideshow, and a marketplace. By the beginning of the twentieth century, the *flaneur*, or artist-pedestrian, had gained unprecedented access to the colonized cultures once the exclusive purview of the explorer, the settler, the missionary, or the trader. There is something of this "holiday fool" in Bishop's traveling persona. When she lived in Lota's luxury apartment in Rio, Bishop viewed the miserable hillside slums of the city from the *flaneur*'s perspective. From that height the poet could survey the vast fairground of Rio, teeming with all the "out-o'-th'-way, far-fetched, perverted things," all the "moveable wonders," and all the filth and excess of an overpopulated metropolis. Standing on her balcony, binoculars in hand, she resembles Wordsworth in his response to the pandemonium of London. Adopting the perspective of the "Showman," Wordsworth climbs atop the platform of his art to escape the "press and danger of the crowd" (*Poetical Works* 6: 254).

In a letter to her Aunt Grace Bowers in October 1964, the poet identifies herself as "one of the 'rich with binoculars' watching from their tall apartment buildings as the police hunt down "The Burglar of Babylon" in the *favela* below them. The sheer spectacle of Brazil often encouraged a poet who distanced herself from others almost by instinct to exaggerate that tendency even further. Four years earlier, Bishop assured her North American friends that, despite her new address with all of its "accumulation of exotic or picturesque or charming detail," she would preserve her identity as a "New Englander-herring-choker-bluenoser" and keep herself from falling into "solid cuteness" as a poet even as she learns how to "use everything" for her art (letter to Robert Lowell, 22 April 1960, HL).

Bishop calls on her New England fortitude, reserve, and wit most conspicuously when she confronts Brazilians from the stage-managed distance of Wordsworth's "Showman's Platform." On saints' days or during Carnival, for instance, the populace appeared to her as a single body, an anarchic throng whose laughter seemed disruptive, liberating, and scandalous. In her early letters to Joseph Summers from Samambaia, she constructs a clean ideal sphere of good taste, defining it in opposition to a masked and muddied, irreverent and irresponsibly protean crowd. The crowd is described in terms of its atrocious "taste," a word whose meaning is complicated by the poet's other references to the outsized body of the multitude, its "weight" and prodigious appetite:

The Eucharistic Congress is under weigh [*sic*; Bishop circles this word]—
a million pilgrims, I think. The papers have been running warnings about
watching out for pickpockets while you pray (with illustrations) and items
like "Half a Ton of Host Required," and "Cocquetail before Cinema for
Eucharist," that surprise my protestant eyes. . . . [There is a] beautiful altar.
But as an added attraction for the pilgrims the Paris Wax Work museum
has been imported . . . mixture of good taste and atrocious taste seems to
be very Brazilian. (Letter to Joseph Summers, 18 July 1955, VC)

The poet's "protestant eyes" feast on the crass vitality of Brazil's
celebrants. *Quae negata, grata*—"what is denied is desired." And
what is desired may be wrongfully "pocketed," as any cutpurse
knows. This awareness spills over into most of the Brazilian poems,
particularly "Questions of Travel," in which she asks, in the name
of all displaced persons,

> Should we have stayed at home and thought of here?
> Where should we be today?
> Is it right to be watching strangers in a play
> in this strangest of theatres?
> . . . .
> Oh, must we dream our dreams
> and have them, too?
> And have we room
> for one more folded sunset, still quite warm?
>
> (*CP* 93)

The last query rebounds on both poet and reader, compelling the
communal "we" to examine our urge to collect relics, "folded"
moments pocketed in an effort to overcome our nagging sense of
dispossession. Savoring this souvenir we call a poem, we as readers
share the poet's misgivings about the genuineness of human sympa-
thy. Staring at her words resting on the page like

> some inexplicable old stonework,
> inexplicable and impenetrable,
> at any view,
> instantly seen and always, always delightful
>
> (*CP* 93)

the reader (a tourist in the alien topography of the poet's mind)
must ask herself whether she has room for one more image, for

one more demand on her sympathy. Will our careful observation help any of us—help the poet or her reader, or the world we ponder "blurr'dly and inconclusively"? (*CP* 94).

Unlike the *flaneur*, a traditionally masculine figure, the poet of "Questions of Travel" cannot remain comfortably aloof from the madding crowd. As Lois Cucullu observes, the woman who dares to travel alone is in a far different position than the male adventurer. The female *flaneuse*, or pedestrian, Cucullu reminds us, may be mistaken for a common streetwalker ("Above All I Am Not That Staring Man", *CP* 4). Even though Bishop's sexual preference alienated her from the marriage market, she nevertheless knew as a woman what it felt like to be on exhibition. For this reason, she might be expected to question the ethics of tourism with a greater urgency than her male counterparts.

The Dream of Possession

As a *flaneuse*, Bishop occupied a liminal position: she was both artist and woman, exhibitor and commodity. Her affinity for Clarice Lispector's prose may stem in part from the way the Brazilian fabulist speaks to the difficulties of this position. Lispector's "The Marmosets," for instance, seems tailored to Bishop's private and professional concerns: her asthma and her accompanying fear of being suffocated by the attention of others, her dread of making a spectacle of herself or appearing ridiculous, and her understanding of the role ridicule plays in the history of relations between the colonizer and the colonized.[2]

The story of a tiny female monkey "wearing a skirt and earrings, necklace, and bracelet of glass beads" like "a woman in miniature," "The Marmosets" serves as something of a companion piece to "The Smallest Woman in the World," which concentrates on a miniature woman "black as a monkey" ("Marmosets" 510; "The Smallest Woman" 504). In "Marmosets," a well-to-do woman (she is accustomed to having a maid) buys a sickly monkey called "Lisette." Lisette "could almost fit in one hand" and wore her bangles and beads with the air of "an immigrant just disembarking in her native costume" (510). But one day, while the woman and her children are out on the terrace "admiring Lisette and the way she was ours," the marmoset appears more listless than usual. Near death, the monkey must be rushed to a hospital where she is given oxygen. With "the breath of life," Lisette changes, growing "more secretive, more laughing, and in the prognathous and ordinary face a certain ironic haughtiness. A little more oxygen and she wanted to speak so badly she couldn't bear being a monkey; she was, and she would have had much to tell. . . . The diagnosis: she wouldn't live unless there was oxygen at hand, and even then it was unlikely" (511). Lisette dies the next day. A week later, the older child tells the mother, "You look so much like Lisette!" and she replies, "I like you too" (511).

What does it mean to resemble Lisette? The answer may lie partially in the history of the marmoset as an export conveyed to Europe from the colonies for theatrical exhibition. Taught to dance, "[a] little Marmoset from the East Indies . . . is now brought to that perfection, that no Creature of his Kind ever perform'd the like; he Exercises by Word of Command, he dances the Cheshire Rounds he also dances with 2 Naked Swords, and performs several other Pretty Fancies"; "a little Black Hairy Pigmey [presumably a monkey], bred in the Deserts of Arabia, a Natural Ruff of Hair about his Face, two Foot high, walks upright, drinks a Glass of Ale or Wine, and does several other things of admiration"; a "Man-teger . . . lately brought from the East Indies, is astonishing not only for its teeth and colour but because 'twould drink out of a Cup as Man does with his lips and not lap with his Tongue" (qtd. in Stallybrass and White 41).

Lisette, like these other trained monkeys, is regarded as remarkable for her ability to imitate the polite, well-bred European. As Stallybrass and White observe in their study of the eighteenth-century fairground, well-mannered monkeys made handsome profits for their importers and handlers because they would "amusingly transgress, as well as reaffirm, the boundaries between high and low, human and animal, domestic and savage" (41). Like the trained monkey, the savage is "civilized" or brought into accordance with European forms of politeness. But the savage is never truly the same as the citizen. In the pages of European travel diaries and accounts of discovery, we find native women uniformly described as vulgar in habit and speech—and "black as a monkeys." Like the marmoset who dances or the manteger who drinks out of a cup, the savage's imitation of European decorum is "treated as absurd, the cause of derisive laughter, thus consolidating the sense that the civilized is always already given, the essential and unchanging possession that distinguishes the European citizen from the West Indian and the Zulu as well as from the marmoset and manteger" (Stallybrass and White 41).

Yet derisive laughter cuts both ways when a monkey apes his betters. The pretensions of well-mannered man are deflated by the marmoset's playful approximation of them. Like the mother who narrates "Marmosets," Bishop sympathizes with the tiny trained primate who suffocates in captivity, the diminutive "immigrant in native costume" displaced in a foreign world. Like Bishop, the little marmoset has a secret side: she is able to deflate pomposity with laughter and irony. This sense of humor was something Bishop felt she shared with the people of Brazil. She once observed that the wit of the poorer Brazilians "is really all that keeps this country bearable a lot of the time . . . the political jokes, the words to the sambas, the nickname[s] etc. are brilliant and a consolation— unfortunately mostly untranslatable" (letter to Anne Stevenson, 8 January 1964, WU).

We find the same capacity for dry humor in Lispector's "Little Flower." When the French explorer studies "the little belly of the smallest mature human being," he "felt sick." An "idealistic man" raised in the courtly tradition, the explorer is stymied by the sheer materialism of this big-bellied "thing" ("The Smallest Woman" 502, 505). At that very moment, as though she sensed his revulsion, "Little Flower" begins to laugh. Her desire "not to be devoured" is matched only by her appetite for pretty things: "It is good to own, good to own, good to own" ("Smallest Woman" 506). She looks up slyly at her captor relishing his ring and his pretty boots— coveting these polite refinements and baffling the French explorer with her "bestial laughter . . . as delicate as joy is delicate" (505). The good humor of "Little Flower," bursting from a body brimming over with fertility, may remind us of Bakhtin's carnival laughter, a laughter of the people that comes from the flesh, folk humor "directed at all and everyone" so that "the entire world is seen in its droll aspect, in its gay relativity" (11–12). But it is dangerous to romanticize her triumphant drollery. To do so would be to participate in that long Western tradition of fabrication: whether demonized as vicious or idealized as noble, the "savage" remains a screen on which to project our repressed fears and utopian illusions.

The Frenchman would like to see his "Little Flower" as a noble savage uncontaminated by avarice. Her laughter and her eye for profit degrades and materializes an encounter he would have preferred to have seen as unsullied. Lispector seems to be following Frantz Fanon's advice when she creates the character of "Little Flower." In *The Wretched of the Earth*, Fanon strikes down the fantasy of the native who retains his innocence in the face of European encroachment: "The look that the native turns on the settler's town is a look of lust, a look of envy; it expresses his dreams of possession—all manner of possession . . . for there is no native who does not dream at least once a day of setting himself up in the settler's place" (39). Seven years after translating Lispector's stories, when Bishop lived for a time in San Francisco, she interviewed Kathleen Cleaver, secretary of the Black Panther Party, and in the course of this odd encounter, the poet mentions Fanon whom she calls an "impressive" and a "wonderful" writer ("Transcript: Discussion with Kathleen Cleaver," box 53, folder 9, VC). Bishop was obviously drawn to Lispector's brand of irony and Fanon's demythologizing for the same reasons she appreciated the deflating humor that characterized the Brazilian approach to life. Comic deflation was an effect she aimed for in her own writing. In the process of honing her skills as a translator, she also learned to clarify her difference as a poet.

The Delights of Crossbreeding

For Bishop, translation at its best became an almost eucharistic act during which the translator and the translated partake of each other's substance and together create the communal body of the poem. In her translations, Bishop re-creates the delights of Santarém, that lovely town at the "conflux of two great rivers," where the people, like their waterways and "mongrel" riverboats, are the striking products of crossbreeding (*CP* 185). "I liked the place," the poet says, " I like the idea of the place" (*CP* 185). Here, translation becomes a form of communion made possible by the translator's sympathy and restraint.

Bishop tested her skills as a "literalist," or self-effacing translator, on material that was itself grounded on the literal, selecting Portuguese poems whose narratives revolve around food, family, and flesh. Her most successful translations paired the poet with Carlos Drummond de Andrade, a man she did not personally like, but a poet she greatly admired. When she has to construct a brief biography of the Brazilian for the introduction to her translation of "The Table," Bishop traces the Andrade family tree. Her genealogy pays homage to the poet's unabashed earthiness and fascination with kinship ties. Her portrait of the poet should be read side by side with a passage from her translation of "Family Portrait" in which an old photograph reveals "the strange idea of family / travelling through the flesh":

> Family features remain
> lost in the play of bodies.
> But there's enough to suggest
> that a body is full of surprises.

(CP 261)

Carlos Drummond de Andrade, according to Bishop's biographical sketch, "is considered to be the best of the older generation of Brazilian poets." After this neutral pronouncement, Bishop trails off into matters more idiosyncratic and interesting: "He was born in the little town of Itabirito, in the state of Minas Gerais. As his name indicates, he has Scotch blood, and oddly enough, *mineiros*, people from the state of Minas or 'the mines' are often compared to the Scots. It is high, harsh, and rocky (and the rocks are full of minerals. Itabirito has one of the largest iron deposits in the world) and life is hard, narrow, religious, and often fanatical." "The Table," Bishop informs us, "appears in his collected poems in a section of other poems about his early life and birthplace, 'The Family I gave

Myself.' They evoke the immediate past even more than Frost evoked the New England past, or possibly they strike a foreign reader that way because so many details of landscape, and of Brazilian family life, manners, foods, and interiors, are still almost unchanged" (box 58, folder 11, VC).

"The Family I Gave Myself" might very well have appeared as a section in Bishop's own collected poems, and her comparison of Andrade to Frost shows how her mind is working to forge a family resemblance between her New England past and her Brazilian home. Andrade's Scottish blood sets some sort of precedent for the "cross-breeding" ("The Table," *CP* 252) on which his many poetic portraits of kinship, constancy, and community are founded. At the same time, the "disagreements of blood" running divided in his body ("The Table," *CP* 253) make him a cultural go-between and mirror for Bishop herself as she takes up the task of translation. In Andrade's case, Old World blood has mingled, "oddly enough," with New World blood of the same type—the *mineiros*, like the Scots, live where life is "hard, narrow, religious, and often fanatical." Bishop might just as easily have said that there is something of the original Nova Scotian and New England flintiness in the *mineiro* way of life. Nostalgia for her own childhood in the community of Great Village, circumscribed by the Baptist church on one side and the Presbyterian church on the other, may fuel her love of "Brazilian family life . . . still almost unchanged" (box 58, folder 11, VC). The writings of Andrade will help her to recover the intimate interiors of her own past in poems like "Manners," "Sestina," "First Death in Nova Scotia," and the autobiographical story, "In the Village."

In her English version of "The Table," Bishop let four words stand untranslated in the original Portuguese: *mineiro, tutu, farofa, cachaca.* All save *mineiro*, which refers to the state of Minas Gerais, are dishes and drinks you would typically find at a big *mineiro* ("miner's") dinner. These are the sacraments of family life, and though their piquancy is untranslatable, they are universal in their meaning. The meal, after all, is as elemental as it can be—beans and flour, with liquor from sugar cane. And it is served on an occasion of remembrance in honor of the father who has just been buried. The poem evokes the regrets of love unspoken and words that can no longer be retracted (can no longer be "eaten") all within the frame of religion and folklore. Particularly vibrant throughout the work is the old custom of dining on a dead man's sins. The tradition recalls the words of the song sung by the South American Indians as the ate the flesh of the dead—words translated by Montaigne: "Know you not that the substance of your forefathers limbes is yet tied unto yours? Taste them well, for in them shall you find the relish of your own flesh" (169).

The dead man's eleven sons and his one daughter (a single "Rose") sit around the table "of wood more lawful than any / law of the republic" (*CP* 257). The Portuguese phrase for hardwood, Bishop informs us in a note, is *madeira de lei*, "lawful wood": In her Time/Life book on Brazil, she traces the very name "Brazil" back to the brazilwood loaded onto the first European ships that were sent back from the continent of South America (25). The distinction Andrade makes is especially resonant for his own republic: The family table with its law of unbroken succession and the "strange idea of family / travelling through the flesh" is sturdier and more legitimate than Brazil itself. His poem reaches back to tribal bonds that precede constitutions and covenants and returns us to Montaigne's notion of civilized cannibalism, the moral economy of a community that knows no borders between self and other—to eat the other is to eat the self, and the self is composed of the others one has eaten.

The twelve family members partake in a last supper of unprecedented proportions, nourishing themselves on recrimination, the pain of opportunities lost along broken lines of communication. Eleven of the children are now "great boys in their fifties," forming a "gluttonous brotherhood" of men who are

> bald, who've been around,
> but keeping in our breasts
> that young boy's innocence,
> that running off to the woods,
> that forbidden craving,
> and the very simple desire

> to ask our mother to mend
> more than just our shirts,
> our impotent, ragged souls.

(CP 250)

Mending souls begins, it seems, with feeding bodies:

> . . . Does eating
> hold such significance
> that the bottom of the dish
> alone reveals the best,
> most human, of our beings?
> Is drinking then so sacred
> that only drunk my brother
> can explain his resentment
> and offer me his hand?
>
> . . . .
> Due to the disagreements
> of our blood in the bodies
> it runs divided in,
> there are always many lives
> left to be consumed.
> There are always many dead
> left to be reincarnated
> at length in another dead.

(CP 251, 253)

The pure, elemental pleasure of eating returns these unmended
souls ("all lower-case, / all frustrated"[*CP* 255]) to their childhood
selves. As the poem draws to a close, the surviving members of the
family seem to be joined by a crowd of angels—"forgotten ones"
who were never born, children who were lost, or children yet to
come:

> Count: fourteen at the table.
> Or thirty? Or were there fifty?
> How do I know—if more
> arrive, daily, one flesh
> multiplied and crossed
> with other loving flesh?
> There are fifty sinners,
> if to be born's a sin,
> and demonstrate, in sins,
> those we were bequeathed.

The procession of your grandsons,
lengthening into great-grandsons,
comes to ask your blessing
and to eat your dinner.

(*CP* 255)

The bonds of family are immensely satisfying and infinitely irritating. Flesh of my flesh, bone of my bone, says the father to his offspring, and the family dinner reenacts the equivocal relationship that obtains between father and child, child and sibling, self and other. When the sins of the father—the sins of the flesh—are consumed by the son, the act eloquently expresses the basis of most Native American civilization: kinship. In this way, Drummond de Andrade's poem is the fruit of a crossbreeding between tribal culture and Catholic rites of communion.

The poem closes with the admission that all human rituals feed a hunger for love, a void in the soul. Each time we "summon" absent loved ones to the table of life we "delude ourselves" for an hour or an evening that our life, and our table, is complete (*CP* 257). Bishop approached translation with these thoughts in mind. It became for her a rite of communion, a declaration of kinship with poets who shared her own equivocal understanding of family. In turn, the act of translating another writer's work reinforced features of her own poetic, confirming the sanctity of a world, a people, a literature she could commune with, but never consume or master. Bishop faced a hard fact that so many other writers sought to avoid: estrangement is our lot in life, and so the most we can do is treat a world of strangers with the respect they deserve. She reserved her greatest criticism for the writer who shirked this responsibility by dreaming of some brighter future while ignoring the irreducible reality of the present: "I'm thunderstruck by the helplessness, ignorance, ghastly taste, lack of wordly [worldly] knowledge, and lack of observation, of writers who are much more talented than I am" (letter to Stevenson, 8 January 1964, WU).

Bishop's requirements for translation were her requisites for poetry, as well. The poet, like the translator, must faithfully render the material before her eyes. Both must be wary of preying parasitically on the scene or the text they hope to memorialize. And, finally, both must be able to recognize and take advantage of those rare moments when some kind of communion or crossbreeding is possible. Separated from her Brazilian neighbors by language and upbringing, Bishop nevertheless recognized the universality of the "strange idea of family" (*CP* 261) and its rituals of remembrance. She found in translation one more gesture of rapprochement to add to her poetic repertoire. With no parents, siblings, or children of her own, Bishop relied on poetry to perform the rites of reproduction. Translation allowed her to partake in the play of bodies ("one flesh / multiplied and crossed with other loving flesh" [*CP* 255]) that provides us all with our only taste of immortality.

6 *"Whispering Galleries"*
The Visual Arts and the Incarnation of Memory

This study has focused thus far on the ways in which Elizabeth Bishop translated physical conditions and sensation into poetry. But Bishop was also adept at expressing nonphysical, or mental, states in bodily and spatial terms. During her extensive travels she came across objects capable of evoking long-forgotten ideas or feelings, and they became the stuff of her art. In the working notebook she kept between the years 1934 and 1937, Bishop wrote of her love for these relics, mementos that retain "an existence *strong* enough to produce these ghosts" ("Recorded Observations," 1934–37: 37, VC). While searching for these objective correlatives, Bishop defined herself in relation not only to the poetic imagism of Pound and Eliot but to the visual arts as well, where emotional disturbance is regularly conveyed through a somatic shorthand. The pictorial arts provided her with a set of graphic analogues for her own poetry of recovered bodies and salvaged things. This was particularly true in the later stages of her career after her initial happiness in Brazil released a flood of childhood memories, freeing the poet to write with increasing power about her accumulated losses.

The rite of passage from disembodied thought to visceral expression is one that Bishop enacts and reenacts throughout the whole of her life as a poet. The temporal is converted into the spatial, the mental into the material, in Bishop's architectonics of memory. In "Dimensions for a Novel," an essay she wrote during her senior year of college, Bishop describes with a Cocteau-like whimsy the influence that the present moment has on memories of the past:

"We live in great whispering galleries, constantly vibrating and humming, or we walk through salons lined with mirrors where the reflections between the narrow walls are limitless, and each present moment reaches immediately and directly the past moments, changing them both." In the mental arena Bishop describes, the time traveler cannot re-create the past "exactly as it was," because memory invariably reflects the intervening years, and the changes they have wrought. As her readers have been well aware of for some time, Bishop's life was marked by a series of abandonments, each of which she took to be a repetition of a prior tragedy, as though the past were indeed a hall of mirrors. Her metaphor of the whispering gallery or the mirrored hallway makes the dynamic process of re-membering concrete, an architectural feat of legerdemain involving the marvels of acoustic and optic illusion—as if to say, "Look, the work of the mind is all done with mirrors."

From midcareer forward, Bishop honed her approach to the memory poem ("First Death in Nova Scotia" and "Sestina") and story ("In the Village," "The Primer Class," "The Country Mouse," and "Gwendolyn"). In his study of her artistic development, Thomas Travisano traced the way Bishop increasingly turned to the subject of public and personal history as her career unfolded and her range of reference expanded "out toward actualities that are at once homely and surreal" (Travisano 41). Her earliest poems tended to convert private anxieties into detached allegories, but slightly later poems like "The Fish" sought to overcome isolation by attending to the natural world with "self-forgetful" interest. This middle phase of her career is dominated by what Travisano thinks of as a poetic "voice that might be called the impersonal I." It is the meditative voice that we hear in "The Fish," where the poet attempts to comprehend a natural object as fully as possible before letting it go (Travisano 175–76). The "impersonal I" refuses to possess what it observes, in part because possession necessarily leads to deprivation, and at this interim stage in her development as an artist, Bishop is not yet willing to confront and to chronicle the necessity of loss.

Bishop's poems and stories of childhood surfaced after she moved to Brazil, where she expanded her vocal range to include the personal and the elegiac. But long before she found within herself the voice of controlled pathos that animates the poems of her last collection, *Geography III*, Bishop's working diaries show that she struggled with the problem of objectifying loss. In her early symbolist poetry ("Paris, 7 A.M." and "Quai d'Orléans," in particular), memory is a potentially petrifying faculty, one capable of imprisoning the memorialist in nostalgia, as Bonnie Costello has rightly noted (*Elizabeth Bishop* 176). Before she could learn to regard memory as a liberating rather than a stultifying faculty, Bishop first had to accept the emotional risk of reaching out to others and reaching back into the past. To borrow a phrase from "One Art," "So many things seem filled with the intent / to be lost" (*CP* 178). In the years leading up to *Geography III*, Bishop studied the art of renunciation.

Costello and others have written well on Bishop's ability to convey the "constant re-adjustment" (*CP* 10) between past and present that goes on in the course of remembering. My interest lies in the way Bishop projects primal longings and fears onto the belongings and appurtenances she carries with her over time, tangible objects that bear the burden of otherwise inexpressible feelings. Bishop's unpublished papers uncover the relationship between her personal history and her frequent use of metonymic substitution (by which objects move and speak in lieu of people). The poet views her own mind as a storehouse crammed with furniture, most of which might be found in her grandparents' turn-of-the-century homes or in the pages of a Sears, Roebuck catalog. And she often likened a mind deranged by sorrow or guilt to a home overrun by insects and collapsing from within. Several of her early poetic dreamscapes resemble surrealist collages in which monsters spring up uninvited in the bourgeois salon.

Bishop's longing for memory-rich objects intersected with her long-standing love of the visual arts. Gravitating toward certain objects associated with childhood fears and desires, Bishop is initially attracted to the surrealist aesthetic and its various fetishes. Although she retained, from first to last, a preoccupation with oneiric imagery, her flirtation with this Freudian-influenced aesthetic was brief. Wary of the way surrealism simulated and celebrated mental derangement and leery of the oracular role that the movement promoted for the artist, Bishop turned to other pictorial analogues for her poetry. In the canvases of so-called folk or primitive artists and the boxes of Joseph Cornell, Bishop found a visual language far more suited to her own sensibility. With their modest devotion to the "thingness of things" these artists were able to suggest the strangeness of the everyday without glorifying madness and irrationality.

The "Store-room" of the Mind

The emblematic memento became a fixture of Bishop's explicitly autobiographical work, particularly those pieces that stepped gingerly around the figure of the departed mother. But quite apart from any direct role her mother's hysteria might have played in her artistic effort to embody mental states (a subject that will be taken up in the next chapter), Bishop's interest in the relation between writing and objectifying was intense. She made and collected pictorial art throughout her life, and her curiosity was piqued by the large cargo of associations that accompanied certain familiar things. In pursuit of these associations, Bishop turned first to the familiar mail order catalog, the early twentieth-century equivalent of the old-fashioned dry goods store. This source of inspiration reflects Bishop's predilection for the dadaist aesthetic of found objects, where the past speaks disjointedly through the souvenir.

In the back of a travel diary from the 1930s, Bishop tucked an article called "Eden in Easy Payments," a review by Lovell Thompson of *The Sears, Roebuck Catalogue: Spring and Summer 1937* for *The Saturday Review* (3 April 1937). Thompson's portrait of depression-era America reimagining itself in the pages of the mail order catalog sets the New York reader (sophisticated, thoughtful, postlapsarian) against Sears's wholesome rural idyll, "Eden before the fall." The Sears, Roebuck consumer paradise is not only a guide to the dreams of rural America but a model for the "art of the moment" that "owes much to the spirit of Sears' Eden" (16):

Here within its thousand-odd pages is the unrefined ore of much of current regionalism. Here is what Faulkner hopes to startle, and what Lewis once tried to awaken. The sophisticated seaboard laughs at it as a land of butter and eggs, but secretly envies its peaches and cream, its certainties, as of Eden before the fall.

Accordingly, out of this 1937 catalogue, you can buy everything you need for living in the garden of Eden—and nothing else. . . . You can have whisk-brooms and whistling tea kettles, but not whisky. . . . You can have a book on The Rhythm, maternity gowns, life insurance, but not a coffin. . . .

Besides the raw material for novels, Sears offers free to American writers, "even though they may never purchase from us," a model of style. Sears is conscientious, frank, direct; it is hard to doubt the truth of what is said. When the right word is found, it is used wherever needed; there is no coyness about repetition. Good concrete words, lost to the working vocabulary of most men, give hard, well-trained precision. (Thompson 15)

The mail order catalog, as Thompson described it with a mix of amusement, wistfulness, and condescension, is a made-to-order American Gothic, where things are endowed with the gift of tongues, a pure language that needs no translation: without "coyness," without equivocality, the Sears caption is itself tangible, made up of "good concrete words." It accords perfectly with the pictured object, and the object truly embodies the idea.

Living in a world after Babel, Bishop's mind gravitated toward the pleasant assurances of the Sears, Roebuck guide to "health and happiness." On the *Konigstein*, bound for Europe in the summer of 1936, she was overcome by a wave of homesickness ("overtaken by an awful, awful feeling of deathly physical and mental illness"), and her diary entries from the time suggest that she turned to old Sears, Roebuck catalog for relief ("Recorded Observations, 1934–37: 36–37, VC):

I should like to write a series of short delightful poems that would give me the same satisfaction as the pictures and description in the old mail-order catalogues. They—the catalogues—must enter prominently into the "novel" [that she was planning at the time]. I must get a French one, too. Many of the advertisements, the shop windows, the kinds of things for sale here, cheap candies, children catching flies in bottles, pencil "scribblers," Sunday coats and shoes make me think of the Village. I'd like to go and buy a pair of child's white pumps—they are exactly the same, even to the nasty little celluloid buckle.

THE MAIL ORDER CATALOGUE—particularly toy-department,

musical instruments, appliances like trusses and syringes, etc.—filled me with horror. The same effect as the little legs, kidneys, hearts, made out of silver they stick up around the altars in churches here.

The promissory notes (*promessas*, in Portuguese) that Catholics offer God (little legs or hearts of silver offered in hopes that a palsied limb or a broken heart might be miraculously cured) never failed to interest Bishop. Like the gray-green soot of mold and mildew, they conveyed a certain "attractive morbidity," a general odor of hope mixed with futility (*CProse* 228). Above all, she was intrigued by the animistic power of the object as fetish, powerful enough to open the floodgates of memory: "That an object has an existence *strong* enough to produce these ghosts, distortions, funeral, en-graved nightmares of itself—with prices and writing underneath—this is very hard to get to the bottom of" ("Recorded Observations," 1934–37: 37, VC).

Quite apart from the buttons, brassieres, tea kettles, and curtain rods hawked within its thousand-odd pages, the hefty Sears, Roe-buck catalog itself—like her grandfather's heavy family Bible and farmer's almanac or her grandmother's Little Marvel stove—proved endlessly evocative. Perhaps in Lovell Thompson's sly characteriza-tion of "Mrs. Fred Sparrow," the Sears buyer who will brook no deception in advertising, Bishop saw the sturdy features of her own Nova Scotian stock: "She is firm of mouth, a long-faced, long-headed Yankee" (Thompson 15). While summering on Cuttybunk Island in Massachusetts, Bishop linked Thompson's "long-faced" Yankee with her own New England and Canadian relatives—all of whom used "concrete words," or a clipped no-nonsense vocabulary. This was the "Nova Scotia way of talking": "It sounds, to outsiders, resentful & angry . . . harsh and *inverted*?" ("Recorded Observa-tions," 1934–37: 3, VC; Bishop's emphasis). Her grandmother's cooking was as "concrete" as her speech, with "heavy cooking and all the black tea—which you think was delicious till you go back to it. Curds for tea—puddings, dumplings, the method of eating cereal with a cup of milk at the side" (3). Throughout her diaries, the past returns to Bishop in weighty words with a shape and a taste all their own. She even closes her last book of poems, *Geography III*, with a parting glance toward the stubborn weight of the past.

In "Five Flights Up," a little black dog greets the morning as though it were his first, without a need to ask what he has done before, without a need for words, without a "sense of shame": "Yesterday brought to today so lightly! / (A yesterday I find almost impossible to lift)" (*CP* 181).

While under the influence of T. S. Eliot in college, Bishop played with relatively rarefied, Europeanized images for the capacious hold-all of the mind: a whispering gallery, a salon. But gradually she began to think of more homely similes for her overstuffed brain where ideas accumulated like so many static icebergs or pieces of furniture in constant need of reshuffling (letter to Marianne Moore, 11 September 1940, RM). For Bishop, the mind was a mansion of many apartments, its hidden recesses crammed with belongings that jogged the memory:

> Sometimes I wish I had a junk-room, store-room, or attic, where I could keep and had kept; all my life the odds and ends that took my fancy. The buffalo robe with the moth-eaten scalloped red-flannel edges, my Aunt's doll with the limp neck, buttons, china, towels stolen from hotels, stones, pieces of wood, beach-toys, old hats, some of my relatives' cast-off clothes, toys, liquor labels, tin foil, bottles of medicine to smell, bottles of colored water, things which please by their neatness, such as small lined blank-books—*Everything and Anything*! If one had such a place to throw things into, like a sort of extra brain, and a chair in the middle of it to go and sit on once in a while, it might be a great help—particularly as it all decayed and fell together and took on a general *odor*. ("Recorded Observations," 1934–37: 36, VC)

Once again, as with trusses and syringes pictured in the Sears, Roebuck catalog, Bishop's own idiosyncratic family album is funereal, monumental, and subject to decay, when it will give off a "general odor"—the fierce odor of mortality. In one of several notebooks she kept during her twenties, Bishop muses under the heading "Relatives": "I have bought a town in the Middle West and I mean to monument it thoroughly. In the square, confronted by the county hall and the apothecary,—Uncle Jack, etc. marbled, master of himself. . . . By this way I shall get them off my mind. 'Dead or Alive' " (box 72A, folder 2, VC).

Harold Bloom once remarked that *Geography III* could be distinguished from Bishop's earlier collections by its "language of personal

loss," a language "nobly 'postponed' " until then (29–30). But look-
ing back over her unpublished writings, we discover just how strong
the poet's desire had always been to get her relatives off her mind
by giving them, once and for all, some concrete and lasting shape.
In a sense, memorializing or marbleizing her Uncle Jack meant
mastering him as well. But throughout her first two collections of
poetry, the strain of such an enterprise was apparent. In her late
twenties and early thirties, when she fell under the influence of
French surrealism and placed herself temporarily under the care of
a New York psychoanalyst, Bishop's longing to lay her past to rest
became evident both in her private journals and in the Parisian-
inspired poems that filled her first volume of verse.

Souvenirs and Surrealists

Bishop's special interest in the souvenir must have been at least
partially responsible for her early attraction to the surrealists. After
all, Adorno and his fellow surrealists were the first artists to fully
capitalize on bizarre images that bore witness, in the Freudian
sense, to repressed pain and confusion. A fundamental principle of
surrealism held that we do not sense ingrained desires and anxieties
directly; when childhood traumas return to haunt us, they do so
in the guise of an object or fetish to which the repressed experience
and emotion had long ago attached itself. The theoreticians and
practitioners of surrealism—André Breton, de Chirico, Max Ernst,
among others—created a form of painting and writing that could
"reveal in sudden bursts of shock the images of our childhood past
still crystallized within us" (Wright 268). Breton, for one, insisted
that there be no rational explanation given for the strange gathering
of images flung on the page or the canvas. He underlined this
absence of order in a recurrent image: " 'the street car of dreams'
ventures onto the 'demolished bridge' (*Oeuvres complètes* 1: 519). Like
dream imagery, the elements of the surrealist collage are "rationally
unbridgeable" (Adamowicz 92).

Bishop might very well have had Breton's "street car of dreams"
in mind when she speaks in "Sleeping Standing Up" of "the armored
cars of dream, contrived to let us do / so many a dangerous thing"

(*CP* 30). And certainly, Bishop's odd collection of insomniacs and narcoleptics hanging from ceilings, sitting on masts, or impaled by weeds invite comparison with a dadaist aesthetic that strove to imitate the mechanism of dreams. The same Freudian processes of condensation and displacement that produce the surrealist monster, or hybrid creature, seem at first to be behind Bishop's man-moth, her fish with skin like ancient wallpaper ("The Fish"), her loaves of bread like yellow fever victims ("Going to the Bakery"), her fire balloons that splatter like eggs ("The Armadillo"), and her giant snail whose "white bull's head was a Cretan scarehead" ("Rainy Season; Sub Tropics"). By now, Bishop's reliance on surrealist-inspired dreamscapes, shifts in scale, dissociations, and personified bestiaries has received its share of critical attention. But most of her readers agree that her grotesque and often humorous concatenations simply do not fit the surrealist mold.

For one thing, her monsters are the result of her gift for adroit associations, whereas the surrealist monster is essentially a product of dissociation, as Richard Mullen was the first to realize (64). Her imagination synthesizes, conflates, and marries objects to one another, while the surrealist imagination dislocates, dismembers, and detaches objects from their familiar surroundings, signaling a derangement of consciousness. While the surrealists liked to simulate a sense of mental instability by upsetting our assumptions about reality, Bishop showed us that familiar objects were weird enough when left in their customary settings. In her poetry and prose, the object is not reduced to a mere prop in the poet's psychological drama but maintains its own independent integrity.

Given the history of mental illness in her immediate family and among her closest companions, Bishop did not look kindly on surrealist efforts to simulate mental disturbance through uncanny effects in painting or syntactical breakdown in poetry and prose. Surrealism's glorification of the unhinged mind held little attraction for her, as a comment in one of her Key West notebooks makes clear: "Semi-surrealist poetry terrifies me because of the sense of irresponsibility & [indecipherable] *danger* it gives—of the mind being 'broken down'—I want to produce the opposite effects (KW1 193). In another entry, Bishop mulled over her distaste for Crevecoeur's "Letters from an American Farmer," where the farmer leaves a hornets' nest hanging from the ceiling of the parlor so that he can observe his children's reactions as they are stung: "The whole story of the wasp-nest is fantastic, surrealistic, we'd say now. Is surrealism just a new method of dealing bold-facedly with what is embarrassing? Only for sadism, accounts of atrocities, etc., *embarrassing* as well as horrifying? (KW2 12). In her notebook for the years 1934 through 1937, Bishop had described family life as a breeding ground for torture: "families seemed to me like 'concentration camps'—where people actually let out their sadistic natures" ("Recorded Observations," 1934–37: 29, VC). Something of this attitude lingers in her response to Crevecoeur, in which she so obviously empathizes with the farmer's children, who have been shamed and betrayed by their father's insensitivity. The farmer's scientific detachment reminded her of the surrealist's nonchalant and amoral probing of the unconscious mind.

Surrealism's repertoire of sadistic, erotic, and scatological images repelled Bishop for reasons that were at least in part connected to her gender. In Whitney Chadwick's words, "The ravaged female, denied her normal sexual, emotional, and procreative functions," her ovum, breasts, and genitalia dismembered and bizarrely relocated, becomes "the theoretical basis of the surrealist object and of the word images of Magritte" (107). And while the torn and reconfigured body of the female supplied surrealist art with its basic vocabulary, the woman's disintegrating mind became a primary object of scientific and poetic inquiry. According to this aesthetic movement, when men simulated madness it became a source of male creativity. But women's only source of power, by contrast, lay in real madness, a passive, powerless surrender to the forces of the unconscious (74). Needless to say, the male surrealists were far more comfortable with the exploitation of madness and sadism than their female companions and contemporaries. Madness was simply too close to home and too "embarrassing" a prospect for Bishop to look favorably on Breton's mingling of Freud and Sade. The male surrealists, to her way of thinking, seemed to have no conscience, no ethical moorings. In this, Bishop took a position quite similar to that of Leonor Fini (whose exhibition Bishop attended in New

York in 1936) and the other women surrealists who, according to Chadwick, slighted the sadistic or erotic domain while their male counterparts reveled in it (126).

When Bishop did experiment with hallucinatory figures, she tended to abort the project, as is the case in the unfinished poem, "In a Room," where a phantomlike object lurks in a seemingly safe visual space. Recalling Max Ernst's collages and Breton's monsters, the fragmentary work focuses on a creature that springs up uninvited in a bourgeois setting, exposing the bestiality and sexuality that lives within the decor. Ernst's chair legs become murderous claws, his ladies' dresses grow dragon tails, and the folds of his curtains suggest the female vulva. In much the same way, Bishop's "In a Room" transforms a discoloration on the ceiling into a bizarre hunting trophy:

> there was a stain on the ceiling
>   over the bed
>   shaped like a rhinoceros head
> with a horn in his mouth, hideous up in air
>   and his trumpet blew without feeling
>
> all this gilt plaster work out
>   from his jaw
>   in the morning we saw
> him over our heads and plaster hanging
>   coarsely ornate
>   coarse-toothed and gold-toothed
>
>   (Draft C, KW2 16)

Like Leonor Fini's sphinxes and Man Ray's minotaurs, Bishop's rhinoceros is born out of a verbal as well as a visual pun: hers is a rhino with a horn/trumpet. This unmistakably phallic image is generated from "stains" and "gilt" (or guilt) and conveys a certain Daliesque sexual aggression and paranoia.

But aside from this sketchy experiment, Bishop displayed little interest in surrealism's symbol-laden eroticism. More typically, surrealism simply reinforced her appreciation for visual or verbal accidents, including the newspaper misprint that inspired "The Man-Moth." Although tempted at times to express her loneliness in surreal terms, Bishop largely refused to indulge the impulse. And when she did, her feelings were displaced onto a succession of personae. For this reason, an unpublished prose piece like "Mrs. Sullivan Downstairs" offers us a rare opportunity to catch Bishop in the act of manufacturing grotesque images out of her own private traumas. The story recounts that period in Bishop's childhood when she was abruptly removed from her paternal grandparents' Worcester mansion, where she lived in luxurious isolation, and taken to her Aunt Maude's noisy, Boston tenement. The child Elizabeth has difficulty falling asleep and projects all her fears onto the white wall of her new room.

The room's blank wall resembles Breton's notion of the screen, that material reality onto which the surrealist artist projects his private grammar. Breton's screen, in turn, recalls Leonardo da Vinci's "ancient paranoiac wall" (Breton, *Le Surréalisme et la peinture* 129) from which "bizarre inventions" emerge so long as the hallucinating eye is predisposed to find them there. The episode Bishop recounts contains all the elements of surrealist psychodrama:

When I lay in bed at nights the light threw the shadows of the leaves uphill and greatly magnified on the white wall. The leaves looked gigantic—only a dozen or so—and on nights of strong wind, in the late summer, before they fell, or when some had fallen—then shadows would move agitatedly, frantically, wagging chop-chopping—I half [con]sciously frightened myself watching them. I looked at them and saw a group of [wom]en in lively conversation in an argument, threatening each other, emacing, interrupting, insulting, roaring—and all in silence—Horrible wide opening mouths, waving hands, gnashing jaws thrown back heads, contemptuous laughs. . . . I watched and watched and terrified myself—what were they talking about? Would they fight. Used to violence in the neighbors and a certain amount threatened even in my own apartment. ("Mrs. Sullivan Downstairs," box 54, folder 6, VC)

A certain class snobbism can be detected, of course, in Bishop's response to the close quarters of Boston's immigrant world. But perhaps more to the point is how readily this snobbery is mixed with a fear of violent women. Much of the child's horror and repugnance centers on the overwhelming femaleness of this uncensored world. In her hallucination, the shadows of gigantic leaves dissolve into gaping mouths and waving hands, synecdoches for the irrational female—and reminders of the child's own hysterical mother.

Bishop may have abandoned "Mrs. Sullivan Downstairs" because she had not yet discovered how to represent irrationality in a way that did not compromise her own sense of mental control. By laying the story aside, she also parted company with the surrealists who nonchalantly and unquestioningly associated all women with the feral and the insane. But above all, she seems to have turned her back on the work because, in it, she resorted to a surrealist device that terrified and repelled her. She had scanted and distorted the contours of the real world—here represented by the tree outside her window—in an effort to express the shadowy workings of her own mind. In this, she broke faith with her true subject: the "always-more-successful surrealism of everyday life" that can only be captured through patient, "self-forgetful" observation (letter to Stevenson, 8 January 1964, WU). Just as she rejected the psychoanalytic concept of therapeutic closure and cure, she felt little sympathy for the surrealist claim that art could revolutionize and transcend the particulars of ordinary experience. For her, no amount of surrealist divination could resolve the contradictions of life.

The Whited Sepulcher

Although Bishop used the dissociative techniques of surrealism only sparingly in her own work, she retained a surrealist's interest in the life of the unconscious mind. Not surprisingly, this preoccupation was particularly strong when she struggled with surfacing childhood memories. In her early published and unpublished writings, the many images of monuments, masks, and other tamed exteriors express her desire to control the past. But these carefully prepared facades are inevitably undermined by the unconscious life burrowing beneath. This secret infection (the *unheimlich*, or hidden, reality) is sometimes figured as a horde of insects tunneling behind delicately papered walls. Bishop's insect-ridden structures hearken back both to the biblical parable of the whited sepulcher (a shining surface belying the corruption beneath) and the visual vocabulary of Freud so favored by the surrealists. Ever the realist, Bishop could not ignore the inevitable, and valuable, role that accident and illogic played in creativity, and this forced her to take a second look at Wallace Stevens's "idea of order" ("The Idea of Order at Key West," *The Collected Poems* 129).

Bishop's youthful experiments with surrealism, in which she strove to subvert logical control, culminated in "The Monument." At least in part, the poem was written as an antidote to a central image employed by Stevens in "Old Woman and the Statue" and "Mr. Burnshaw and the Statue," two works from *Owl Clover* (published in 1936) that seemed to glorify the artist's rational mastery of his material. Writing to Marianne Moore, Bishop explains that she cannot help reading *Owl Clover* as Stevens's "defense of his own poetic position," and the ubiquitous statue as his "conception of art," a conception that struck her as moribund, "confessing the 'failure' of such ART . . . to reach the lives of the unhappiest people," the people most hard hit by the depression, the people whose ideas of health and happiness are shaped largely by the mail order catalog (5 December 1936, RM). Stevens's notion of art, like Yeats's Platonic tower, stands as the last outpost of genteel minds, a fortress besieged by craven women and the uncouth poor, who represent the forces of irrationality at work in the world. If the statue is Stevens's icon for the sanity and grace of a culture on the wane, the hysterical woman signals encroaching cultural dissolution.

In a Key West notebook, Bishop uses the Freudian-laced terms of surrealism to argue that poetry should include traces of its unconscious origins and a hint of the uncontrollable depths from which the writing has sprung: "What I tire of quickly in Wallace Stevens is the self-consciousness—poetry so aware lacks depth. Poetry should have more of the unconscious spots left in" (KW2 89).[1] A year after telling Moore of her misgivings about *Owl Clover*, Bishop started to form a clear image of her "monument," one that would employ the hallucinatory techniques of Max Ernst to expose the darkness and turmoil carefully excluded from Stevens's conception of art. A pen-and-ink drawing of a structure ready to collapse, with several limp ornaments hanging from its summit, appears in a Key West notebook; above it a caption reads, "Take a *frottage* of the sea" (KW1 100). The instruction refers to Max Ernst's practice of laying a piece of paper over a leaf or a wooden plank and taking a pencil rubbing. The texture of the natural object would suggest to the willing eye a host of forms—fragments of bodies, landscapes, chimeras dredged up from the artist's own psyche.

For the surrealist, these creations of chance emerge out of a larger reality, one that encompasses the space of dreams and obsessions. Bishop owned a copy of Max Ernst's *Histoire Naturelle*, studied the effects of *frottage*, and agreed that art must make contact with this larger reality.[2] "The Monument" centers on a rubbing taken from a wooden plank and the shapes suggested to the poet's mind by the swirls and ridges of the grain formed by the stratified fibers of the growing tree. After wood has been cut, planed, and converted to lumber, the grain still denotes change, since dried wood will begin cracking and splintering from these natural fissures. The long history of the wooden plank, its origin in the organic world and its ongoing state of decomposition, come together to produce an impression in the poet's mind—an image of a monument set against a wooden seascape.

But as Bishop's notes for the work indicate, the poet is attempting something more complicated here. Her aim is to take a *"frottage* of the sea." Whatever she is describing in "The Monument," it is not simply a scene evoked by the texture of a wooden plank. Instead, it is a scene evoked by the texture of the psyche. Impossible as it may seem, the poet has taken a rubbing of the sea, a force as dimensionless and mercurial as the unconscious mind that produces a work of art. We have in "The Monument" one of the first instances of what would become a common genre for Bishop—the poem that consciously reflects back on the processes of artistic creation. In the poem's final passage, we are told that the "monument" is the "beginning of a painting, a piece of sculpture, or poem" (*CP* 25), and, like any product of the imagination, it was engendered by an amorphous sea of associations. As the dialogue structure of "The Monument" suggests, the poet is trying to reconstruct the process by which associations give rise to a work of art, whether that artifact is a construct of wood or of words.

Bishop's poem, like her monument, cherishes "all the conditions" of its existence that make it "homelier than it was" (*CP* 24). The rough sea winds that erode the wooden structure represent all the conscious and unconscious wishes that shape any creation, including the cultural and the personal conditions of the artist's life. A poem built out of the poet's own experience is doubtless "homelier" or more *heimlich* than it would be otherwise—and more haunting. As Freud taught us, the most disturbing apparitions are the ones closest to home. In Bishop's "homely" monument, the comforting assemblages of the conscious mind are forced to confront the *unheimlich*, or the unsettling powers of the subrational.

Bishop will return in later work to the homeliness of the sea and the primal knowledge it carries. Compared in "At the Fishhouses" with milk flowing from a "rocky breast," the sea is subtly feminine in its implications. Looking back at "The Monument" from the vantage point of "At the Fishhouses," we can see that Bishop's "temple of crates" is an early attempt to pin down the nature of the larger, more threatening reality associated with the maternal. Her monument stands at the center of her vision much as the dark wedge of Mrs. Ramsay stands at the center of Lily Briscoe's painting in Woolf's *To the Lighthouse*. "One needs at least fifty eyes to get round that woman," Lily says of her surrogate mother as she tries to capture her mysterious depths on canvas (294). The same may be said to hold true for any artist who tries to take a *frottage* of the unconscious mind and for the onlookers who are invited into the process. As readers of "The Monument," we are asked to accompany the speaker on this mission. Like the sun, we "prowl" around the structure while the poet cautions us to "watch it closely" (*CP* 24). Weaving a circle around it, we step back with "holy dread." Bishop, in Coleridgean fashion, has brought us face to face with the very source of creative energy and psychic unrest.

The monument gives concrete shape not only to the idiosyncratic dreams of the poet but to the collective obsessions of a whole culture. It is a vast image out of the *spiritus mundi*, the universal reservoir of memories, eternally flowing and flown, which we will encounter again in "At the Fishhouses" (*CP* 66). There is, after all, something all-inclusive about the culture-laden monument. Its crowning fleur-de-lis is a relic of glory and conquest, a moldering sign of human history. Though the particular occasion commemorated by this cenotaph may have long ago died out of human memory, the desire to commemorate lives on and is embodied in the monument's sagging but surprisingly durable form. It seems to stand for the reconstructive spirit of art itself.

Still, the history that this pile of wood recounts, with its royal and ecclesiastical ornaments, is fundamentally elitist and, like the high modernism of Eliot or Stevens, removed from the lives of the unhappiest people. The two voices of the poem vacillate in their responses to the monument's modernist ambiguity, oscillating between interest and antipathy. The question for Bishop seems to be whether poetry can remain true to itself while touching the lives of a wider audience and whether that goal might be accomplished by showing that audience how flexible and accommodating art can be once it makes room for the arbitrary and the accidental. Reacting against Stevens's overly polished "statues," Bishop proposes a makeshift structure to which remnants of history have been "carelessly nailed" (*CP* 24). In a constant state of revision, growing, unfolding, changing, it is alive to possibility, always wanting "to cherish something." In the end, we as readers are enjoined to share in the collective enterprise by "decorating" the monument with our own impressions and contributing to the communal meaning of the *frottage*.

"The Monument" may have helped Bishop articulate her attitude toward Wallace Stevens, but the poem did not relieve her of the disquiet and disorientation she felt when looking into her own mind's abyss. As she continued to write surrealist-inspired works like "Paris, 7 A.M." or "Sleeping on the Ceiling," Bishop experienced a macabre resurfacing of buried memories. In a notebook entry written in 1935 just before sailing for Europe, she calls these repressed "incidents out of the past" her "family monuments" ("Recorded Observations," 1934–37: 31, VC). She was particularly susceptible to this resurfacing of the past when she tried to paint, as a diary entry from the summer of 1950 indicates (1950 diary: 23 June, VC; my emphasis):

I think when one is extremely unhappy—almost hysterically unhappy, that is—one's time-sense breaks down. All that long stretch in K[ey] W[est], for example, several years ago,—it wasn't just a matter of not being able to accept the present, that present, although it began that way, possibly. But the past and the present seemed confused, or contradicting each other violently and constantly, and *the past wouldn't 'lie down'* (I've felt the same thing when I tried to paint—but this was really taught me by getting drunk when the same thing happens, for perhaps the same reasons, for a few hours.)

Later in life, Bishop would confidently contend that she found "no split" between the conscious and unconscious mind, but as a young artist she was troubled by the disjunction between interior and exterior realities. For a brief period in her mid-thirties, Bishop even saw a New York psychiatrist, in part because she was plagued by dreams. An unfinished poem entitled "From Halifax" and addressed to her doctor touches on the difference between the coded intelligence of dreams and the frustrating vagueness of memory:

> Dear Dr. Foster,
> yes dreams come in color
> and memories come in color
> though that of dreams is more remarkable,
> particular & brighter,
> like that intelligent green light in the harbor.
> which must belong to a society of its own
> [made up of similar lights somewhere peaceful & clean]
> and watches this one [just for] now unenviously
>
> (KWI 157)

Living on her own in New York just after graduation from college, Bishop was especially disconcerted by the way nightmare images regularly intruded where they did not belong, superimposing themselves on everyday experience. She began, for instance, to dream of masked men and women, their emotions concealed and somehow deadened. Eventually, the pedestrians she encountered during the day seemed to take on the same numbed appearance, victims of a general neurasthenia. In her notebook Bishop drew on the mechanized figures in a de Chirico dreamscape and the "hollow men" of Eliot's "unreal city" to convey the horror she felt as she sat in a subway car staring at a nearby woman. With justification, David Kalstone (19) sees in this lifeless subway rider a precursor of Bishop's man-moth:

A woman sat at right angles to me in the subway last night, very close, so I could look directly into her face. Her clothes, her shoes and handbag, everything about her had died, and her face was dead too. Her blue straw hat was pulled and sodden all over her head and her clothes showed that she had forgotten to think of them as clothes for a long time. She sat with her eyes shut, and her face was dead white, the wrinkles looking stiffened, except over the eye-balls where they still had the soft creepy appearance of live flesh, but there too thin. I couldn't see the eyebrows, but the lashes were absolutely the only live thing about her: perfectly black, stiff, and shiny, like those on a sleeping-doll. There was even a little unwholesome looking iridescence shifting along them. Margaret [Miller] told me a dream she had a while ago in which she looked into the inside of a small mask someone had pulled from his face, and caught in it all around the eye-balls were the little hairy eye-lashes. This woman's face made me think of that— its expression was a concave one like an empty interior expression, and its only markings were all the little eyelashes. It is rather strange the way the eye is surrounded with this. . . . hair grows, I've heard, even on the dead. ("Recorded Observations," 1934–37: 16, VC)

In 1950, during one of the most difficult periods of her life, she returned to this image of the mask as a facade or "whited sepulcher" concealing inner corruption. In a diary entry from October of that year, she writes, "A perfectly ghastly brief nightmare—I was looking at a head, showing it to someone—no one's I recognized, white and neat like a statue and very perfect. Then I said 'See' and opened the mouth to show that the inside was corrupt and running with ants." To this description, Bishop attaches a parenthetical comment: "Early surrealism influence here!" (1950 diary: 24 October, VC). Here Bishop is struck, as Bakhtin was in *Rabelais and His World*, by the difference between the body as represented in classical statuary, static and monumental, and the grotesque physical body represented by Bosch or Bruegel. The classical statue has no openings or orifices and is placed on a pedestal to be admired as the image of symmetry, reason, and purity, whereas the grotesque body, with its gaping mouth, designates all that rationalism attempts to contain—the mad, the criminal, the sick, the unruly, and the irrational. Once again, as in "The Monument," Bishop challenges Stevens's vision of the poem as "white and neat like a statue and very perfect," uncontaminated by the unconscious.

In Bishop's nightmare, the return of the repressed is symbolically figured in the image of ants crawling from the mouth of Orpheus. Her dream enacts the strange etymology of the word *mask* and its connection with the word *larva*. The insect's first stage is called a ghost, specter, or mask (disguise) of its last one. In *Masks, Transformation, and Paradox*, A. David Napier traces the history of this linkage:

From the Stoics, for example, we have inherited the logical paradigm called the larvatus, the "masked man." According to this paradigm, I do not know the identity of a certain masked man; I know well the identity of my father; the masked man, therefore, is not my father. . . . [and] Melville's Aristotelian metaphor for character—that of a caterpillar becoming a butterfly—would have been especially unacceptable in the Middle Ages, when the word Larva stood for all that was insidious and deceitful. For the Middle Ages, the body itself became a persona—a mask that its wearer only escaped in death. (Napier 226 n. 15)

In some respects, Bishop's "Man-Moth" resembles the larvatus, or "masked man," for whom the body itself is a mask that its wearer escapes only in death. At the same time, he is the mask or persona of the poet as she explores the compelling difference between the classical ideal and the grotesque physical body, the conscious and the unconscious mind.[3]

"Sleeping on the Ceiling"

Perhaps Bishop's most telling use of the crawling or tunneling insect as a figure for the grotesque irrationality lurking beneath the surface calm occurs in the Parisian poem, "Sleeping on the Ceiling." Like the woman narrator of Charlotte Perkins Gilman's *The Yellow Wallpaper*, the speaker in this poem is troubled by insomnia and mesmerized by the floral arabesques covering the walls of her apartment, which seem to break down the boundaries between interior and exterior space, the domestic and the strange, the rational and the irrational. Planning the poem in a working notebook, Bishop writes,

The wallpaper is the Jardin des Plantes. Tunnelling insects. Photographs hanging on it—The Walrus, etc. The Chandelier is the Fountain in the Place de la Concorde (the ceiling) The fountain casts long shadows—how quiet it is up there. The water has been turned off and the fountain is dark—The insects in the heavy foliage of the Jardin des Plantes rattle and rustle a bit.

> battle the gladiator-insects with net and trident
> Sleep—rediscoverer of old claims
> The excavator, the Miner, Re-Staker-Out
> (KW1 51–52)

Bishop may have come up with her image of the "gladiator-insects" rustling under the wallpaper's painted leaves after studying the hallucinatory "insects" Tanguy or Max Ernst generated from the texture of leaves through the process of *frottage*. Whatever their origin, the presence of these adversarial insects literally undermines the room's illusion of comforting domesticity and tidy control. In these first notations, Bishop is uncertain about whether to mine or to do battle with the resources of her unconscious mind. As we can see in the final stanza of the published version of the poem, Bishop treats the irrational finally as a menace that cannot be ignored. Dislodged from its place of concord, the mind must meet the enemy:

> We must go under the wallpaper
> to meet the insect-gladiator,
> to battle with a net and trident,
> and leave the fountain and the square.
> But oh, that we could sleep up there.
>
> (CP 29)

Even after completing "Sleeping on the Ceiling," Bishop still could not free herself from the specter of corruption and instability represented by insects and their unchecked invasion of the home. In a diary kept during her first lonely months in Florida, she again focused on drawing a line between the safety of voluntary, crafted expression (represented by wallpapered rooms and unlittered writing desks) and the involuntary sources of creativity that leave the writer feeling exposed and vulnerable: "The *ants* have scaled the desk. . . . It gives me a horribly naked, Daliesque feeling to see them filing across an unfinished poem" (travel diary, 1937–38: 58, VC). In this instance, the insect armies work against the poet's effort to complete her poetic designs, and the white page of the poem becomes a field of battle (an idea she would later literalize in "12 O'Clock News").

The wallpapered walls of "Sleeping on the Ceiling" figure in other published works, including "In Prison," "Faustina, Or Rock Roses," and "In the Village." Like Charlotte Perkins Gilman before her, Bishop associated the labyrinthine designs of wallpaper with the patterns and circumscriptions of the domestic world. In Bishop's writings, too, wallpaper that has been eaten, ripped, or burned away signals the onset of madness. This is doubtless true in part because wallpaper loomed large in Bishop's memory of the night that separated her from her mother forever. An uncomprehending child, she was awakened in the middle of the night by a fire that she imagined to be there in the room with her, burning the wallpaper beside her bed (*CProse* 270). The next morning she learned that her mother, too, had been startled by the flames, and the fire had triggered the mental breakdown that would lead to Gertrude Bulmer Bishop's permanent hospitalization. For the child of such a mother, sanity was linked with the surface securities of an undisturbed domestic life—"peaceful ceilings," wallpapered walls, unmarked writing paper, and a tidy desk. But lurking always amid the familiar bric-a-brac were monsters waiting to emerge. The insects of irrationality tunneling beneath the calm veneer inevitably crawled out of the woodwork.

"Objects and Apparitions"

We see little evidence of the Daliesque in the autobiographical "In the Village," in her Brazilian work, or in her late poetry. Bishop took pains to disassociate her art from that of Max Ernst (whose paintings she found "dreadful") and the other male surrealists with whom she was compared after the appearance of her first book of poems. Steadfastly refusing the mantle of prophet, she was indebted to surrealism only for the "air of imminent danger" or imminent surprise in her later work. Her respect for the natural object led to a disdain for the surrealist's self-conscious sophistication. She recoiled from surrealism's analytic approach, with its symbols and codes and waited instead for those "unexpected moments of empathy" when

familiar things seemed somehow magnified, heightened, and sug-
gestive (letter to Stevenson, 8 January 1964, WU).

In some ways, her childhood hero, Nate, the blacksmith of Great
Village, embodies both the alluring and the disquieting characteris-
tics of the surrealist, for his artistry "is the elements speaking: earth,
air, fire, water," and "it turns everything to silence" (*CProse* 274).
A self-proclaimed alchemist, the surrealist takes a cavalier approach
to the natural objects that Bishop handled with care. In the alche-
mist's alembic furnace, all elements are converted into the same
substance. And all things express the nature of man, that *prima
materia* of romantic, symbolist, and surrealist art. In an effort to
escape the tradition of the artist-virtuoso, Bishop adopted a calculat-
edly naive vision based in part on amateur, or primitive, art.

Next to folk artists like her great-uncle George and Gregorio
Valdes (a Key West primitive painter who first caught her eye when
she saw his work hanging in a barber shop on Duval Street in a
block of "cheap liquor stores, shoeshine parlors and poolrooms"
[*CProse* 50]), the larger-than-life dimensions of surrealism appeared
overstated. In "Large Bad Picture" and again in "Poem," Bishop
paid tribute to her uncle, an unpretentious picture maker who never
earned any money for his drawings in his life. By painting the
Nova Scotia he knew—the tiny cows, minuscule white geese, and
a specklike bird ("or is it a flyspeck looking like a bird?")—on a
canvas the size of "an old-style dollar bill," he took perfect measure
of "the little we get for free,/ the little of our earthly trust": "Nothing
much" for any of us to crow about (*CP* 177). She found inspiration
in the "captivating freshness, flatness, remoteness" of the primitive
artist's canvas where "life and the memory of it so compressed /
they've turned into each other" (*CP* 177). These works of "unwit-
ting" heroism were painted purely for the love of modest observa-
tion, and Bishop recognized in them the "self-forgetful, perfectly
useless concentration" on objects both homely and curious that she
strove for in her own writing (letter to Stevenson, 8 January 1964,
WU).[4]

Bishop's respect for the quotidian struck Randall Jarrell as deeply
moral in its implications: "[Bishop's] poems are quiet, truthful, sad,
funny, most marvelously individual poems; they have a sound, a feel,

a whole moral and physical atmosphere, different from anything else I know. They are honest, modest, minutely observant, masterly" (198). But for all their studied simplicity, they did not pander to a simple-minded readership. When Anne Stevenson compared her to Andrew Wyeth, Bishop took offense, proving that she was just as suspicious of the populist appeal in Wyeth's brand of American Gothic as she had been of surrealism's pseudosophistication: "The only thing I didn't like very much, and you guessed I wouldn't before I saw it, was the Wyeth comparison. I know what you mean by it, of course—but I dislike what he stands for in American painting. . . . Wyeth has an anti-intellectual appeal; the kind of person who believes in John Canaday admires him—and there are days, when I get letters from two nuns in the same mail, when I'm afraid I might have that appeal! (I read that Kennedy hadn't wanted to give Wyeth that medal—He wanted to give it to Shahn—and even said 'Next time we'll go abstract.')" (letter to Stevenson, 14 November 1964, WU).

Perhaps only Joseph Cornell could combine worldliness and naïveté in a way that Bishop found emotionally satisfying and inspiring. Each of Cornell's box theaters displayed a miscellany of objects that were brought together not in order to induce a surrealist shock of dislocation and breakdown but to reveal what Bishop called "unexpected moments of empathy" (letter to Stevenson, 8 January 1964, WU). Bishop shared Cornell's sensibility, which was rooted more in laconic New England than in the diabolic straits of surrealism. Art critic Robert Hughes might well have been talking about Bishop's poetry when he described Cornell's art as a reinvention "of the past in the full light of what modernism entailed: a formal strictness, a banishment of rhetoric, and an almost unequaled power to slip down through the mind's strata" (67).

In her translation of "Objects and Apparitions," Octavio Paz's tribute to Cornell, Bishop declared her own attachment to the narrative power of "marbles, buttons, thimbles, dice, / pins, stamps, and glass beads" (*CP* 275). "Objects and Apparitions" draws together the images Bishop intuitively associated with memory. In it, she returned to her old notion of the whispering gallery with its "skein of voices": "Memory weaves, unweaves the echoes: / in

the four corners of the box / shadowless ladies play hide-and-seek."
Cornell's art also preserved certain residues and traces of childhood
when objects seemed animated with magic powers: "A comb is a
harp strummed by a glance / of a little girl / born dumb" (*CP* 276).
How companionable this image must have seemed to Bishop, who
remembered a time in her own childhood when, "dumb" with
longing and sadness, she helped to dress her grandmother's hair
with silver combs. Bishop recounted the episode in "In the Village":
"I pretend to play a tune on each [of the combs] before we stick
them in, so my grandmother's hair is full of music" (*CProse* 260).
Bishop struggled against the troubling ephemerality of her lan-
guage, of words which so readily turned to invisible music, to
viewless breath, to apparition.

Resembling souvenir cases themselves, Bishop's homes in Sa-
mambaia and Ouro Prêto and her last home in Boston, the reno-
vated condominium at Lewis Wharf, were full to brimming with
things that she thought of as the "tales of the time" (*CP* 275): rows
of books (and hundreds in storage), ancestral paintings, wasps'
nests, bird cages, a boatman's paddle painted with the flags of Brazil
and the United States, Venetian blackamoors, and a large ship's
figurehead. Like Cornell, her souvenirs were paperweights that
ground the lost past in the material present but only for a moment:

> The apparitions are manifest,
> their bodies weigh less than light,
> lasting as long as this phrase lasts.
>
> Joseph Cornell: inside your boxes
> my words became visible for a moment.
>
> (*CP* 276)

Bishop made a sandbox in homage to Cornell. Two shocks of
color occupy the lower half of the box: a large morpho butterfly
from the tropics, its wings a brilliant blue, and below the morpho,
a smaller butterfly with bright yellow wings. In her early career,
when Bishop's imagination was most susceptible to surrealism's
vision of the broken down mind, these objects in close proximity
with one another were enough to induce in the poet a quiver of
dissociation and disorder. But earlier images of the larvatus, or

masked man, whose surface calm disguises the madness beneath, undergo a metamorphosis in Bishop's Cornell-inspired box, where the brilliant butterfly replaces the disturbing ants and burrowing insects that once haunted her imagination.

While living in Florida, Bishop considered the role that brilliant butterflies might play both in the resurgence of childhood memories and in the mind's restoration. She copied into her journal a lengthy passage from Clifford Whittingham Beers's *A Mind That Found Itself*, an autobiographical account of the author's recovery from madness. Describing the symptoms of his paranoid schizophrenia, Beers remembers how he imagined a "magic lantern" projecting and gory heads and handwritten messages on the blank walls and white sheets of his hospital room. But then he recalls how these terrors were dispelled by other visions of "vivid beauty." In one instance, "swarms of butterflies and large and gorgeous moths appeared on the sheets." Their appearance is linked to another pleasing fantasy that he could trace directly "to impressions gained in early childhood" and "the quaint pictures by Kate Greenaway—little children in attractive dress, playing in old-fashioned gardens" (qtd. in KW2 25). Passages like these from Beers's book helped launch The Connecticut Society for Mental Hygiene in 1908 and a larger public health movement in New England.

In her sandbox, Bishop's butterflies, like Beers's, are set beside images from Kate Greenaway illustrations. Filling the upper portion of the box are shells and an infant's pacifier, objects marked by longing. But the space is dominated by row after row of paper dolls, little children in attractive dress clipped perhaps from a Sears, Roebuck catalog. This parade of angelic faces, all alike, all wearing smocks with collars that extend on either side like wings, seems to represent the kind of girl child that might inhabit the catalog's manufactured Eden. Since Bishop's paternal grandmother had been sorely disappointed to find that her tomboyish granddaughter could not, or would not, live up to this ideal, the box may have given the poet a chance to come to terms with all the cultural pressures exerted upon her both as a lonely child and a nonconforming adult.

The components of this collage were enough to summon up a long-cherished dream of home—a dream deferred. But where the bricolage activity of a Max Ernst or a Dali provoked in the viewer a sense of disorientation, even paranoia, Bishop's Cornell box produces an opposite effect. Breton insisted that his viewers walk "a dangerous plank" when they ventured into his world of disconnected images (*Oeuvres Complètes* 534). Bishop's works of memory, by contrast, were feats of engineering, offering herself and her audience lifesaving bridges across the expanse of time. Surrealism unmasked the sexual component, the irrational impulse, lurking in our transcendental or romantic aspirations (Wright 270). Bishop, instead, worked to rescue and renew the beleaguered mind.

7 *"In the Village"*
Madness and the Mother's Body

In her book, *On Longing: Narratives of the Miniature, the Gigantic, the Souvenir, the Collection*, Susan Stewart explains the human desire for "belongings or appurtenances" (xi). The mental baggage we carry with us expresses a "yearning desire" for the mother's body and is therefore "emblematic of the nostalgia that all narrative reveals—the longing for the place of origin . . . for the point of identity with the mother" (xii). As such, the souvenir recalls Freud's description of the fetish: a part of the body that is substituted for the whole or an object that is substituted for the body whose absence inspires longing. If it is evoked fetishistically, however, the souvenir suggests a certain ambivalence about that maternal place of origin; the souvenir holder may have mixed feelings about returning to that primal embrace. The portable knickknack is less of a threat than the absent mother with whom it is tenuously connected. A relic of an "authentic experience," the souvenir is a kind of contraband, removed from its potentially dangerous, "natural location" (135). No longer tied irrevocably to a source of pain or frustration, the memento now offers the sense of distance and control over "yearning desire" (ix) that is the motive force of autobiography—and the motive force of Bishop's brilliant memoir, "In the Village," where objects are magically animated and speak in lieu of people.

In this tale, the poet deliberately shifts her focus away from the looming central figure of the dark mother to the objects and people surrounding her, a form of misprision as protective gesture. The child narrator of "In the Village" does all she can to deny her attachment to the screaming woman by repressing any awareness of a mother-daughter bond. Though the events of the story are recounted through the eyes of the young Elizabeth, the child is never named and her relationship with the central, screaming woman must be deciphered by the reader as the story unfolds.[1] Fearful of the resemblance between herself and her mother, the child nevertheless reinforces that resemblance by showing signs of hysteria herself, including her willingness to endow inanimate objects with magical powers of speech.

More an apparition than a tangible being, Gertrude is seen through her young daughter's eyes as a set of nervous mannerisms, fleetingly glimpsed, and a collection of belongings and appurtenances—a purple dress, a group of black and white handkerchiefs, a cracked set of china, a bundle of crumbling postcards. Unable to acknowledge the grave danger her mother's instability represents, the child displaces her fear onto a series of talismanic things, which become leading actors in this domestic drama. She regards the purple material for her mother's new dress, for example, with all the wariness, the anxiety, that she cannot afford to direct at Gertrude herself. The textiles and perfumes and other "stuff" threaten to "echo" what they have heard, and yet every attempt is made to ignore their oracular speech (*CProse* 258–59). Forced to "look away" before the "purple stuff" can speak of what it knows, she learns to concentrate instead on the more innocuous and distracting sounds, sights, smells, textures, and tastes of her village (*CProse* 258–59).

Warding off the revelation of her mother's madness, Bishop's narrative technique actually mimics the kind of deflection associated with hysterical conversion symptoms. The screaming woman and her poet daughter, each in her own way, tries to give voice to what is unspeakable, yet irrepressible, about the past. Both suffer mainly from reminiscences, but as a writer, Bishop possessed the power to control and to time the uncanny reemergence of the past or the return of the repressed. An intense attachment to determinate objects is the principle trait that Bishop's writing shares with the hysteric's symbolic speech. Like the hysteric whose bodily tics, speech impediments, or involuntary gestures encode a pain she cannot bring herself to express directly, the writer uses signs, similes, and metaphors drawn from the corporeal world to convey otherwise inexpressible feeling. The narrative reenacts the hysterical disorder it presents and turns out to embody what Mary Jacobus has called "the repressed (because disruptive, unassimilable, and contradictory) aspects of all narrative" (202), since "one might say that the fetishizing of signs is the occupational hazard of writing" (217).[2]

"In the Village" exposes the mind of a child shying away from, yet compulsively drawn to, the maternal body. The five-year-old has not yet acquired the language to describe the mother's intense physical reality, which has become for her a primal scene of terror. The mother embodies the strange disorder that Bishop's story draws on yet seeks to domesticate. Gertrude's hysteria remains as threatening and fascinating to the poet as her own primordial imagination. Bishop's most primitive mental world is re-created in her short story, where all things are uncannily attuned to the human emotions that hang in the air. As Elizabeth Wright explains, "The uncanny is the projection of our inner fears onto the external, creating *objects* of love and hate" (272; my emphasis), and it is a vestige of the child's imagination carried over into adult experience.

According to Freud, the fantasy world of the infant is a world "intimately connected with . . . the belief in the omnipotence of thoughts":

Our analysis of instances of the uncanny has led us back to the old, animistic conception of the universe. This was characterized by the idea that the world was peopled with the spirits of human beings; by the subject's narcissistic overvaluation of his own mental processes; by the belief in the omnipotence of thoughts and the techniques of magic based on that belief; by the attribution to various persons and things of carefully graded magical powers, or "mana"; as well as by all the other creations with the help of which man, in the unrestricted narcissism of that stage of development, strove to fend off the manifest prohibitions of reality. It seems as if each one of us has been through a phase of individual development corresponding to this animistic stage in primitive men, that none of us has passed through it without preserving certain residues and traces of it which are still capable of manifesting themselves, and that everything which now strikes us as "uncanny" fulfills the condition of touching those residues of animistic mental activity within us and bringing them to expression. (Freud, "The Uncanny" 219)

The calculatedly naive perspective Bishop adopted in "In the Village," and the sense of the *unheimlich* erupting out of the familiar, which is so characteristic of her poetry as well as her prose, accounts for the way Bishop's writing seems to "vibrate," in Helen Vendler's words, "between two frequencies—the domestic and the strange" (32).

Although the strangeness of the village and its inhabitants threatens to permanently upset the child narrator's equilibrium, she turns to that very strangeness for emotional support. If certain bodies or gestures bear the weight of the child narrator's anxiety, other magical objects delight and absorb her. In an effort to escape her own dark thoughts, she immerses herself in the wonders of a finely observed world. Buoyed up by the collectibles she finds along the way, the child keeps her spirits aloft like a sugar ball hung from an elastic band: "I know I don't even care for the inside of it, which is soft, but I wind most of the elastic around my arm, to keep the ball off the ground, at least, and start hopefully back" (*CProse* 268).

Like her child self, Bishop works to keep her spirits and her story aloft. In her characteristic way, she eschews the emotional core, the soft, crumbling "inside" of her tragic past, preferring to focus on the hard outer shell of circumstance. Her oblique style takes considerable poise to pull off. Like the child that she once was, Bishop performs a delicate balancing act that, in the face of destabilizing realities, ensures survival. Still we sense that the adult writer's hurt cannot be assuaged. The five-year-old Elizabeth could not extricate herself from her family's "skein of voices" and untangle her own from all the others. More than forty years had to pass before she could gain the confidence to cast her own net over the past and catch its meaning.

Hysteria and the Modern Artist

Bishop was always sensitive to the ways that other respected artists deflected attention away from wounding personal matters. In a letter dated 19 October 1967 (VC), and sent to her friend, Joseph Summers, Bishop considers the psychological dimension at work in Marianne Moore's "meticulous attention" to the phenomenal world, noting that such extraordinary powers of observation must stem in part from "intolerable pain." Certainly "intolerable pain" is at the root of the ambivalence that Bishop expresses toward the figure of the screaming woman at the center of "In the Village" and the intensity with which she tries to disguise both the woman's identity and the biographical connection between the woman and herself. But it is also consistent with the standards of high male modernism with which Moore identified and to which she tried to hold her protégée Bishop (with only partial success).

Bishop's reliance on a succession of images that build to some intellectual and emotional truth through their sheer accretion became her own method of extending Pound's theory of imagism. In his preface to *Imagist Poetry,* Pound says he sought that fugitive moment "when a thing outward and objective transforms itself, or darts into a thing inward and subjective' " (Jones 40), and Bishop's narrative technique expands the possibilities of Pound's method. But Bishop's oblique approach to emotion stems more from personal circumstance than political agenda. The male modernists, on the other hand, were forthright about their desire to rid poetry of its pathological femininity, which they linked with sentimentality, lethargy, and effeteness. Many postmodern men of letters, including Bishop's great friend, Robert Lowell, continued to fight the good fight against the hysteria they associated with literary women. In the poem "Statue of Liberty," Lowell characterized the spirit of his society as militantly, annoyingly female, noting "the thrilling, chilling silver of your laugh, / the hysterical digging of your accursed spur" (*History* 147).

Private trauma and the standards of her day combined to produce in Bishop's mind a similar fear of the pathologically feminine. Bishop's conspicuous effort to suppress her narrator's gender works to suggest a lingering terror of identifying herself with the feminine. Women and hysteria (from the Greek word for "uterus") have long been linked in Western culture, so much so that hysteria had come to be regarded in early psychoanalytic circles as the defining feature of woman, insofar as the woman's thought processes were believed to be inherently unstable, riddled with detours, gaps, and omissions.

That Bishop shared her fear of the female hysteric with the dominant male modernists of the preceding generation raises interesting interpretive issues. For instance, scholars have recently approached a seminal text like *The Wasteland* as a case study in repression and have come to view Eliot as a personality haunted by hysteria. Wayne Koestenbaum, for one, has pointed out that Eliot's sexual frustrations and nervous breakdown leave behind "hysterical discontinuities" in the poem's narrative that reveal his "uneasy sympathy" with the "pathology of femininity" (124), and "the hysterical technique of the poem [with its famous ruptures, gaps, and fractures] results from his only fitful ability to speak directly from painful experience." Pound, as editor of *The Wasteland*, took it upon himself to turn Eliot's emotional weaknesses into aesthetic strengths.

"If a woman had written a text with the properties of *The Wasteland*," Koestenbaum concludes archly, "its incoherence might not have been judged successful" (136). By the time "In the Village," Bishop's scaled-down, unassuming prose poem, appeared, sandwiched between the Brazilian and the Canadian halves of her third collection, *Questions of Travel* (1965), narrative disjunction and discontinuity no longer conveyed the shock of the new, and her experimental prose could hardly have been condemned for its nuanced, "feminine" obtuseness. At the same time, Bishop's "hysterical technique" is never solely, or even primarily, a method of dissociating her own art from the incompetence or weakness so long associated with the feminine. As a woman writer, Bishop could not deny the reality and the pain of her kinship with the female hysteric. And unlike her male predecessors, she could not make a denial of the feminine the virtual foundation for her poetic. Although she valued a depersonalized tone even in her most self-revealing work, Bishop was never quite able, or quite willing, to detach herself from her feminine, or maternal, legacy.

"True Confessions"

The trappings of feminine domesticity were uppermost in Bishop's mind when she sat down to compose "In the Village." She wrote the story while living with her Brazilian lover Lota in a house still under construction. The makeshift atmosphere reminded her of Great Village, which had always been "50 years or so backwards" (letter to Stevenson, 6 March 1964, WU). To Anne Stevenson, Bishop wrote, "When I came to live in Samambaia and we had oil lamps for two or three years, etc. a lot came back to me," including the practical knowledge to design the sitting room stove, baking bread, and making marmalade. "When the need arises," she said with a touch of pride, "apparently the old Nova Scotian domestic arts come back to me!" (6 March 1964, WU). Along with the old "domestic arts" came reminders of the old domestic tragedies, glimpsed before only in disjointed images.

Although Bishop was customarily squeamish about disclosing the details of her mother's mental collapse, she did so in a letter dated 5 May 1964 (WU) that she sent from Rio to her biographer. Doing research for her book on the poet, Stevenson had tried to contact Great Village's Chamber of Commerce. In a community so small that "everyone knows everyone else," the letter was handed over to the poet's favorite relative, Aunt Grace. Bishop appreciated Grace as an "active, strong, humorous woman" who "believes in living in the present." "She is almost eighty years old now," Bishop explained, "and apparently she was baffled and a bit put out [by Stevenson's inquisitiveness]—She had never wanted to discuss the past with me at all, although she was more concerned with my mother than anyone else, and I think now, almost fifty years later, she has almost succeeded in burying it completely." In her letter, Bishop went on to say that Grace "was the only daughter of that family who 'went back home' " and "by now she has many grandchildren and dozens of step-grandchildren—and so has a great deal of 'life' to have buried the past under."

Disinterring the past did not come any more easily for Bishop than it did for her Canadian aunt. Both women had been raised to be ashamed of their hidden selves and actual circumstances. Bishop offered to "answer for the 'Chamber of Commerce' " and supply Stevenson with the information requested. The result is a bland rehearsal of the "official" facts:

It has always been said that what set off my mother's insanity was the shock of my father's death at such an early age, and when they'd only been married three years. (He was 39, she was 29). It is the only case of insanity in the family, as far as we know. She had undoubtedly (*I* think) shown symptoms of trouble before—perhaps traits that in our enlightened, etc. days might have been noticed and treated earlier. As it was, she received the very best treatment available at the time, I feel sure. She was in McLean's sanitarium outside of Boston (you must have heard of that)—once maybe twice. Aunt Grace herself went with her, and also, I think, though I'm not positive, took her to doctors in N.Y.—At any rate, the Bishop family 'spared no expense.' Since Aunt Grace was so involved with it all she naturally does not like to remember it, I suppose. That generation took insanity very differently than we do now, you know. *My father did not beat her* or anything like that—really! I am telling you the facts as I have always been given to understand them, and a lot I remember pretty well. (Of course I may have distorted it; but as I'm sure you know, children do have a way of overhearing everything.) The tragic thing was that she returned to N[ova] S[cotia] when she did, before the final breakdown. At that time, women became US citizens when they married US citizens,—so when she became a widow she lost her citizenship. Afterwards, the US would not let her back in, sick, and that is why she had to be put in the hospital at Dartmouth, Nova Scotia.

Well—there we are. Times have changed. I have several friends who are, have been, will be, etc. insane; they discuss it all very freely and I've visited asylums many times since. But in 1916 things were different. After a couple of years, unless you cured yourself, all hope was abandoned. (Letter to Stevenson, 5 May 1964, WU)

Bishop's reserve, in this instance, is understandable. But she had little need for tact when writing for herself alone. A verse fragment scribbled on a sheet of stationery bearing the letterhead "Penzance Causeway/Woods Hole, Massachusetts" and tucked away in the back of a Key West notebook, questions "the facts" as she had always been given to understand them. Long an observer of organic decay, Bishop struggled in her journals to accept her mother's mental erosion:

> Laying flowers on my mother's grave
> those colored circles sink
> · through earth
> flowers that appear
> when you press hands over the eyes
> worlds and suns
> decay and thought and disintegration.

(KW2 39)

In the first years of her life, Bishop saw more of Gertrude (Bulmer) Bishop than commonly believed. During an interview with Ashley Brown in 1966, Bishop clearly established that she had stayed only briefly in Great Village as a child: "I didn't spend all my childhood in Nova Scotia. I lived there from 1914 to 1917 during the First World War. After that I spent long summers there until I was thirteen. Since then I've made occasional visits" (Brown 6). Here she disproved the common assumption among scholars that she had lived in Great Village from the end of 1911 to 1916 and was separated from her mother long before Gertrude's final breakdown parted them forever. Intermixed, then, with recollections of her hymn-singing aunts in Nova Scotia are darker images of her mother in New England.

In the unpublished "True Confessions," Bishop gave a surreal twist to her very first home, the Worcester, Massachusetts, apartment house she shared with her mother:

I was born there, sort of in the middle but slightly to the left and rather inset—a tiny, almost invisible baby. I could see it under a magnifying glass—a tiny, almost invisible baby, a small dark haired mother upstairs in a tiny toy wooden apartment house painted grey. Years later, when it was visible to the naked eye, but still not very big, I saw it from a trolley car, someone said, "That's where you were born" and I turned around to stare and saw briefly through its gray walls and a vague fierce picture of myself being born hanging on one of them and then it receeded [receded] behind [my shoulder] and up a curve to the left, and vanished. (Box 55, folder 5, VC)

As a child in Great Village, the poet used to train her grandfather's magnifying glass on bright illustrations of the Bible stories where people were dressed in robes of many colors. But her own life, drab by comparison, receded from view almost immediately. This "invisible baby" self "hanging" vaguely but fiercely on the walls of memory prepares us for the "invisible" child of "In the Village," who knows how to "vanish" at opportune times. In the opening pages of the memoir, Bishop's child self is swallowed up by the avalanche of belongings associated with her mother and shunted aside by the entourage of womenfolk working to keep Gertrude on an even keel. For the tiny Elizabeth, invisibility comes as something of a relief. Her childhood instinct for self-effacement and the reasons for it doubtless lay the groundwork for her famous reticence as a poet, but the connection, however suggestive, remains elusive. Much of the tension that animates "In the Village" stems from the ingenious balance Bishop maintains between confession and denial or forthrightness and repression.

Encrypting Mother

Bishop wrote "In the Village," her masterwork, in a "single stretch straight off the typewriter—the first time she had ever done such a thing." She was given too much cortisone for asthma, and "sat up all night in the tropical heat," she later told Elizabeth Spires. "The story came from a combination of cortisone, I think, and the gin and tonic I drank in the middle of the night. I wrote it in two nights" ("The Art of Poetry" 73). But many years of thought prepared her for this burst of creative energy. For one thing, she had already written a prose sketch of her reminiscences from which she culled material. The manuscript is now a part of the Elizabeth Bishop Collection held at Vassar College Libraries and provides an uncensored and unpolished account of arguably the most decisive event in Bishop's life:

The hardest thing about it now . . . is to realize that it has happened. Sad things, sadder things, awful things, seen always a minute afterwards, so unnecessary, so unreasonable. What I had done before, & have done since, and what has happened to us all—it is understandable—if you thing [think] about it long enough it makes sense and you feel, like a light moving behind a window pane at night, a certain reason, to it—an illumination— like an inscrutable aloof force, lit up by a smile. But this—what happened to her—throws the picture off—the music all out of key . . . . Gran, at the end of her life, thought suddenly it had all been wrong—and Aunt Grace could look ahead thinking whatever came could be all wrong. . . . Grandpa thought God might step in between. ("Reminiscences of Great Village" 9, box 54, folder 10, VC)

Bishop once said that the incidents of "In the Village" were all "accurate—just *compressed* a bit" (letter to Anne Stevenson, 2 October 1963, WU; my emphasis). And certainly the narrative's atmosphere feels "compressed" from the very start. In the story's brief overture, Bishop minimizes the scale of the village itself, accommodating it to the naïveté of a child's perspective: the lightning rod atop the church steeple becomes a tuning fork set to the pitch of "my village," a place of the subjective mind. Bishop's image of the mind as a "great whispering gallery" in which we live, a chamber "constantly vibrating and humming" returns in her portrait of the village. The hymn-singing town of her childhood is not a place of stone and mortar but a psychic arena of furtive whispers and indelible screams.

The story opens with a primal scene of Bishop's childhood: "The large front bedroom with sloping walls on either side, papered in wide white and dim-gold stripes" where a woman is being fitted for a new dress (*CProse* 251). Featureless, nameless, the woman has come from Boston and is identified only as the bearer of the scream—a scream that is anticipated throughout the story, a cry that will "hang over that Nova Scotian village" long after her departure, living forever in memory, like "a slight stain in those pure" picture postcard skies. As the events of this summer day unfold, the threat of the woman's imminent collapse is described through a complex synaesthesia. The hysteric's lament—"the sky is falling, the sky is falling"—hovers just out of hearing range but enters the tale through many apertures as the contents of the woman's trunk are unpacked: the darkening stain that spreads "over the woods and waters as well as the sky" over the village is repeated in the "awful brown stains" from a leaking perfume bottle that ruin the woman's delicate, white handkerchiefs. And then there are the postcards "from another world . . . the world of sad brown perfume" and mourning: the buildings pictured on them are outlined in metallic crystals "in a way buildings never are outlined but should be—if there were a way of making the crystals stick" (*CProse* 255). But nothing adheres as it should in this imploding world: There are "words written in the skies with the same stuff, crumbling, dazzling and crumbling, raining down a little on little people who sometimes stand about below: pictures of Pentecost? What are the messages?" (*CProse* 255).

The "messages" are clear in Bishop's "Reminiscences of Great

Village," her preliminary notes for "In the Village." An early version of the story's opening scene, for instance, is all raw emotion and exposed nerve:

That afternoon I tapped on my mother's door and went in. Easter [her mother] was standing in the middle of the room with Miss O'Neil [the dressmaker, renamed Miss Gurley in the final version] kneeling at her left and Aunt Grace at her right. The tiny fan of shiny needles in Miss O'Neil's starved looking mouth might well have been a sacred host. She stared up at Easter with fear and wonder, and I thought to myself "Oh, she knows. . . ." Miss O'Neil picked up a large pair of shears & took hold of the extra cloth, to cut it away. *At once Easter fell to her knees and snatched the cloth away from her. "Oh Oh!" she cried, "You hurt me. You mustn't cut it. . . . It's mine . . . so take the scissors away. Grace! make her stop. It will bleed. I shall bleed."* . . . She jumped up & ran to the other end of the room trailing the cloth in a wonderful swirl behind her. She stood there and screamed." (11–12, box 54, folder 10, VC; my emphasis)

A relatively realistic account of the episode, this passage nevertheless attempts a certain metaphoric heightening, less effective certainly than the ambiguities of the final version. From the mother's pseudonym, "Easter," to the dressmaker's role as supplicant and witness, her mouth fed by "shiny needles" that "might well have been a sacred host," we find Bishop experimenting with a motif of martyrdom and transubstantiation. Her mother excites the dressmaker's "fear and wonder" as though she were what the French call a "sacred monster," but there is no redemption in her holy madness. In its final incarnation, the story will no longer identify the mother by name or by alias, but a subtle association between the mother and the "sacred host" remains in the story's emphasis on a child's longing for her mother's body and the nurturance only she can provide.

Emerging from a prolonged period of mourning, Gertrude feels that she cannot embrace life without betraying the memory of her late husband. Her histrionics underscore the theatricality of her position as a woman alone, living in a culture of proprieties. She is being asked to choose between what are, for her, two equally unacceptable roles (cloistered widow or nubile woman) and two unwearable costumes (the armor of austerity and social obligation or the apparel of invitation and desire). Her body becomes the stage on which this drama is acted out. The "bleeding" purple color of the cloth becomes linked in her mind with her woman's body, fertile, desirable, and vulnerable to passions both transformative and wounding. The dressmaker's attempt to cut the cloth, in an effort to make it suitable and "fitting," is taken by Gertrude to be an attack on her person, on her proper self: "Grace! make her stop. It will bleed. I shall bleed."

This opening scene has been substantially altered by the time it appears in the final version of "In the Village." The purple prose and sacrificial imagery are gone, replaced by insinuation. Only the purple cloth retains its original aura of significance. In keeping with Gertrude's own hysterical conversion of her body into a bolt of fabric, the screaming woman of "In the Village" has very little bodily presence of her own, and her power to excite longing and fear is displaced onto the purple swatch of material. To her child she is a textile filled with holes left by the dressmaker's shears; to the reader she is the reason why the text is likewise holey and quietly deranged:

> The village dressmaker was fitting a new dress. It was her first in almost two years and she had decided to come out of black, so the dress was purple. She was very thin. She wasn't at all sure whether she was going to like the dress or not and she kept lifting the folds of the skirt, still unpinned and dragging on the floor around her, in her thin white hands, and looking down at the cloth.
>
> "Is it a good shade for me? Is it too bright? I don't know. I haven't worn colors for so long now. . . . How long? Should it be black? Do you think I should keep on wearing black? . . .
>
> Unaccustomed to having her back, the child stood now in the doorway, watching. The dressmaker was crawling around and around on her knees eating pins as Nebuchadnezzar had crawled eating grass. The wallpaper glinted and the elm trees outside hung heavy and green, and the straw matting smelled like the ghost of hay. (*CProse* 251–52)

There are ghosts moving everywhere within this passage: straw matting that echoes a past life, wallpaper that "glinted" with meaning and malice (from the Middle English *glinten*, "to dart obliquely"), and a child that hovers in the background barely there at all. Even madness darts obliquely into the story, entering through the biblical allusion to King Nebuchadnezzar who ate grass the way a dressmaker eats pins—crawling on all fours. Insanity tunnels its way through the wallpaper and across the floor of the large front bedroom, though its presence is displaced from its source and materializes only in bric-a-brac and kneeling seamstresses.

A striking comment in one of Bishop's working journals sheds new light on this opening scene. In her preparatory notes for "Sleeping on the Ceiling," Bishop writes: "The bodily equivalent to insanity is = To go through life on all fours—hands and knees as an insect, too" (KW1 51). We have already had occasion to touch on the ways in which Charlotte Perkins Gilman's famous chronicle of her own descent into madness sets a precedent for Bishop's depiction of a bourgeois world disrupted by the irrational. Here again, Bishop's choice of metaphor recalls Gilman's nameless female narrator, reduced by the end of *The Yellow Wallpaper* to a dehumanized creature creeping on all fours. As a hysterical conversion symptom, crawling appropriately reminds us of her cringing status as a subjugated wife and mother. Bishop may have remembered this singular image when it came time to settle on a set of "bodily equivalents" for her mother's psychic unrest, her distinctly "female" hysteria.

Carefully, the child narrator refuses to be named as a girl, an "Elizabeth." At the same time, the child avoids speaking of her relationship to the screaming woman, as though madness might be catching, a genetic and environmental legacy. In fact, the story suggests that in the mind of the child, madness is something communicable, something in the drinking water, something that can be eaten. At the story's end, the front room is empty, the screaming woman is in a sanitarium, and there she receives packages from home that spell out, ruefully, why she can never return: "cake and fruit . . . Fruit, cake . . . Fruit. Cake" (*CProse* 272).

"A bosom full of needles"

The sacramental meal of the dressmaker's pins (the "sacred host") introduces a concern with eating, sucking, ingesting, and transmuting that will be repeated throughout the story, becoming associated primarily with the child's need for maternal succor. The foods of infancy, candies and soft-textured pabulums (porridge and potato mash) are used to pacify the "screaming woman" and distract her anxious child. Yet everything carries a bittersweet taste that lingers "wonderful but wrong" (*CProse* 259). Crying into the potato mash, her grandmother gives the child a spoonful that tastes like tears (*CProse* 259). The next morning her grandmother hopes to get the child out of the house before her mother comes downstairs ("Hurry up and finish that porridge"), but the child dawdles, not feeling very hungry. Although she says, "I think I've had enough," the child must wait while her mother feeds her the rest, before she can take the cow to the pasture. On her way home later that morning, she passes the Hills' general store. Along with the Moirs chocolate she offers her (*CProse* 265—66), Miss Ruth Hill gently tries to extract information from the child about her mother's "illness" ("How is she? We've always been friends. We played together from the time we were babies."). While at the dressmaker's home, the child finds among Miss Gurley's cards of buttons "little glass ones delicious to suck" (*CProse* 258). Later that day, while her mother is being fitted again for her new purple dress, the child is sent to Mealy's candy store for some "humbugs" that her mother can suck on, but before she can leave, she is spotted in the mirror by her mother who tells her "Stop sucking your thumb!" (*CProse* 267).

For child and mother, sucking becomes a symbolic expression, both of their unmet need for succor and their suppression of emotion. The cultural ideal of the mother as "sacred host," as sacrificial offering, places impossible demands on the mother and arouses impossible expectations in the child, expectations that are doubly tormenting in the context of "In the Village." Luce Irigaray, in her prose poem, "And the One Doesn't Stir Without the Other" (62), articulates what remains unspoken in Bishop's memoir of her mother's disappearance from her life. Irigaray speaks in the voice of a daughter confronting her mother's body: "Will there never be love between us, the daughter asks, other than this filling up of holes"—this filling up of "my mouth, my belly?" Is your only desire to "close off and seal up everything that could happen between us, indefinitely?" The mother's hunger to make her child literally "flesh of her flesh" fills the daughter with dread and the bitter understanding that there can be no other way for intimacy between the two so long as the mother "metamorphoses into a baby nurse" at her daughter's approach.

Examining the "oral relations" central to the mother-daughter bond, Jane Gallop remarks that it "ought to be one in which the daughter absorbs (from) the mother," and yet as often as not, "that transaction is confused with the mother's absorbing the daughter, since the difference between the two is not stable and since absorption is precisely a process which undermines boundary distinctions" (114). As Patricia Yaeger notes in her provocative reading of "In the Village," small things tend to be absorbed, ultimately disappearing into the story's dangerously capacious female world (140). So many things seem filled with the intent to be lost in this story, particularly the child whose voice we hear. At the bottom of "a thick white teacup," for instance, the child finds what appear to be "pale blue windows" formed by grains of rice that were "put there just for a while" before they disappear, leaving something—some trace—behind them, making those pale blue lights (*CProse* 256).

A small and innocent thing herself, the child views these ghost grains with wonder: "What odd things people do with grains of rice, so innocent and small!" The seamstress's home becomes a primary locus for this engulfing female energy. As a character, Miss Gurley, the dressmaker, absorbs much of the unacknowledged desire and fear that the child feels for her mother. Her bosom is "full of needles with threads ready to pull out and make nests with"; an Arachne who absentmindedly kills as she weaves, Miss Gurley has been known to entangle and capture small things in her web. A "gray kitten once lay on the treadle of her sewing machine, where she rocked it as she sewed, like a baby in a cradle" until it "got hanged on the belt," while another kitten "lies now by the arm of the machine, in imminent danger of being sewn into a turban" (*CProse* 258).

Stories of children who suffer from having been sewn inextricably into the woof and warp of their parents' lives were always a particular preoccupation of Bishop's. The diaries and notebooks Bishop kept after college are stuffed with newspaper clippings about strange infant deaths. One clipping found in the back of her journal for the years 1934 through 1937 tells of a four-year-old separated from his ailing mother who is himself seriously ill, mysteriously wasting away:

Four-year-old Emmie Wilson, who "can't stop talking," carried on his childish prattle today, growing weaker from a strange malady which baffled his doctors. His body wasted away to twenty pounds and his hair turned snow white. . . . the boy had a slight stroke two weeks ago which affected his face. One eye remains open; one side of his mouth is drawn. . . . Throughout his waking hours Emmie talks—of home, childish desires and his mother . . . herself seriously ill at her Munford (Tenn.) home. Always he seems to be afraid to be alone, especially at night. Busy nurses passing his room hold a handkerchief to their eyes when they hear his plea: "Come on in! Please come on in! ("Recorded Observations," 1934–37, VC)

Bishop may have seen her childhood self ("scabby body and wheezing lungs") in the bedridden Emmie Wilson. In 1935, having borrowed the diary of Margery Fleming from Marianne Moore, she read and reread this story of a Scottish girl, born in 1803, who began keeping a journal from the age of six and was dead before she was nine. But most of the newspaper clippings that she collected describe violent deaths. One tells the story of an apparent "mercy killing" by a father of his incurably imbecilic infant son in Perth, Australia. In another newspaper report, this time from Lyon, France, a mother is judged to be indirectly responsible for her child's murder: "Eight-year-old was stoned to death by his playmates because they did not like his long hair. . . . They battered Paul's skull with rocks, police said. His mother had refused to cut his hair" ("Recorded Observations," 1934–37, VC). Bishop turns yet another newspaper report into "The Farmer's Children" (first published in 1948), a short story about two boys whose mother tells them to spend the night watching over the farm machinery in the barn while their father is away on "business" ("probably mostly drinking") (CProse 194). In the harsh cold of December, they freeze to death. In the same journal where these clippings are gathered, Bishop makes a record of a conversation she had with her close friend Margaret Miller on 1 July 1935: "[We] sat in the funeral parlor rooms of Luchow's and had ice-cream. I said that families seemed to me like 'concentration camps'—where people actually let out their sadistic natures" ("Recorded Observations," 1934–37: 29, VC).

Bishop, who counted Hans Christian Andersen among her favorite writers, records her thoughts about the fairy tale, its magical, often brutal, compressions: "Sometimes a children's book—a fairy tale might be made to hold things that could only be put into poetry in three life-times." In one of her Key West notebooks

Bishop tries to come to terms with the capacious powers of the fairy tale in an untitled poem that she dedicates to her doctor, Anny Baumann ("For A. B."):

> The pale child with silver hair
> Sat on the sofa all afternoon
> And in the softest Southern accent
> Read Hans Christian Anderson [Andersen],
>
> And laughed half-scared and too high-pitched
> Showing pallid little gums;
> Cried because the Snow-Queen came,
> Her temples hollowed with bad dreams,
>
> Wept for the interrupted story:
> The woodsman's child who grew so weary,
> The princes dressed in white, the orphan,
> The child who died and lay in the white coffin.
>
> (KWi 233)

"In the Village," like the poem "First Death in Nova Scotia," which Bishop composed about the same time, both confront the jarring interruptions in a child's beautiful dream of life. The entrance of the "Snow-Queen / Her temples hollowed by bad dreams" heralds a rude awakening. In "In the Village," the seamstress Miss Gurley ("girly") bears the weight of this fairy tale tradition, with its ambivalence toward the powerful female figure. Alternatively infantilized (she sleeps, like Thumbelina, "in her thimble") and demonized ("she has a bosom full of needles"), Miss Gurley and her disorderly, unsettling house are hollowed out by the child's bad dreams.

At the same time, however, the dressmaker represents the only pattern within the female realm for creative expression and artistic recuperation. The woman weaver (Penelope at her loom, Ariadne and her thread, Arachne and her web) has become a focal point for scholars who concern themselves with the relation between text, tissue, and *textus* ("textile"), something woven or made from threads, patches, grafts. Nancy K. Miller cautions us to remember that this tropology of the loom cannot and must not be disentangled from the woman who weaves and the material conditions that give rise to her art. Miller grounds her arguments in Virginia Woolf's famous image of art as a spider's web "attached to life at all four corners." When it is "pulled askew, hooked at the edge, torn in the middle, one remembers that these webs are not spun in mid air by incorporeal creatures, but are the work of suffering human beings, and are attached to gross material things, like health and the houses we live in" (*A Room of One's Own* 43–44). In the workshop of Arachne, art is spun out of the body itself; it is a matrix born out of the material world.

Subtly but insistently, Bishop associates the dressmaker with her own suffering mother. Gertrude uses her body, as Penelope uses her tapestry, to give loss and absence some definable shape. In her outbursts and her attachment to objects that can never take the place of what has been lost, the madwoman registers the way her life has been "pulled askew" by nature. The echo of a scream is woven into the very texture of their art, just as it seems to be woven into the purple fabric that Bishop's mother associates with her own "bleeding" body ("Reminiscences of Great Village" 12, box 54, folder 10, VC). The mother's ivory embroidery tools inspire in her child the same mixture of desire and trepidation she feels while watching her mother undress. Absconding with one of these ivory wands, she buries it for safekeeping "under the bleeding heart" (a garden plant with drooping heart-shaped flowers) by the crab-apple tree (*CP* 257). The buried tool, partnerless and unusable even if it could be recovered, "is never found again." It is as irretrievable finally as mother-love (*CP* 257) and lies buried still, under the sign of empathy beside the tree of sullen complaint.

Central to the story is Bishop's fear that she will be condemned to spin art out of her body. To do so would be to repeat her mother's madness in her own life, echo what she has heard, and create a future that turns back on the past. Miss Gurley now assumes the status of a wizened Fate at her spinning wheel. Like a kitten sleeping on a treadle, the child is in imminent danger of being woven into a design not her own, a design seemingly set by nature herself. What would it mean to be caught in the mother's "skein," reabsorbed into the mother's body? The prospect is a terrible one for the child of "In the Village" who "slides out from under" her mother's hands when they settle on her head, "pushing [her] down"

(*CProse* 261). Throughout the story, the mother remains an erratic, intimidating, and generic "she . . . [who] gave the scream."

"Vuillard's Sister in the Wall-paper"

The same atmosphere of "imminent danger" that pervades the dressmaker's shop in "In the Village" may be found in the paintings of the nineteenth-century symbolist, Édouard Vuillard, for whom Bishop felt an affinity. His canvases often center around the commanding image of his mother surrounded by the seamstresses she employed in her corset-making business. While other symbolist painters made art more emotionally expressive by exaggerating, attenuating, and deforming exotic or otherworldly subject matter, Vuillard looked for the deeper meaning in familiar, domestic settings. Vuillard specialized in "the always-more-successful surrealism of the everyday" (Bishop's letter to Anne Stevenson, 8 January 1964, WU). "Poised in a state of controlled panic," like Bishop's "sandpiper" combing the beach for something lost and unrecoverable, Vuillard traces and retraces the dimensions of his childhood home in canvas after canvas. Lavishing attention on the bric-a-brac of domestic life where objects can come to dominate people, Vuillard created a mood of airlessness and potential violence.

Randall Jarrell once said of Bishop's poems that "even their most complicated or troubled or imaginative effects seem, always, personal and natural, and as unmistakable as the first few notes of a Mahler song, the first few patches of a Vuillard interior" (198). Bishop appreciated the comparison with Vuillard. To her biographer, Anne Stevenson, she wrote, "Randall [Jarrell] has said Vuillard—and that is more what I feel like, I think—but I can't put words or ideas in your head, after all" (14 November 1964, WU). It is not surprising that Bishop discovered a kindred spirit in Vuillard. When he shifted his attention to the members of his family in the 1890s, Vuillard conveyed the often ambiguous and troubled relations among them. In her study of the French painter's "intimate interiors," Elizabeth Easton refers her readers to the "sense of intense privacy, almost of a secret language, that hangs over the

Vuillard family [that] addresses the symbolist aesthetic as eloquently as the decorative language of the paintings of seamstresses" (58).

Like Bishop, Vuillard relies on disquieting discrepancies in scale to evoke "a peculiar psychological tension" that can be attributed to his point of view (Easton 83). As Easton explains, "The notion that an object takes on a particular appearance when seen from a certain point of view and a certain state of mind is at the center of Vuillard's approach to the depiction of a particular space" (82). The bric-a-brac of his domestic interiors—a dining table, a chest of drawers, a wallpaper pattern, a purple bolt of cloth—often dwarf the people within them who stand isolated from one another, caught in their own private space. Vuillard may have been inspired by the Dutch Masters, but he introduces a claustrophobia and airlessness into his depictions of family life that distinguish his perspective from the "logically organized" interior scenes of Jan Vermeer and Jan Steen (Easton 58).

Bishop's "In the Village" seems full of the same uneasy portents that make Vuillard's canvases a gripping psychological experience for the viewer. Bishop's eye is particularly drawn to the tense mother-daughter drama visible in Vuillard's intimate interiors. Though these paintings often revolve around a meal, they convey a family's failure to provide emotional nourishment and focus primarily on the psychological strains visible between Madame Vuillard and her daughter. Bishop uses the phrase, "Vuillard's sister in the wall-paper" as a shorthand to express the kind of fear she associates with her childhood—a vertiginous sense of being "consumed" by overwhelming circumstance. The phrase occurs in an unpublished draft titled "Back to Boston (Just North of Boston)," where an old farmhouse dwarfed by the modern highway with its miles of advertising ("screaming letters") seems to

> have given up not quite the ghost—the ghost is there—
> (like Vuillard's sister in the wall-paper)
> weak, stunned, dazed, pale, pining
> "gone into decline" "consumptive" consumed, all right.
>
> (Draft 1, box 66, folder 10, VC)

The image of this consumptive creature progressively being absorbed into her obtrusive surroundings remains a vivid one for

Bishop and makes a brief appearance in the published poem "The End of March." As the speaker and her companions walk across a beach at Duxbury on a cold and windy day, they come on "lengths and lengths" of white string, a bit of Ariadne's thread. Following this looping line back to its source, they find it ends at the ocean's rim in a "thick white snarl, man-size, awash, rising on every wave, a sodden ghost, / falling back, sodden, giving up the ghost. . . . / A kite string?—But no kite" (*CP* 179, Bishop's ellipsis). Vuillard's sister may have been lost in the transition from unpublished to published poem, but the idea of "giving up the ghost" remains as a metaphor perhaps for the aura of movement and power that continues to surround the "perfectly useless" or unobtrusive thing.[3]

In alluding to "Vuillard's sister in the wall-paper," Bishop reveals a deep personal identification with one Vuillard canvas in particular, *Mother and Sister of the Artist* (ca. 1893). Mme Vuillard, dressed in black, demands the viewer's attention by sitting squarely in the center of the painting, while her daughter seems to disappear into the wall's decorative pattern, nearly forced out of the frame entirely by her mother's dark and portentous shape. The painting is small and the air of claustrophobia is exacerbated by the contracting room; a radically pitched perspective causes the floors of the room to appear to rise and the walls to close in on Vuillard's hapless sister, Marie. The effect is heightened by the decorative flatness of Marie's plaid dress, which gives no sense of a substantial body beneath; her dress and the wallpaper bleed into one another while the bottom corner of the window and the walls press down on her collapsing form. Marie bends over awkwardly as if to defend herself against effacement. The contrast between mother and daughter is extreme: while the mother is seen head on and dominates the space, her daughter virtually vanishes, consumed finally by her living arrangements. *Mother and Sister of the Artist* is only one of a series of family portraits where a pallid, ghostlike Marie fends off the mother's assaults on her independent identity. Marie's identity is completely effaced by, and yet entirely dependent upon, her mother's presence.

A typical Vuillard canvas, according to Easton, "focused not on the features or even the psyche of his subject but rather on the figure's *absorption* into her environment, using color and form as metaphors for that relationship" (85; my emphasis) so that "perhaps the most striking aspect of Vuillard's facture [the manner in which the art work is made] is what he chose not to paint in his canvases." (130). The same may be said of Bishop's facture as an artist of intimate interiors—the areas of the canvas that she leaves blank play as important a role in her compositions as do the delineated areas, producing ambiguities of space and meaning. Where Vuillard often leaves the features of his mother and sister blurred and indefinite, while concentrating instead on the world of textiles into which their bodies are absorbed, Bishop likewise introduces us to a world in which figures are strangely marginalized within the setting and yet central to the meaning of the scene.

The screaming woman of "In the Village" is featureless (even bodiless), and yet her presence, like that of Mme. Vuillard, forms a black hole at the center of the picture into which all other figures seem to disappear. Marjorie Perloff stresses that "everyone else is named . . . but the mother remains always a pronoun," and this creates a figure centered in the story's pictorial frame but as amorphous and imageless as Shelley's "deep truth" (178). In the opening scene of "In the Village," the child, like "Vuillard's sister in the wall-paper," is in imminent danger of vanishing into this spatial abyss. From the start, we see the child poised for flight, ready at any moment to bolt an interior realm concentered on an erratic and intimidating "she." The child stands watching the woman from the doorway, half inside and half outside the frame of the picture, hoping for release from the front bedroom with its "glint[ing]" walls papered "in wide white and dim-gold" bars (*CProse* 251). She listens for the saving sound of the blacksmith's "clang" (*CProse* 253):

> The pure note: pure and angelic.
> The dress was all wrong. She screamed.
> The child vanishes.

The Mother's Body and the Blacksmith's Hammer

The child of "In the Village" finds release from female intimacy in the Stygian darkness of the blacksmith's shop, where Nate, the demiurge—all sooty, sweaty, and triumphant—forges beauty from despair and meaning from chaos. The story establishes an antithesis between the child's mother, a woman who screams, and this surrogate father, a man who creates beautiful sounds, rhythmic and consoling speech. While the womenfolk whisper and fret as they practice their bittersweet salvage crafts—cooking, darning, embroidering, patching holes, picking up unraveled threads only to find them unraveling again—the men gather laconically, stoically, around the village blacksmith who signals quiet competence and confidence in every blow of his hammer as he forges his imperturbable order. Nate's wheel rims and horseshoes permit men to see the world, to travel (and escape), to circulate (and disseminate), to transport (and transcend), leaving behind the stationary feminine realm. Patricia Yaeger argues that the blacksmith's rings of metal are fashioned "in a peculiarly antagonistic relation to the feminine" (138). Yaeger finds vestiges of the female body in the hot, pliable horseshoes, "bloody little moons" that drown, "hissing and protesting," in the smithy's "tub of night-black water" (*CProse* 253). As the moonlike rings of metal "sail through the dark," following each other into the black water, the child feels as though the scream is finally "settling down" (*CProse* 253–54). Thus, Nate's forge represents both a refuge from the mother's frightening voice and presence and a crucible for the violent reshaping of her maternal "matter" and its significance.

Nate's world is filled with titanic forces. The only beings who are "perfectly at home" there are grown men who tower above the child and a horse whose rump reminds her "of a brown, glossy globe of the whole brown world" (*CProse* 257). While she is not ignored or effaced in this world of men, the child seems even more of an auslander here than in the diminutive and diminishing world of women. Though the child tries to pump the bellows, it is Nate standing behind her who really does it all (*CProse* 257), and the ring he fashions at her request is too big. With this outsized ring about to slide off her small finger, she presents herself at Miss Gurley's shop; the dressmaker gives the child a shiny five-cent piece (with King George emblazoned on it) commonly called a "fish scale." It is no wonder, given the precarious position of Nate's ring on her tiny finger, that the "fish scale" would remind her of fishes who swallowed lost rings and carried these treasures inside them for lucky fisherman to find. The chain of association—from magic ring to five-cent piece to fish to magic ring again—shows her active mind pursuing the pleasures of transmutation, even before she decides to swallow the coin (King George and all) so that it will transmute "all its precious metal into my growing teeth and hair" (*CProse* 259). Perhaps this strange diet will immunize her against loss, instill in her growing body the mettle (the strength of spirit, the stamina) to translate woe into joy. Above all, she may be hoping to acquire the blacksmith's sublimating powers.

Swallowing the five-cent piece with the law of the father (King George) imprinted on it, the child expresses her longing for legal tender—that is, for a warrantable language. What form of expression does Nate offer her? The lyricism with which Bishop evokes the blacksmith's "beautiful pure sound," a sound that "turns everything else to silence" (*CProse* 274) encourages us to think of Nate as an avatar of the artist translating the mother's elemental cry of pain into transcendent song. Nate's forge is a hub, a reassuring point of origin and telos for all things. As a wheelwright, Nate gives literal shape to what Emerson calls "the circular or compensatory character of every human action" (*Complete Essays* 279). Emerson finds his image for man's "continual effort to raise himself above himself," in the "generation of circles, wheel without wheel" (*Complete Essays* 282, 280). This ceaseless sublimation, as Thomas Weiskel defines it, is "in fact . . . the transubstantiation of what Marx called 'individualities' and Blake called 'minute particulars' into an abstract medium of exchange" (58–59). The price of this "enhanced sense of self," Weiskel explains, "is alienation from particular forms of primary experience." Sublimation "melts the formal otherness of things" and reduces them to the material of art, "the money of the mind," and the means of self-expansion (59).

The sublimating imagination that Nate represents "recoils from everything but the plastic, the pliant, and the indefinite" because, according to Weiskel, "too great an attachment to determinate objects makes sublimation impossible, as Freud points out" (59). Shaping disorganized matter into circles of metal, Nate resembles the Freudian analyst who imposes on the hysteric's narrative a sequence (and a consequence) that eliminates the gaps in memory, leading simultaneously to closure and cure. The cure is accomplished only when the patient is weaned of her "too great attachment" to the found objects she substitutes for lost friends and absent lovers.

The art of Bishop's blacksmith cannot bring an end to this "fetishizing of signs," cannot guarantee comfort and closure. After all, Nate creates unclosed circles, horseshoes, little crescent moons. These semicircles cannot wholly contain and explain loss or close the gap between what is and what ought to be. While the voice of Nate's hammer commands earth, wind, and fire, it cannot still the "unexpected gurgle" of the river (*CProse* 274). The disagreeables will not evaporate, the formal otherness of things will not disappear, and neither will the cries and whispers of women. Nate works to transmute raw emotions and their bodily equivalents, the many objects, the obtrusive furniture that accumulates in the capacious bedrooms and attics of the female mind. But female handiwork, however ephemeral, and female voices, however frightening, remain visible and audible alternatives to the steady rhythms of the forge.

Ultimately, Bishop loves the memory of Nate yet cannot embrace the blacksmith as a model of the artist she will eventually become. After all, the smithy's consolidating fire would swallow and drown all the particulars that Bishop studies with all the minute attention of a sandpiper searching for untold meaning in a grain of sand. Vanishing in one domain only to reappear in the other, the child of "In the Village" dramatizes the author's twin allegiances. As an artist, she is, like Nate, a forger of unity (a maker of supreme fictions) and relies on the mystical power of art to make connections. But her method remains determinedly metonymic, focusing on the irrevocable separateness of things.

In her memory poems and stories, Bishop fashioned a home for herself, furnishing it with longing and desire but knowing all along that poetry could never promise a final sanctuary from pain. After writing the story of her mother's madness, personal revelations came a bit more easily for Bishop. The poet's rapprochement with the past culminated in her last, and most personal, collection of poems. "In the Village" paved the way for *Geography III* and for its saving sense of place.

8   *Shipwreck and Salvage*

In the last years of her life, Elizabeth Bishop wrote poems that reflected a new belief in naturalistic narrative, stories that weave together dream states and old conversations, and a return to the ancient riddles of identity and human isolation. Published three years before her death in 1979, *Geography III* sounds something of a valedictory note, and yet it rehearses a familiar theme with renewed vigor: the tonic value of dreams. Practicing a secular form of re-memberment and salvage, the poet initially looks backward to a child's first unsettling awareness of her body and then forward through evocations of lost love, to rueful intimations of mortality. Midway in this lyrical journey, Bishop stops to remember the way grandparents "talked / in the old featherbed" about "deaths and sicknesses," about friends who "died in childbirth" or "took to drink" or lost their sons "when the schooner foundered." The voices that first found their way into her dreams now find a place in her art, and they go on and on, "talking in Eternity" ("The Moose," *CP* 171–72).

The foundered schooner, the shipwrecked life, or troubled mind is the burden, the ever-present bass line that runs through the poet's compositions. Against this central theme, Bishop introduces the sound of quiet affirmation and endurance. Muted, it can be heard in every crafted line, in each preserved detail from the past, but it comes through clearly, unmistakably, in "The Moose," a poem twenty years in the making:

> "Yes . . . " that peculiar
> affirmative. "Yes . . ."
> A sharp, indrawn breath,

half groan, half acceptance,
that means "Life's like that.
We know *it* (also death)."

(*CP* 172)

Many metaphors for the relation between life and art recur in
Bishop's writings, but one predominates, particularly in her last
years: shipwreck and salvage. Her own aging body, subject now
to broken bones and inflammations of the jaw, along with the
ancient ailments—asthma and alcohol-related depression—re-
minded her with greater frequency of her stoic ancestors and their
acceptance of life's inevitable defeats. Their stories and her own
would come together in *Geography III*, where Bishop perfects the
understated narrative technique she had first used years ago for her
most anthologized poem, "The Fish." There, she presented the
complications and mysteries of nature in the simplest possible way,
avoiding mastery and discovering courage in the battered body of
another being. In what would be her final book of poems, Bishop
continues to rely on a succession of images strung together, building
toward a "dramatically delayed recognition" of their "symbolic
value" (Travisano 71). But by this late date, she shows more interest
in recognizing the symbolic value of human-centered stories, the
kind grandparents talk of in their featherbed at night: motherless
children, shipwrecked Crusoes, the unsalvageable and the homeless.

The hope of asylum runs through *Geography III*, drawing the
collection together. *Asylum* was a charged word for Bishop: her
mother died in a sanitarium, her friend Lowell committed himself
regularly to the famous McLean's hospital for the mentally ill,
and her duties as poet-in-residence at the Library of Congress had
included visiting the notorious Pound in his ward at St. Elizabeth's.
As the years took their toll, she tried to keep her own mind fit,
while preserving the sanity of her closest companions. This salvage
mission contributed a new urgency to her last poetic narratives.
Always concerned with capturing the drama of the human mind
as it sought to make sense of itself and its world, Bishop had come
to think of herself as a Dorothea Dix for the literary world, an
architect of asylums and a rescuer of shipwrecked souls.

Doctoring the Spirit

Bishop's own life nearly foundered after her lover Lota committed suicide in 1967. This catastrophe intensified her resolve to save someone, if only herself. While supervising the construction of an urban park, Lota's mind broke under the strain of dealing with the Brazilian bureaucracy. At the height of the crisis, fearing for her own health, Bishop accepted a temporary position teaching in Seattle, Washington, where she became involved with a young woman— a relationship she took great pains to hide from Lota. When Bishop returned to Brazil, Lota was in desperate shape and blamed Bishop for abandoning her, while the poet, for her part, battled against the urge to drink. During this period, Bishop fears that her letters to Dr. Baumann (now referred to more familiarly as "Dr. Anny") sound "hysterical." On 25 September 1966, she writes:

I never felt so helpless and ignorant in my life, and unfitted to cope with my life or hers—you must surely know how a situation can get so that everything one does or says seems to be wrong, or is taken the wrong way. . . . There isn't much point in writing this—but I feel there is no one this side of the equator I can talk to or who understands me in the slightest if I try to—I wanted to get to New York just to see you, chiefly—but I was afraid that you, too, might not understand, and then—I hoped that things would be better when I got back, not much worse, as they are. . . . The simple truth is that my darling Lota whom I still love very much if she'd give me a chance to show it—has been simple hell to live with for five years now—and I am not exaggerating—everyone has found her "difficult"—and no one else lives with her all the time the way I do. The work is a sort of obsession—and I seem to have got to be one, too—and I am not very good under these prolonged strains and don't know how much longer I can hold out, really. . . (& some of it is my fault). (VC)

Unable to "face 15 or 20 years more of being made to feel guilty, etc.," Bishop tells Baumann that she is "determined to enjoy life a bit more, even if it *is* awful." A week later, she writes Baumann again, apologizing for her "hysterical letters" and describing her plan to help Lota by taking her to Amsterdam and from there to London where they will stay with Ilse and Kit Barker whom Bishop calls "almost my dearest friends, and both very soothing to be with." Bishop continues: "I think that possibly a few weeks of Dutch stolidity (if they really are that way) and English stoicism will be good for Lota after all this Latin hysteria. . . . WHY do they carry on so. . . . I am sick of it, and I think it exhausts L[ota] without her realizing it, she is so accustomed to it" (3 October 1966, VC).

The European respite did not have the desired effect, and Bishop's letters to Baumann upon her return are increasingly frantic. By 20 January 1967, Bishop is writing of Lota's hospitalizations and her "insulin shock treatments." Bishop careens helplessly between self-recrimination and defensiveness: "I *do* know my own faults, you know,—but this is really not *because* of me, although now all her obsessions have fixed on me—1st love, then hate" (VC). Forbidden by Lota's psychiatrist to see or get in touch with Lota in any way for at least six months, Bishop is effectively stranded in Brazil: "I haven't a home any more—actually nothing but 2 suitcases and a box of old papers, all the wrong ones." The apartment in Rio and the house she and Lota built near the mountain resort of Petrópolis were closed to her. And at the end of her letter to Baumann, she expresses the fear that she will have to give up the baroque house she restored in Ouro Prêto and christened Casa Mariana in honor of Marianne Moore. Bishop eventually took up temporary residence in New York. Lota came to visit the poet in the early fall of 1967. Bishop awoke to find that Lota had sunk into a coma after overdosing on prescription pills. She would never regain consciousness.

Lorrie Goldensohn writes sympathetically of this time in the poet's life, cautioning us to remember that "no one should underestimate this loss of both a person and a world for Bishop." As Goldensohn explains, Bishop's "severance from Brazilian ties even after Lota's death was complex, long-drawn out, physically and emotionally wrenching" (*The Biography of a Poetry* 233–34), and she would not leave her house in Ouro Prêto until 1971, when severe illness and troubling personal entanglements forced her northward once again. On the verge of turning sixty, Bishop was still haunted by her mother's breakdown, made palpable to her once again by Lota's nervous collapse in 1967 and by the mental instability that she felt had overtaken the young woman she began to live with directly following Lota's death. During the teaching stint at the University of Washington in Seattle, Bishop became friends with

Dorothee Bowie, to whom she would later confide her feelings about the succession of losses in her life:

I was alone with my mother until I was 4½ or so . . . and no father. . . . But some loving aunts and grandparents saved my life, and saved me—a damaged personality, I know, but I did survive. . . . My life has been pretty darkened always by guilt-feelings, I think, about my mother—somehow children get the idea it's their fault—or I did. And I could do nothing about that, and she lived on for 20 years more and it has been a nightmare to me always. I feel I should have been wiser about Lota, too, somehow, and maybe, maybe, I could have saved her—*But she is lost to me forever, and, by God, I am going to save someone, if I can.* Schizophrenia CAN be cured—my mother was too early a case, historically I mean. . . . Look at Robert Lowell (all my friends are mad)—with a new drug, he hasn't had a breakdown for over three years, I think—no psychiatry or anything, just PILLS." (14 June 1970, VC; my emphasis)

The poet relived the nightmare of her mother's collapse each time a friend or companion succumbed to mental illness and was quick to reassure those who supported her through these crises that her own sanity was intact. After Lota's death, she writes openly to Bowie about the isolating circumstances in her life, conditions of body and mind that she normally refused to speak about: "You needn't spare my unstable personality—queer, drunk, and all the rest. I am sane and I've never felt saner. I have no children and no real responsibilities except myself—and I am putting everything I have when I die into a 'Foundation' in Lota's memory—for Brazilian girls to study in the US. . . . I thrive on suffering" (14 June 1970, VC).

When Bishop found Lota comatose in her apartment, she phoned the woman whom she knew as "my Dr. Baumann" (letter to Bowie, 3 October 1967, VC). Six months after Lota's death, Bishop writes to tell her old friend Frani Blough Muser, "I spoke to Dr. Baumann on the telephone Sunday last and she said she thought my 'New England' character had triumphed. Well, when she is talking it is hopeless to try to correct her—but I must tell her the only real New Englander was my Bishop grandma, who was pretty, but totally incompetent and helpless—it must be my English Tory ancestry, I think" (4 January 1968, VC). "Dr. Anny" became an increasingly active presence in her life when Bishop accepted a teaching position at Harvard in the mid-seventies and found a new home on Lewis Wharf in Boston Harbor. Bishop began moving into her apartment in the renovated 1853 warehouse even before she was able to sell the house in Ouro Prêto. Though she was worried about the financial straits she would be in if Casa Mariana could not be sold, Bishop was still delighted with the Lewis Wharf home and its view of a harbor where ships from Nova Scotia once docked, perhaps even her great-grandfather's. All the granite for the building had been quarried in Quincy, the home of Bishop's ancestors on her father's side of the family.

At some point in the mid-to-late seventies while living for the first time in decades near the home of her English Tory ancestors, Bishop began a poem for Anny Baumann that she calls "Belated Dedication." In the aborted work, she tries to mingle her long-standing concern over "family monuments" with the images of engraved angels staring from the gravestones in Harvard Yard cemetery or the Copps Hill graveyard in Boston. Bishop looks inward, down through the years of emotional and physical anguish back to the origin of her pain. This self-examination takes the lid off her relationship with Baumann to reveal the depths of Bishop's self-disgust and of her gratitude:

> I looked through
> two stove-lids
> and saw the flames below,
>
> I looked down, through
> the graveyard angel's eyes
> blind circles without lids
> as in the past I'd stared
>
> down through the identical eyes
> of the privy
> at the sad muck
>
> The blue tides had withdrawn
> and left the red-veined mud carved into flames
> The gusts of rain lifted only to show
> > Avernus
> outwards, outwards and down,
> in pairs like tears
>
> . . . .

Under the rainbow's caress.
It's colored fingers are kind
within it is the clean honest blue of your eyes.

(box 65, folder 8, VC)

Looking down into the "blind circles" of depression and addiction
that marked so much of her life (and formed the subject of so many
minutely detailed letters to Dr. Baumann), the poet is afraid of
seeing her own eyes staring back at her, lidless and "red-veined"
from too much observation. But whenever she seemed trapped in
a cycle of shame and self-loathing, Dr. Baumann's "clean honest
blue" eyes helped her to see herself in a new light.

Dorothea Dix

If she seemed to gravitate toward brilliant, witty, troubled people
who too often self-destructed, Bishop was also careful to surround
herself with healers like "Dr. Anny." In fact, she reserved her highest
praise for physicians and other pioneering figures in the crusade to
save the mentally ill from inhumane and ineffective treatment. As
she explains to Bowie, "Everyone I have ever loved, practically
(except for Lota) has been in McLean's [Asylum] . . .—starting
with my mother" (14 June 1970, VC). McLean's sanitarium on the
outskirts of Boston was a new facility when Gertrude Bishop might
have been admitted for treatment. Although there are no hospital
records confirming Gertrude Bulmer Bishop's hospitalization there,
Bishop thought Gertrude had been taken to the Belmont, Massa-
chusetts, facility after her husband's death in 1911. McLean's Asylum
established the character and the principles of a new state-supervised
approach to the insane that stressed liberty and personal responsibil-
ity over restraint and force. Before Dorothea Dix's campaign, the
asylum was nothing more than a prison; but after her movement
gained momentum and spread throughout the country and the
world, the publicly funded asylum began to be thought of as a
"retreat." Perhaps it is Dorothee Bowie's first name that inspires
Bishop to reveal to her a long-standing desire to write a book about
Dorothea Dix, founder of a vast network of sanitariums for the
mentally ill modeled after McLean Asylum: "I am typing electrically

full tilt—many mistakes no doubt—and telling you all, Dorothee. The only prose book I ever thought I wanted to write is a book about the life of Dorothea Dix—her real name—a wonderful young woman who devoted herself to the insane, and the awful asylums in the US, in the 19th century—she died quite young, shipwrecked, I think" (14 June 1970, VC).

Bishop is a bit confused about the facts of the case: Dix did not die young in a shipwreck, but (despite ill health all her life) lived well into old age. Bishop had read *The Life of Dorothea Lynde Dix* by Francis Tiffany, and Dix's efforts to aid the insane and the shipwrecked had apparently become conflated in her mind with an image of self-sacrifice and early death. In the preface to her biography of the crusader, Francis Tiffany draws a parallel between Dix, a woman who founded "vast and enduring institutions of mercy in America" and St. Theresa of Avila who founded "great conventual establishments" throughout "European Christendom" (iii). Dorothea Dix displayed the same "balance" Bishop admired in St. Theresa's prose, which "swings quickly from most inebriated sort of rapture to practical affairs and explanations" ("Reading Notes, New York Public Library" 9, box 74, folder 11, VC). A St. Theresa for the nineteenth century, Dix persuaded state legislators to fund her system of asylums for the mentally ill through the technique of memorials—compositions that described the inhumane conditions under which the insane suffered at the time.

Reading the life of Dorothea Dix, Bishop must have been struck by the parallels between her own family background and that of the indefatigable reformer. Dorothea, like Elizabeth, overcame the grimness of a New England childhood marked by lengthy periods of illness. Dix was born in Maine, but like Bishop, spent most of her early years in Worcester, Massachusetts, and Boston. Her father was subject to episodes of "fanatical religious excitement," during which he wrote endless tracts that Dorothea was set continuously to pasting and stitching together (Tiffany 2). She ran away from her father's house in Worcester to her paternal grandmother's residence in Boston. Also like Bishop, Dorothea Dix was raised in New England by wealthy paternal grandparents so stern that "no threat of penal fires would have betrayed [them] into the weakness of kissing [their grandchild] good-night" (8). Although it would have made the poet squirm to be thought of in such sentimental terms, Dix's biographer might well have been speaking of Bishop's predicament when she writes, "The child Dorothea owed [to her grandparents], on the one hand, a debt of lasting obligation, and, on the other, years of acute suffering and heart-starvation . . . in a grim and joyless home" (9). And she would never know the meaning of home. Dix drove herself relentlessly, despite being an invalid for most of her life, suffering from consumption, pulmonary weakness, and severe inflammations. Like Bishop, Dix found relief in poetry, science (particularly natural history), biography, and travel. She made exhaustive studies of nature in the tropics and wrote out full extracts from the saints on the subject of right conduct and discipline.

Quite apart from the similarity of their upbringings, there was another reason for Bishop's enduring personal interest in Dorothea Dix. Bishop's great-grandfather on her mother's side was lost at sea in a famous storm off Sable Island, lying some thirty miles southward from the eastern end of Nova Scotia and aptly named "the Graveyard of Ships." No stone lighthouse could stand on the ever-shifting sands of the shelterless island, and no wooden structure could withstand the storms. By the late sixteenth century, the island had become a penal colony for the French settlements of Arcadia. Later, it became the home of "wreckers" who scavenged foundered ships for loot. In June 1853, while Dix was engaged in asylum work at St. John, Newfoundland, she was caught up in a storm that caused several deadly shipwrecks, one of which might well have been the wreck that claimed Bishop's ancestor. Dix turned her considerable organizing abilities to the rescue of sailors by raising funds for the construction of metallic lifeboats equipped with the most modern salvaging apparatus. Around 1949, Bishop herself made a trip to Sable Island on a Canadian Lighthouse Service boat, and her notes from the book *Sable Island: Its History and Phenomena* by the Reverend George Patterson are filled with references to "Miss D. L. Dix." Bishop is most intrigued by one fact in particular, which she picks up from her reading of Patterson's history: from 1850 to 1860, the island was the home for a population of the mentally insane, who were sent out to help the coast guard rescue the crews of shipwrecked vessels. And she dutifully records the names of the lifeboats Dix commissioned—the *Victoria* of Boston, the *Grace Darling* of Philadelphia, and the *Reliance* and the *Samaritan* of New York, with a life car called the *Rescue* ("Notes and Observations," 1951, box 72B, folder 7, VC).[1]

"The Deadly Sandpile"

Dorothea Dix's evangelical mission of salvage was translated by Bishop into a secular poetic of reclamation and recovery. When the poet first approached the subject of Dix's efforts on behalf of the insane and the shipwrecked with the intention of writing either a full-length study or a series of short poems, she was experiencing great turmoil in her own life. From 1949, when she visited Sable Island, to 1951, when she began taking notes for the project on Dix, Bishop was emotionally at sea, adrift in her personal life and finding it difficult to control her drinking and depression. Among her miscellaneous notes from the time is a fragment entitled "The Deadly Sandpile" that appears to combine her interest in Dix's asylum work and the Sable Island episode. Bishop imagines an asylum "all on a vanishing sandbar." Beneath the heading, "poor madmen confined in their gigantic sand-box," she makes a list of the inmates' maladies:

1. death
2. insanity
3. alcoholism

(box 53, folder 16, VC)

And just below this, Bishop prescribes a cure, which is "first and most and always the diminishment of their fearful echoes—resounding [screams]." The "deadly" sandpile becomes an allegory of what life was like for Bishop at a time when she suffered chiefly from reminiscences and an inherited susceptibility to disease.

In the course of the projected poem, Bishop intended to incorporate images from George Herbert's "Church Monuments" and Gerard Manley Hopkins's "The Wreck of the Deutschland," works to which she would turn again and again for solace and inspiration. A quotation accompanying her notes for "The Deadly Sandpile" suggests the direction in which her allegory might have developed: "I am the soft sift / In an hourglass" (box 53, folder 16, VC). Compare this to the conclusion of Herbert's "Church Monuments":

> And wanton in thy cravings, thou mayst know,
> That flesh is but the glasse, which holds the dust
> That measures all our time; which also shall
> Be crumbled into dust. Mark here below
> How tame these ashes are, how free from lust,
> That thou mayst fit thy self against thy fall.
>
> (*Works* 65)

Because Bishop's images of childhood appeared to her like "monuments" sinking deeper and deeper into the shifting sands of memory ("Recorded Observations," 1934–37: 31, VC), Herbert's "Church Monuments" held a special place in her imagination. The speaker of Herbert's poem sends his body to "school" in a cemetery, a deadly sandpile where he finds his genealogy "written" in "dustie heraldrie and lines." For Joseph Summers, Bishop's close friend and her favorite interpreter of Herbert, "the figure of the hourglass summarizes what 'thou mayst know' from the contemplation of monuments": from them, the flesh learns its "stemme / And true descent" from ashes to ashes, dust to dust (131). But there is hope in this message, for the knowledge that the flesh has gained may "serve as bridle to 'tame' its lust," and so the flesh "may 'fit' itself 'against' its 'fall' in that, in preparation for its known dissolution, it may oppose its 'fall' into pride and lust." (132). Bishop particularly admired Summers's analysis of how the extraordinary use of enjambment and Herbert's unusually loose syntax contributes to the poem's thematic preoccupation with form and its dissolution: "The sentences sift down through the rhyme-scheme skeleton of the stanzas like the sand through the glass; and the glass itself has already begun to crumble" (134–35).

For Bishop, the "flesh" of poetic form gave structure to her life, but she introduced just enough looseness into the frame of a poem to suggest the fragility of human order. "Life and the memory of it [are] cramped" within the small expanse that the skeleton of her stanzas allows, but within that space they breathe for a moment, long enough to show "the little we get for free, the little of our earthly trust" and "size of our abidance" ("Poem," *CP* 177). Here the pathos of the human condition is seen most clearly—in the patient process of finding a shape in the sand. Bishop would never complete her 1940s Sable Island piece, "The Deadly Sandpile," but a patient and prolonged sifting of that material would allow her to complete a poem it took her nearly twenty years to write, a poem that pivots gently on an "indrawn breath."

"The Moose"

Although the first extant drafts of "The Moose" date from the fall of 1956, Bishop most likely began thinking about the poem in 1946 after a short trip to Nova Scotia. In a letter to Marianne Moore dated 29 August 1946, she describes her strange encounter with the woodland animal. Late at night she hailed a bus as it passed her relatives' farm and began her journey back to Boston. As darkness fell, the bus entered the New Brunswick woods, and with the first hint of morning, it stopped suddenly for a big cow moose wandering down the road (RM). Early in the process of poetic recovery, Bishop had settled on the meter (largely three-stress) and the skeleton of the poem (short, six-line stanzas), but the accumulating details of the landscape—the long tides where the bay leaves the sea, the tidal river meeting the bay, the setting sun casting its "silted red" on the sandflats, creating "burning rivulets" and "veins" of lavender—remain suspended for years in a succession of drafts, waiting for the bridge of narrative to give them meaning.

Narrative is the great blessing of the poem, and its agency seems to have come to Bishop during her years in Brazil. Indrawn for so long, the breath of the poem is released as the poet finds a satisfying way of hailing and boarding the passing bus and joining its passengers as they journey west toward the end of day. She enters the poem almost invisibly as a "lone traveller" saying "good-bye to the elms, / to the farm, to the dog" (*CP* 170). Leaving the "narrow provinces / of fish and bread and tea" for a world of incoming mist, the poem might seem at first to venture with Coleridge's mariner into the realm of the Gothic, "below the kirk, below the hill, / Below the lighthouse top" (*The Rime of the Ancient Mariner*, ll. 23–24). But the traveler seems to carry some faint echo of the homely with her as she enters the well-worn body of the bus with its "dented flank" that moves forward with a rocking, lulling motion and "waits patiently" for new arrivals. The connection to home is tenuous at best. Still, like the "iron bridge" that "trembles" and the "loose plank" that "rattles" as the bus passes, it shivers "but doesn't give way," even when the bus and its unromantic pilgrims enter the New Brunswick woods, "hairy, scratchy, splintery," unmistakably feral.

It is narrative itself that provides the bridge in this journey between night and morning, between uncertainty or weariness and an unexpected "sweet sensation of joy." Mortality has not been banished and flesh will crumble, but there is comfort in motion and the gentle art of conversation. In her notes for the poem Bishop writes, "Our nature consists in motion; complete rest is death" (box 59, folder 4, VC). But the unfolding movement of the poem did not come easily. In its journey from birth to completion through many different drafts, "The Moose" (more akin to fairy tale than Dantean allegory) stalls time and time again at the point when the bus enters the dark woods. But in the final version of the poem, Bishop achieves a natural transition into the world of dreams:

> The passengers lie back.
> Snores. Some long sighs.
> A dreamy divagation
> begins in the night,
> a gentle, auditory,
> slow hallucination. . . .
>
> In the creakings and noises,
> an old conversation
> not concerning us,
> but recognizable, somewhere,
> back in the bus:
> Grandparents' voices
>
> uninterruptedly
> talking, in Eternity:

names being mentioned,
things cleared up finally.

(*CP* 171)

In one of her Florida notebooks Bishop recommended the medicinal properties of dream work: " 'To sleep perchance to dream.' Freud's theories should be carried a step further—we sleep only in order to dream. God found the man he had created unequal to the conditions of the world he's created him for, & so he gave him sleep . . . dreams, as a kind of medicine to keep him going—a medicine that hides its necessarily unpleasant taste in a sweet syrup,—but the taste comes through now & then" (KW119). Caring little for narrative as Freudian "talking cure," Bishop nevertheless found respite from dissolution in dreams. She also found a measure of salvation in the framing of "gentle, auditory" spaces. She regarded them as her "little, soluble, / unwarrantable" arks for the preservation of sound (*CP* 95).

The voices in the back of the bus blend with those of her own grandparents, and Bishop's "dreamy divagation" on eternity begins and ends with the stories of this world, the pillow talk that lulled her to sleep as a child—"what he said, what she said," and then " 'Yes . . .' / A sharp, indrawn breath, / half groan, half acceptance, that means 'Life's like that' " (*CP* 172). And it is here that the story of "The Moose" and the story of Sable Island meet, in the sound of grandparents talking "in the featherbed, / peacefully, on and on," making it "all right" even now to fall asleep just as one had done as a child. Musing in the 1940s on "The Deadly Sandpile" and those lives claimed by the engulfing waters off its shores, she writes

Anyone familiar with the accent of Nova Scotia will know what I mean when I refer to the Indrawn Yes. In all their conversations Nova Scotians of all ages, even children, make use of it. It consists of, when one is told a fact—anything not necessarily tragic but not of a downright comical nature,—"yes," or "yeah," while drawing in an acceptance of the worst, and it occurred to me as I walked over the fine, fatalistic sands, that Sable Island with its mysterious engulfing powers was a sort of large-scaled expression of the Indrawn Yes. (box 53, folder 16, VC)

In "The Moose," the indrawn breath of resignation is balanced by the indrawn breath of surprise and sudden delight. The grandparents' voices talking in the eternal "now" bathe the passengers in peace and safety. Just when a jolt is least expected, the moose appears, "towering, antlerless, high as a church, homely as a house (or as safe as houses)" (*CP* 172–73). "It's awful plain," whispers one passenger, "childishly, softly," too polite to call undue attention to the creature's homeliness.

Out of the "impenetrable wood" the moose comes and "sniffs at the bus's hot hood." A wood "impenetrable" to humans may yet be crossed by this peculiar animal without the benefit of roads, bridges, or headlights. The similes accumulate as those aboard the bus struggle to translate the "otherworldly" creature into the familiar language of their "narrow provinces." The passengers have at their disposal the language of transcendence ("high as a church") and domestication ("homely as a house"), but the moose's undeniably alien presence escapes the engulfing powers of human expression. As they watch this creature, so fully at home in a place so impenetrable to them, while she sniffs their bus inquiringly, they are reminded that they too are "curious creatures," both inquisitive and strange.

> Taking her time,
> she looks the bus over,
> grand, otherworldly.
> Why, why do we feel
> (we all feel) this sweet
> sensation of joy?
>
> (*CP* 173)

The passengers cannot greet her arrival with their customary resignation because her presence sends a jolt of uncertainty running through them and their slow hallucinations about life and death and acceptance. With her arrival, life becomes unpredictable and curious once more, and as she leaves, they crane backwards to watch her disappear into the "moonlit macadam" (*CP* 173). The sudden appearance of the moose at the end of Bishop's poetic journey captures the element of surprise that her poetry always kept in reserve as an antidote to fatalism.

Though leavened in her case by inquisitiveness and an eye for the unexpected, Bishop felt the stoicism of her Sable Island ancestors in her bones. A child of Nova Scotia, Bishop saw "deaths and sicknesses" as the shifting ground on which we all walk, the material condition of our lives. In "The End of March," she dreamed of a hermit's "crypto-dream-house" where the fatalistic sands and mysterious engulfing powers could not touch her (*CP* 179). But, of course, that dream, that house, that avenue of possibility was "boarded up" long ago (*CP* 180). Bishop refused to find release in the isolation of a fine, creative madness. In "North Haven," an elegy for "Cal" Lowell, she describes with pity and sadness her dear friend's attempts to doctor his poems over and over again, rearranging and deranging them, refusing to accept that poems, like lives, have their own inevitability about them. There simply comes a time when one must let go.

Like her beloved Herbert, Bishop was willing to face hard facts, while surrendering mastery over time and circumstance. Over the course of her life, she lost her treasured homes, her health, and most of all, "the joking voices" of those she loved best ("One Art," *CP* 178). But some lingering sense of them lives on in the body of her song.

Notes
Bibliography
Index

Notes

Introduction

1. The matter of gender and its influence on Bishop's stance toward subjectivity, eroticism, and literary tradition has received a great deal of attention in recent criticism. Lee Edelman reads Bishop's work from within a feminist/deconstructionist context in his landmark essay, "The Geography of Gender: Elizabeth Bishop's 'In the Waiting Room'" (1985). In "Bishop's Sexual Poetics," a chapter from her book *Women Poets and the American Sublime* (1990), Joanne Feit Diehl discusses the poet's sexuality in relation to the gender politics of the Emersonian sublime. In *Elizabeth Bishop: The Biography of a Poetry* (1992), Lorrie Goldensohn discusses the eroticized female body as it appears directly in unpublished material and indirectly in the landscapes of Bishop's descriptive poems. Both Goldensohn and David Kalstone in *Becoming a Poet* (1989) refer to the poet's asthma and alcoholism, but only glancingly. Brett Millier's critical biography (1993) treats these subjects at length but rarely probes the relation between the daily burden of the two diseases and Bishop's artistry. My argument differs from other readings in exploring the poet's fascination with medical science, her correspondence with her personal physician, and her somatic history and its impact on her understanding of the physical character of the poem.

2. Although she saw a New York psychoanalyst briefly during the 1940s and often allowed herself the freedom to speculate about the psychology of the creative drive when it pleased her to do so, Bishop refers Anne Stevenson to Arnold Hauser's *The Philosophy of Art History* (1959) and its critique of "psychologism" in literary criticism: "Artistic technique is, in fact, inaccessible to the psychologist altogether, being determined by what is called the 'inner logic' of the work of art and by tradition . . . rather than by the particular mental constitution of the individual artist" (85).

1. "O Breath": Asthma and Equivocality

1. Bishop and Louise Crane made Key West their home through 1943 while Bishop completed the poems that would make up her first book,

North and South. Bishop continued to winter there in the home of her friend Marjorie Stevens until 1949.

2. Bishop published only a handful of poems that describe erotic pleasure overtly. As Lorrie Goldensohn suggests in her consistently illuminating essay on Bishop's erotic imagination, an unequivocal vision of erotic fulfillment may have been blocked in the "rooted sadness of Bishop's childhood" ("Elizabeth Bishop: An Unpublished, Untitled Poem" 46). But however it arose, Bishop's characteristic reticence poses problems for her critics. Just when Bishop is beginning to be given her due as a complex poet, the personal directness of much recent woman's poetry has seduced some commentators into underestimating Bishop's talent once again and returning her to the same niche to which she was relegated during her lifetime. Still, some readers are beginning to recognize that Bishop, in her subtle way, explores the same issues that preoccupy the current, bolder generation of women writers. Joanne Diehl, for instance, warns us that Bishop's poetry "only apparently evades issues of sexuality and gender." Diehl senses an "ominous quality to Bishop's restraint more suggestive than confession" (97) and concludes that a highly erotic imagination is fully present in her poetry: "Verbal masking allows Bishop to preserve the erotic while deconstructing heterosexist categories" (93). Similarly, Bonnie Costello points to the way a woman writer may use "female vantage point" as "the concrete from which the universal is projected" so as to "unite readers before the shared mystery of embodiment" ("Writing Like a Woman" 309). Costello concludes that many other women poets, including Bishop, "have resisted labeling [their artistic vision] as female precisely because they wish to make it available to all readers" (310). I argue that Bishop uses her physical ailments to develop a poetic that confronts cultural labels and their stifling impact on personal and erotic expression.

3. This passage from Bishop's 7 July 1954 letter to Baumann is worth quoting in full: "People's attitude about such things [alcoholism and its treatment] is really quite different from that in the U.S. [The Brazilians] are amazingly tolerant, or indifferent, or ignorant. . . . I suspect one thing that made it harder for me in N.Y. and other places was the more Puritanical outlook that I have inherited myself."

4. As Lee Edelman argues persuasively in "The Geography of Gender: Elizabeth Bishop's 'In the Waiting Room' " (104), what finally "horrifies" the child is the "fundamental affinity" she shares with monstrously disfigured women—with both the deformed mothers who stare back at her from the pages of the magazine and the women who "smile falsely" at her from the other side of the waiting room, their body shapes distorted by corsets and whalebone. She too will be imprisoned within the "awful hanging breasts" and the unempowered body of a woman (*CP* 161).

5. For a fascinating discussion of Bishop's indirections on homosexuality

and erotic fulfillment, see Lorrie Goldensohn's essay "Elizabeth Bishop: An Unpublished, Untitled Poem."

6. From her new home in Samambaia, Brazil, Bishop writes her doctor in a letter dated 21 April 1953: "But an atmosphere of uncritical affection is just what suits *me*, I'm afraid—kisses and hugs, and endearments and diminutives, flying around" (VC; Bishop's emphasis).

2. "*The Queer Land of Kissing*": Sexuality and Representation

1. Merrin's thoughtful essay stresses the playfulness of Bishop's "transmogrifying art" and argues that the poet's "obsession with transmogrification and changeability is inextricable from Bishop's gaiety or lighthearted whimsy," which is "in turn inextricable from her gayness" ("Elizabeth Bishop" 154). Behind Merrin's discussion of the fluid gender boundaries in Bishop's work is a theoretical substrata most directly associated with feminist critics who find in the "eccentric" identity of the lesbian a figure for all that is beyond the categories of sex (woman and man). While my discussion adopts as a framework Merrin's notion of "inversion" and "thirdness" as "powerful psychological gestalts" ("Elizabeth Bishop" 164) in Bishop's work, I employ unpublished letters, poems, and notebook entries to flesh out the story of the poet's preoccupation with hermaphroditism and its relation to her mobile, shape-shifting, and ambivalent vision.

2. As Lorrie Goldensohn argues in her treatment of "Insomnia," "Other readers could complain that inversion is too prejudicial and negative a word to apply to homosexuality, yet Bishop's application of that sense of inversion, rather more usual in the early fifties than now, seems deliberate. . . . Our attention flicked by that reading of 'inverted,' the poem appears to record a constellation of feelings best explained by reference to homosexuality, and its explosive but largely repressed public connection" (*The Biography of a Poetry* 30–31). Evidence also suggests that Bishop knew and on occasion employed the word *queer* in reference to her own homosexuality, despite its stigmatizing connotations. In a letter from 1970 that Bishop wrote to her friend Dorothee Bowie, she refers to herself as an "unstable personality—queer, drunk, and all the rest" (14 June, VC).

3. The exoticism that surrounds this image of the turbaned poet is apparent as well in Bishop's youthful notions of love. A diary entry from the summer before, turns the moon of love and lunacy into a Moorish scimitar: "There was no moon tonight. Instead we "made out" with two white dress shields hung up at the window to dry by a young lady across the street. They glowed through the twilight, doubly, with a Moorish, double-crescent effect (1 July 1935, VC).

4. The mirror world or the "world-upside-down" became the poet's earliest tropes for modeling and legitimating the idea of deviance while showing creative disrespect for the established hierarchies of "life / death, right / wrong, male / female" ("Santarém," *CP* 185). Through playful (and poignant) inversions made possible by the looking glass, the well, the violations of gravity, Bishop defines her culture's lineaments while questioning the usefulness and unassailability of its rigid ordering.

5. For a sustained history of the lesbian figure in literature, see Faderman, *Odd Girls and Twilight Lovers: A History of Lesbian Life in Twentieth-Century America*.

3. *The Rose and the Crystal*

1. In her *Livre de la Cité des Dames*, Christine de Pizan describes a book on gynecology entitled *Secreta mulierum* , which must be hidden from women because, according to de Pizan, "it was done so that women would not know about the book and its contents, because the man who wrote it knew that if women read it or heard it read aloud, they would know it was lies, would contradict it, and make fun of it" (22–23).

2. Bishop's reference to "Faustina II" draws attention to the relationship between her vision of the june bugs thumping against the screen and the insect life of "Faustina, or Rock Roses," where the poet shines an eighty-watt bulb on the forces of erosion that we would like to screen from view but ultimately cannot. In this unsettling poem, a visitor to the home of an invalid "sits and watches / the dew glint on the screen / and in it two glow-worms / burning a drowned green" (*CP* 72). The eighty-watt bulb "betrays" the room to close inspection, "lighting . . . on heads / of tacks in the wallpaper" where pictures once hung—photographs of loved ones, perhaps, who no longer visit. While the bulb "exposes," "betrays," and "discovers," the glowworms (female fireflies) cast a ghastly green, the color of "drowned" corpses, on their surroundings and, in Bonnie Costello's words, "create an uncanny effect of imminent death" (*Elizabeth Bishop* 70).

3. Bishop's notes for "Faustina II" appear to confirm Lorrie Goldensohn's belief that Bishop saw in the old woman's dependency on this powerful black servant a subsumed mother-child relationship (*The Biography of a Poetry* 74) but one in which the comforting breast (with its coat of flaming alcohol) was potentially dangerous. Goldensohn argues that in her depiction of Faustina, Bishop is herself coming dangerously close to "the very old projection throwing white fear onto the figure of the black servant, whose exploited weakness and subjugation is made to grow into a black-lashing vision of frightening power" (*The Biography of a Poetry* 75).

4. Virtually all modernist art forms emerging in the 1920s and 1930s, from futurism to dadaism, from cubism to objectivism, subscribed to a

machine aesthetic and cultivated a stance of ironic indifference. For a thorough discussion of the machine aesthetic and its impact on the poetry of William Carlos Williams, see Henry M. Sayre, "American Vernacular: Objectivism, Precisionism, and the Aesthetics of the Machine" 310–14.

5. See Diana Collecott Surman's "Towards the Crystal: Art and Science in Williams' Poetic" for a history of the crystal "ideal" in the modernist poetic, which "coincided with a breakthrough in the development of the modern science of crystallography" (192–93).

6. Bishop's technique of miniaturization has attracted a great deal of critical attention over the years. For a view of miniaturization as an empowering strategy, see Goldensohn, "Elizabeth Bishop's Originality." But see Costello: "This miniaturization is not finally a stance of power so much as a precarious transference of pity from the self to the world" (*Elizabeth Bishop* 18).

7. An unfinished poem entitled "2 Negroes on Bicycles" from the pages of a Key West notebook is clearly influenced by Bishop's six months in Mexico and her days in Florida and focuses on a slowly melting ice cube that resembles a rock-crystal skull in the moonlight (KW2 185–86):

> . . . Peddling slowly along
> the one with the cake of ice on his
> handlebars having to work harder than
> the one with the large fish—
> laid across the handlebars, sagging a
> little in the middle (they talk to each other)
>
> He will throw a dime into the pot—
> if it turns black, the fish is not fit to eat
> but if it stays bright, all right—
> water-nourished creatures, pure & impure
> light glowing off them, water dripping off them—
> from the faces of the sweating cyclists—
>
> the dripping cube held up in the moonlight
> for a minute like a Mexican rock-crystal skull.
> dropped in a tomb, rapidly pushed forward by a strange
> insect making the sign for "infinity."

Beside the poem, in the margins, the poet has sketched the sign for infinity.

8. It would be misleading, however, to associate this verbal liquidity with some fluid, feminine essence, particularly in the work of a poet who strives to undercut the essentializing spirit wherever it makes its presence felt.

9. Gertrude Stein makes several appearances in the pages of Elizabeth Bishop's personal notebooks from the late 1930s and early 1940s. Writing to Anne Stevenson in 1963, Bishop speaks of having letters of introduction to all the great literary and artistic circles in Paris during the mid-1930s,

but that her "shyness—or whatever is the word now" prevented her from taking advantage of her opportunities (18 March, WU). And yet, despite her reticence, Bishop does establish a correspondence with Stein's companion, Alice B. Toklas: "I did meet a lot of famous people, I suppose [including] G[ertrude] Stein and Alice B [Toklas]—I was invited to tea, with a friend— and the friend went without me, finally. What an idiot! (Since then—just a year or so ago—I've corresponded with Alice B who wanted to come to Brazil, of all places—I discouraged her firmly)" (letter to Stevenson, 18 March 1963, WU).

4. *"Abnormal Thirst"*: Addiction and the Poète Maudit

1. For the first serious discussion of Bishop's indebtedness to Poe's aesthetic theories, see Travisano, especially 69–71.

2. As an undergraduate at Vassar, Bishop had already begun to consider the inherent dangers of regularity and predetermined effect in poetry, and she set down her thoughts on the subject of "intoxicating" rhythm in a series of letters written in 1933 and 1934 to another young poet, Donald Stanford: "I can write in iambics if I want to—but just now I don't know my own mind quite well enough to say what I want to in them. If I try to write smoothly I find myself perverting the meaning for the sake of the smoothness (and don't you do that sometimes yourself?) However, I think that an equally great 'cumulative effect' might be built up by a series of irregularities" (qtd. in Lensing 54).

3. Bishop tried to tackle the compulsive properties of the subway train even before she entered college when she wrote a whimsical poem that mythologizes the origin of the railway car and published it in her boarding school's literary review, *The Blue Pencil*. It was recently reprinted in the *Western Humanities Review*. Reminiscent of Christina Rossetti's "Goblin Market," Bishop's "The Ballad of the Subway Train" focuses on the body's greedy hunger for forbidden fruit. "Long, long ago when God was young," dragons lived happily among the moons until they "chanced to eat / A swarm of stars new-made" (25). This original sin of engorgement is met with a swift reprisal. Once the glory of the heavens, the dragons are metamorphosed into subway cars condemned forever to grope their way in a "narrow hole" carrying their "human loads" (25–26).

4. While I read the notebooks and formulated my approach to them before encountering Barbara Page's perceptive essay "Off Beat Claves, Oblique Realities: The Key West Notebooks of Elizabeth Bishop," I am indebted to its discussion of the poet's metonymic approach to experience. Like Page, I employ the newly uncovered Florida journals to clarify the ways in which Bishop developed her principles of composition through

confrontations with her literary predecessors. But while Page's essay focuses on Bishop's gender and its impact on her artistic principles, this chapter highlights the various connections that Bishop's notebooks forge between her battles with alcohol and her writing style.

5. *"Travelling Through the Flesh"*: A Poetics of Translation

1. My discussion of the influence that contemporary Brazilian poetry had on Bishop's later work is inspired by Elizabeth Spires's brief comments on the subject in her essay, "Elizabeth Bishop: 'The Things I'd Like to Write'": "Reading her brilliant translations of Brazilian poets, which began appearing around 1963, one is immediately struck by how dissimilar, taken as a whole, Brazilian poetry is from Bishop's own through mid-career. It must have been this very dissimilarity, the Brazilian poets' easygoing simplicity, sensuality, and emotional expansiveness, that drew her to them and began to influence her own poetry beginning in the 1960's . . . [when] Bishop's range widens immeasurably" (68–69).

2. If the marmoset's need for oxygen awakened Bishop's sympathies it would not be the first time that she was drawn to a foreign work partially because of it named her private pain. She had translated portions of Max Jacob's "Les Pénitents en Maillots Roses" in 1949 and again in 1950, including Jacob's travel impressions of Antibes where he found "Italian staircases easy on asthma" ("Antibes and Antibes Way," box 56, folder 14, VC).

6. *"Whispering Galleries"*: The Visual Arts and the Incarnation of Memory

1. Interviewed by a reporter for *The Christian Science Monitor*, Bishop speaks about inspiration: "Poetry should be as unconscious as possible. . . . Sometimes an idea haunts me for a long time, though poems that start as ideas are much harder to write. It's easier when they start out with a set of words that sound nice and don't make much sense but eventually reveal their purpose. Again, the unconscious quality is very important" (Johnson 24–25).

2. To Anne Stevenson, Bishop wrote, "You are right about my admiring Klee very much—but as it happens, THE MONUMENT was written more under the influence of a set of *frottages* by Max Ernst I used to own, called Histoire Naturel [Naturelle]. I am passionately (I think I might say) fond of painting. . . . Next time round I'd like to be a painter—or a composer—or a doctor—I seriously considered studying medicine for several years and still wish I had" (18 March 1963, WU). But by the new year, Bishop is anxious to set the record straight, cautioning Stevenson not to

make much of her connection with Ernst: "You mention Ernst again. Oh dear—I wish I'd never mentioned him at all, because I think he's usually a dreadful painter. I liked that Histoire Naturelle I mentioned, and his photo-collages still seem brilliant" (8 January 1964, WU). A few months after that, in a letter to Stevenson, dated 6 March 1964 (WU) Bishop speaks of having met Ernst (and other luminaries) in the 1930s: "What was going on in Paris then was mostly surrealism, that I remember—André Breton & his gallery; I met Ernst, Giacometti, etc.—but—I just looked at them."

3. Masks figure elsewhere in her notebooks. For instance, Bishop compares "washing the face with snow—a saintly process" with "the white masked saints." And in her "Recorded Observations" from 1934 through 1937 (VC), she tucks away something that caught her eye: a sheet of instructions for the use of "Joke Specs with Shifting Eyes (a Spectacle mask with Eyes operated by blowing)": "Tear off the paper ring with the arrow. The mouthpiece with hole situated thereunder is sterilized and can be employed without bear by the wearer of the mask. Put on the spectacles and place the mouthpiece in the mouth. Blow air intermittently; the eyes and eye-brows will then be raised an [and] lowered. When the air pressure is removed these return to their initial position. . . . Celluloid is inflammable! Consequently do not bring the spectacles near a naked flame." Beneath these instructions for use, Bishop attaches a handwritten comment: "If one reads this with the proper care, the fact that it goes with a joke is unapparent, apart from the first word. It might just as well be directions for wearing a truss" ("Recorded Observations," 1934–37: 22, VC).

4. In her tribute to the Key West folk painter, Gregorio Valdes, she writes, "His house was a real Cuban house, very bare, very clean . . . the bareness of a Cuban house, and the apparent remoteness of every object in it from every other object, gives one the same sensation as the bareness and remoteness of Gregorio's best pictures" (*CProse* 54). Bishop's primitive painter is freed of any "classical ideal of verisimilitude" and clings with tenacity to the things about him (*CProse* 58).

7. *"In the Village": Madness and the Mother's Body*

1. In 1977, Marjorie Perloff's essay "Elizabeth Bishop: The Course of a Particular" was one of the first to stress that "the real theme of 'In the Village' " is the exorcising of pain, the disciplining of the mind through an "attentiveness to things" (178). Perloff also emphasizes the fact that the child "detaches the act of screaming from its agent, just as she detaches the objects of her environment from the nameless mother, who is always referred to as 'she' " (178). Finally, Perloff refers to the poet's creative use of "a series of metonymic transfers," although Perloff does so strictly in the context of her reading of "The Monument" (187). Nearly a decade later,

Patricia Yaeger associates the unnameable mother with Lacan's preverbal "maternal discourse," a "writing anterior to speech," from which the child is estranged, for the mother's "word" is dangerous (136). The blacksmith's "shaping sounds," on the other hand, "give the child a sense of orientation and direction, of nonliminality." Thus, the story seems to focus on "the alienating necessity—for the woman writer—of escaping from the mother's scream into the father's speech" (136).

2. Freud conceded that his scientific discourse often spoke in the figures of poetry and that poetic figuration has much in common with hysteria (Bernheimer 11). For a discussion tracing the history and sexual politics of hysteria, including Freud's misgivings about the literary aspect of his case studies, see Charles Bernheimer's introduction to *In Dora's Case: Freud— Hysteria—Feminism* 1–18.

3. In the drafts of "Back to Boston (Just North of Boston)," the returning poet describes her approach to Boston along the hysterical modern highway with its "miles of roadsigns," giant doughnuts, twelve plaster Hereford steers, "a heaven-reaching ice cream cone," and "a cowboy's hat" so high "you could walk inside it." All these objects "scream" their messages of need and deliverance, and together they shunt aside the big old "unobtrusive" farmhouses, which have "gone into decline" (draft 1, box 66, folder 10, VC). The ghost of a genteel, more decorous (and more inhibited) age remains, like Vuillard's sister in the wallpaper, half-consumed by all the mad activity in the world of unabashed consumerism she must now inhabit.

8. Shipwreck and Salvage

1. The fragments that Bishop copied from the Reverend Mr. Patterson's history of Sable Island are here quoted in full:

Miss Dix—1853 "On the prosecution of her lifework of founding institutions for the insane she had come to Halifax & St. Johns, N.F."—"practical and sympathetic nature"—2 days—July 26th—27th, 28th—"In that short period she had the opportunity of seeing a wreck"—"4 1st class metallic lifeboats were built in N.Y.—& were respectively named the 'Victoria' of Boston, the 'Grace Darling' of Phil., & the 'Reliance' & the 'Samaritan' of N.Y., with a car called the Rescue. Ready the 25th of Nov. & publicly exhibited on Wall St. "attracting great attention by their beauty and their strength." Miss Dix's "Life"?—also sent several hundred books. ("Notes and Observations," 1951, box 72B, folder 7, VC)

Bibliography

Primary Published Sources

Bishop, Elizabeth. "The Ballad of the Subway Train." *Western Humanities Review* 65.1 (Spring 1991): 25–26.

———. *Brazil* (with the editors of *Life*). Life World Library. New York: Time, 1962.

———. "Dimensions for a Novel." *Vassar Journal of Undergraduate Studies* 8 (May 1934): 95–103.

———. *Elizabeth Bishop: The Collected Prose*. Edited by Robert Giroux. New York: Farrar, Straus, and Giroux, 1984.

———. *Elizabeth Bishop: The Complete Poems, 1927–1979*. New York: Farrar, Straus, and Giroux, 1979.

———. "Gerard Manley Hopkins: Notes on Timing in His Poetry." *Vassar Review* 23 (February 1934): 5–7.

———. "Love from Emily." Review of *Emily Dickinson's Letters to Doctor and Mrs. Josiah Gilbert Holland*, by Theodora Van Wagenen Ward. *New Republic* 27 August 1951: 20–21.

———. "The Thumb." Reprinted in the *Gettysburg Review* 5 (Winter 1992): 28–31.

———. "Unseemly Deductions." Review of *The Riddle of Emily Dickinson*, by Rebecca Patterson. *New Republic* 18 August 1952: 20.

Bishop, Elizabeth, and Emanuel Brasil, eds. *An Anthology of Twentieth-Century Brazilian Poetry*. Middletown, Conn.: Wesleyan University Press, 1972.

Archival Material

Bishop, Elizabeth. Key West Notebook 1. Box 75, folders 4a and 4b: 1–242. Key West Notebook 2. Box 75, folders 3a and 3b: 1–205. Elizabeth Bishop Collection. Vassar College Libraries, Poughkeepsie, N.Y.

———. "Recorded Observations," 1934–37. Box 72A, folder 3. Elizabeth Bishop Collection. Vassar College Libraries, Poughkeepsie, N.Y.

———. Unpublished manuscript materials (diaries, travel diaries, transcripts, notes, essays, and poems) from the Elizabeth Bishop Collection. Vassar College Libraries, Poughkeepsie, N.Y.

Bishop–Ilse Barker and Kit Barker Correspondence. Elizabeth Bishop Collection. Princeton University Library, Princeton, N.J.

Bishop–Anny Baumann Correspondence. Elizabeth Bishop Collection. Vassar College Libraries, Poughkeepsie, N.Y.

Bishop–Dorothee Bowie Correspondence. Elizabeth Bishop Collection. Vassar College Libraries, Poughkeepsie, N.Y.

Bishop–Robert Lowell Correspondence. 1947–70. Robert Lowell Collection. Houghton Library, Harvard University, Cambridge, Mass.

Bishop–Loren MacIver Correspondence. Elizabeth Bishop Collection. Vassar College Libraries, Poughkeepsie, N.Y.

Bishop–Marianne Moore Correspondence. Papers of Marianne Moore. Series V: Correspondence. Rosenbach Museum and Library, Philadelphia, Pa.

Bishop–Frani Blough Muser Correspondence. Elizabeth Bishop Collection. Vassar College Libraries, Poughkeepsie, N.Y.

Bishop–Anne Stevenson Correspondence. Elizabeth Bishop Papers. Olin Library, Washington University, St. Louis, Mo.

Bishop–Joseph Summers Correspondence. Elizabeth Bishop Collection. Vassar College Libraries, Poughkeepsie, N.Y.

Interviews

Brown, Ashley. "An Interview with Elizabeth Bishop." Schwartz and Estess 289–302.

Cory, Chris, and Alwyn Lee. "Poets: The Second Chance." *Time* 89.22 (2 June 1967): 67–74.

Johnson, Alexandra. "Poet Elizabeth Bishop: Geography of the Imagination." *Christian Science Monitor* 23 March 1978: 24–25.

Spires, Elizabeth. "An Afternoon with Elizabeth Bishop." *Vassar Quarterly* 75.2 (1979): 4–9.

———. "The Art of Poetry, XXVII: Elizabeth Bishop." *Paris Review* 23.80 (Summer 1981): 56–83.

Starbuck, George. " 'The Work!': A Conversation with Elizabeth Bishop." Schwartz and Estess 312–30.

Secondary Sources

Ackerman, Diane. *A Natural History of the Senses.* New York: Random House, 1990.

Adamowicz, Elza. "Monsters in Surrealism: Hunting the Human-Headed Bombyx." Collier and Davies 283–302.

Ashbury, John. "Second Presentation of Elizabeth Bishop." *World Literature Today* 51.1 (Winter 1977): 9–11.

Bakhtin, M. M. *Rabelais and His World*. Translated by H. Iswolsky. Cambridge, Mass.: MIT Press, 1968.

Barry, Sandra. "The Art of Remembering: The Influence of Great Village, Nova Scotia, on the Life and Works of Elizabeth Bishop." *Nova Scotia Historical Review* 11.1 (1991): 137.

Barthes, Roland. *A Lover's Discourse*. Translated by Richard Howard. New York: Hill and Wang, 1978. Translation of *Fragments d'un discours amoureux*. Paris: Seuil, 1977.

———. *The Pleasure of the Text*. Translated by Richard Miller. New York: Hill and Wang, 1975. Translation of *Le Plaisir du texte*. Paris: Seuil, 1973.

Baudelaire, Charles. *Les Fleurs du Mal*. Translated by Richard Howard. Boston: David R. Godine, 1982.

———. *Flowers of Evil*. Translated by George Dillon and Edna St. Vincent Millay. New York: Harper and Brothers, 1936.

———. *The Painter of Modern Life and Other Essays*. Translated by Jonathan Mayne. London: Phaidon Press, 1964.

Beers, Clifford Whittingham. *A Mind That Found Itself: An Autobiography*. Garden City, N.Y.: Doubleday, Doran, 1942.

Belitt, Ben. *Adam's Dream: A Preface to Translation*. New York: Grove Press, 1978.

Bernheimer, Charles. Introduction. *In Dora's Case: Freud—Hysteria—Feminism*. Edited by Bernheimer and Claire Kahane. New York: Columbia Univ. Press, 1985. 1–18.

Bersani, Leo. *Baudelaire and Freud*. Berkeley: University of California Press, 1977.

Blasing, Mutlu Konuk. *American Poetry: The Rhetoric of Its Forms*. New Haven: Yale University Press, 1987.

Bloom, Harold. "*Geography III* by Elizabeth Bishop." *New Republic* 5 February 1977: 29–30.

Breton, André. *Oeuvres Complètes*. Vol. 1. Paris: Gallimard, 1989.

———. *Le Surréalisme et la peinture*. Paris: Gallimard, 1965.

Brogan, Jacqueline Vaught. "Elizabeth Bishop: Perversity as Voice." Lombardi 175–95.

Case, Sue-Ellen. "Tracking the Vampire." *Differences* 3.2 (Summer 1991): 1–20.

Chadwick, E. *Report . . . on an Inquiry into the Sanitary Conditions of the Labouring Population of Great Britain*. London: W. Clowes, 1842.

Chadwick, Whitney. *Women Artists and the Surrealist Movement*. Boston: Little, Brown, 1985.

Chessman, Harriet Scott. *The Public Is Invited to Dance: Representation, the Body, and Dialogue in Gertrude Stein*. Stanford, Calif.: Stanford University Press, 1989.

Cheyfitz, Eric. *The Poetics of Imperialism: Translation and Colonization from "The Tempest" to "Tarzan"*. Oxford: Oxford University Press, 1991.

Cixous, Hélène. "The Laugh of the Medusa." Translated by Keith Cohen and Paula Cohen. Rpt. in *New French Feminisms: An Anthology*. Edited by Elaine Marks and Isabelle de Courtivron. New York: Schocken Books, 1981. 245–64. Translation of "Le Rire de la Méduse." *L'Arc* 61 (1975): 39–54.

Collier, Peter, and Judy Davies, eds. *Modernism and the European Unconscious*. New York: St. Martin's Press, 1990.

Costello, Bonnie. *Elizabeth Bishop: Questions of Mastery*. Cambridge: Harvard University Press, 1991.

———. "Marianne Moore and Elizabeth Bishop: Friendship and Influence." *Twentieth Century Literature* 30 (1984): 130–49.

———. "Writing Like a Woman: A Review of Alicia Ostriker's *Stealing the Language*." *Contemporary Literature* 29.2 (1988): 305–10.

Croll, Morris W. "The Baroque Style in Prose." *Studies in English Philology*. Edited by Kemp Malone and Martin B. Ruud. Minneapolis: University of Minnesota Press, 1929. 427–56.

Cucullu, Lois. " 'Above All I Am Not That Staring Man': Positionality in Elizabeth Bishop's Travel Poetry." MLA Convention. San Francisco, 30 December 1991.

———. "Trompe l'Oeil: Elizabeth Bishop's Radical 'I.' " *Texas Studies in Literature and Language* 30.2 (Summer 1988): 246–71.

Dayan, Joan. *Fables of the Mind: An Inquiry into Poe's Fiction*. New York: Oxford University Press, 1987.

Diehl, Joanne Feit. *Women Poets and the American Sublime*. Bloomington: Indiana University Press, 1990.

Easton, Elizabeth Wynne. *The Intimate Interiors of Édouard Vuillard*. Washington, D.C.: Smithsonian Institution Press, 1989.

Edelman, Lee. "The Geography of Gender: Elizabeth Bishop's 'In the Waiting Room.' " Lombardi 91–107.

Ellis, Havelock. "Sexual Inversion Among Women." *Studies in the Psychology of Sex*. Vol. 2. 1897. New York: Random House, 1936. 261–62.

Emerson, Ralph Waldo. *The Complete Essays and Other Writings*. New York: Random House, 1940.

———. *Nature*. Boston, 1836. San Francisco, Calif.: Chandler Publishing Company, 1968.

———. *Selections from Ralph Waldo Emerson; An Organic Anthology*. Edited by Stephen Whicher. Boston: Houghton Mifflin, 1960.

Ernst, Max. *Beyond Painting: And Other Writings by the Artist and His Friends*. New York: Wittenborn, Schultz, 1948.

Faderman, Lillian. *Odd Girls and Twilight Lovers: A History of Lesbian Life in Twentieth-Century America*. New York: Columbia University Press, 1991.

Fanon, Frantz. *The Wretched of the Earth.* Translated by Constance Farring-
ton. New York: Grove Press, 1968.

Fish, Stanley. *The Living Temple: George Herbert and Catechizing.* Berkeley:
University of California Press, 1978.

Freud, Sigmund. "The Uncanny" (1919). *The Standard Edition of the Com-
plete Psychological Works of Sigmund Freud.* Vol. 17. Edited by James
Strachey. London: Hogarth Press, 1953. 217–56.

Gallop, Jane. *Thinking Through the Body.* New York: Columbia University
Press, 1988.

Genet, Jean. *Our Lady of the Flowers.* Translated by Bernard Frechtman.
New York: Grove Press, 1963.

Giles, Paul. *Hart Crane: The Contexts of "The Bridge."* Cambridge: Cam-
bridge University Press, 1986.

Goldensohn, Lorrie. "The Body's Roses: Race, Sex, and Gender in Eliza-
beth Bishop's Representations of the Self." Lombardi 70–90.

———. "Elizabeth Bishop: An Unpublished, Untitled Poem." *American
Poetry Review* 17 (January/February, 1988): 35–46.

———. *Elizabeth Bishop: The Biography of a Poetry.* New York: Columbia
University Press, 1992.

———. "Elizabeth Bishop's Originality." *American Poetry Review* 7.2
(March/April 1978): 1822.

Hadas, Pamela. "Spreading the Difference: One Way to Read Gertrude
Stein's *Tender Buttons.*" *Twentieth Century Literature: A Scholarly and
Critical Journal* 24 (1978): 57–75.

Hall, Donald. *Marianne Moore: The Cage and the Animal.* New York:
Pegasus, 1970.

Harrison, Victoria. *Elizabeth Bishop's Poetics of Intimacy.* Cambridge: Cam-
bridge University Press, 1993.

Hauser, Arnold. *The Philosophy of Art History.* New York: Knopf, 1959.

Herbert, George. *The Works of George Herbert.* Edited by F. E. Hutchinson.
Oxford: Oxford University Press, 1941.

Hughes, Robert. "The Last Symbolist Poet." *Time* 8 March 1976: 66–67.

Irigaray, Luce. "And the One Doesn't Stir Without the Other." Translated
by Helene Vivienne Wenzel. *Signs* 7.1 (1981): 62.

Jacobus, Mary. *Reading Woman: Essays in Feminist Criticism.* New York:
Columbia University Press, 1986.

Jarrell, Randall. "From 'Fifty Years of American Poetry.'" Schwartz and
Estess 198.

Jolas, Eugene. "The Industrial Mythos." *transition* 18 (November 1929): 123.

Jones, Peter Austin, ed. *Imagist Poetry.* Harmondsworth, Eng.: Penguin,
1981.

Kalstone, David. *Becoming a Poet: Elizabeth Bishop with Marianne Moore
and Robert Lowell.* New York: Farrar, Straus, and Giroux, 1989.

Keller, Lynn, and Cristanne Miller. "Emily Dickinson, Elizabeth Bishop, and the Rewards of Indirection." *New England Quarterly* 57.4 (December 1984): 533–53.

Kermode, Frank. *The Genesis of Secrecy: On the Interpretation of Narrative.* Cambridge: Harvard University Press, 1979.

Koestenbaum, Wayne. "*The Waste Land*: T. S. Eliot's and Ezra Pound's Collaboration on Hysteria." *Twentieth Century Literature* 34.2 (Summer 1988): 113–39.

Lanz, Henry. *The Physical Basis of Rime: An Essay on the Aesthetics of Sound.* Stanford, Calif.: Stanford University Press, 1931.

Lauretis, Teresa de. "Lesbian Representation." *Theatre Journal* 40 (May 1988): 155–77.

Lensing, George. "The Subtraction of Emotion in the Poetry of Elizabeth Bishop." *The Gettysburg Review* 5.1 (Winter 1922): 48–61.

Lévi-Strauss, Claude. *Tristes Tropiques.* Translated by John and Doreen Weightman. New York: Atheneum, 1981.

Lispector, Clarice. "A Hen." Translated by Elizabeth Bishop. *Kenyon Review* 26 (Summer 1964): 507–9.

———. "Marmosets." Translated by Elizabeth Bishop. *Kenyon Review* 26 (Summer 1964): 509–11.

———. "The Smallest Woman in the World." Translated by Elizabeth Bishop. *Kenyon Review* 26 (Summer 1964): 501–6.

Lombardi, Marilyn May, ed. *Elizabeth Bishop: The Geography of Gender.* Charlottesville: University Press of Virginia, 1993.

Lorris, Guillaume de, and Jean de Meun. *Romance of the Rose.* Princeton, N.J.: Princeton University Press, 1971.

Lowell, Robert. *History.* New York: Farrar, Straus, and Giroux, 1973.

———. *Selected Poems.* New York: Farrar, Straus, and Giroux, 1976.

McCarthy, Mary. "Symposium: *I Would Liked to Have Written . . .*" Schwartz and Estess 267.

MacMahon, Candace W. *Elizabeth Bishop: A Bibliography, 1927–1979.* Charlottesville: University Press of Virginia, 1980.

Mazzaro, Jerome. *Postmodern American Poetry.* Urbana: University of Illinois Press, 1980.

Merrill, James. "Elizabeth Bishop, 1911–1979." *The New York Times Review of Books* 6 December 1979: 6.

Merrin, Jeredith. "Elizabeth Bishop: Gaiety, Gayness, and Change." Lombardi 153–72.

———. *An Enabling Humility: Marianne Moore, Elizabeth Bishop, and the Uses of Tradition.* New Brunswick, N.J.: Rutgers University Press, 1990.

Millier, Brett Candlish. *Elizabeth Bishop: Life and the Memory of It.* Berkeley: University of California Press, 1993.

———. "Modesty and Morality: George Herbert, Gerard Manley Hopkins, and Elizabeth Bishop." *Kenyon Review* 11 (Spring 1989): 47–56.

Montaigne, Michel Eyquem de. *The Essayes of Montaigne.* Translated by John Florio. New York: Modern Library, 1933.

Moore, Marianne. *The Complete Poems.* New York: Viking/Macmillan, 1967.

Mullen, Richard. "Elizabeth Bishop's Surrealist Inheritance." *American Literature* 54.1 (March 1982): 63–80.

Napier, A. David. *Masks, Transformation, and Paradox.* Berkeley: University of California Press, 1986.

Ostriker, Alicia Suskin. *Stealing the Language: The Emergence of Woman's Poetry in America.* Boston: Beacon Press, 1986.

Page, Barbara. "Nature, History, and Art in Elizabeth Bishop's 'Brazil, January 1, 1502.'" *Perspectives on Contemporary Literature* 14 (1988): 39–46.

———."Off-Beat Claves, Oblique Realities: The Key West Notebooks of Elizabeth Bishop." Lombardi 196–211.

Parisi, Joseph, ed. *Marianne Moore: The Art of a Modernist.* Ann Arbor: UMI Research Press, 1990.

Parker, Robert Dale. *The Unbeliever: The Poetry of Elizabeth Bishop.* Urbana: University of Illinois Press, 1984.

Paz, Octavio. "Elizabeth Bishop, or the Power of Reticence." *World Literature Today* 51 (Winter 1977): 15–16.

Perloff, Marjorie. "Elizabeth Bishop: The Course of a Particular." *Modern Poetry Studies* 8.3 (1977): 177–92.

Pizan, Christine de. *Livre de la Cité des Dames.* Translated by Earl Jeffrey Richards. New York: Persea Books, 1982.

Poe, Edgar Allan. *Collected Works.* Edited by Thomas Ollive Mabbott. 3 vols. Cambridge: Harvard University Press, 1969.

———. *Essays and Reviews.* New York: The Library of America, 1984.

Raymond, Marcel. *From Baudelaire to Surrealism.* Translated by Raymond. London: Methuen, 1970. Translation of *De Baudelaire au Surrealisme.* 1933.

Rich, Adrienne. "The Eye of the Outsider: The Poetry of Elizabeth Bishop." *Boston Review* 8 (April 1983): 15–17.

Ross, Marlon. "Naturalizing Gender: Woman's Place in Wordsworth's Ideological Landscape." *ELH* 53.2 (Summer 1986): 391–410.

Sayre, Henry M. "American Vernacular: Objectivism, Precisionism, and the Aesthetics of the Machine." *Twentieth Century Literature: A Scholarly and Critical Journal* 35.3 (Fall 1989): 310–42.

Schwartz, Danielle. "Barthes, le langage et le pouvoir." *La Nouvelle Critique* 106 (August–September 1977): 55–57.

Schwartz, Lloyd. "Elizabeth Bishop and Brazil." *The New Yorker* 30 September 1991: 85–97.

Schwartz, Lloyd, and Sybil P. Estess, eds. *Elizabeth Bishop and Her Art.* Ann Arbor: University of Michigan Press, 1983.

Shelley, Percy Bysshe. *The Complete Poetical Works*. Boston: Houghton Mifflin, 1901.

Spiegelman, Willard. "Landscape and Knowledge: The Poetry of Elizabeth Bishop." *Modern Poetry Studies* 6 (1975): 203–24.

Spires, Elizabeth. "Elizabeth Bishop: 'The Things I'd Like to Write.' " *Gettysburg Review* 5.1 (Winter 1992): 62–70.

Stallybrass, Peter, and Allon White. *The Politics and Poetics of Transgression*. Ithaca, N.Y.: Cornell University Press, 1986.

Stanley, Henry Morton. *In Darkest Africa, Or, The Quest, Rescue, and Retreat of Emin, Governor of Equatoria*. 2d ed. New York: C. Scribner's Sons, 1890.

Stevens, Wallace. *The Collected Poems*. New York: Knopf, 1954.

Stevenson, Anne. *Elizabeth Bishop*. New York: Twayne Publishers, 1966.

Stewart, Susan. *On Longing: Narratives of the Miniature, the Gigantic, the Souvenir, the Collection*. Baltimore: Johns Hopkins University Press, 1984.

Stimpson, Catharine R. "The Somagrams of Gertrude Stein." *Poetics Today* 6.1–2 (1985): 67–80.

Sullivan, Karen. "At the Limit of Feminist Theory: An Architectonics of the *Querelle de la Rose*." *Exemplaria: A Journal of Theory in Medieval and Renaissance Studies* 3.2 (Fall 1991): 435–66.

Summers, Joseph. *George Herbert: His Religion and Art*. London: Chatto & Windus, 1968.

Surman, Diana Collecott. "Towards the Crystal: Art and Science in Williams' Poetic." *William Carlos Williams: Man and Poet*. Edited by Carroll F. Terrell. Orono: National Poetry Foundation, University of Maine at Orono, 1983. 187–207.

Thompson, Lovell. "Eden in Easy Payments." *The Saturday Review* 3 April 1937: 15–16.

Tiffany, Francis. *Life of Dorothea Lynde Dix*. Boston, 1918. Ann Arbor: Plutarch Press, 1971.

Travisano, Thomas. *Elizabeth Bishop: Her Artistic Development*. Charlottesville: University Press of Virginia, 1988.

Vendler, Helen. "Domestication, Domesticity, and the Otherworldly." Schwartz and Estess 32–60.

Wagley, Charles. *Amazon Town: A Study of Man in the Tropics*. New York: Macmillan, 1953.

Wagoner, David. "Poem about Breath (*a memory of Elizabeth Bishop, 1950*)." *Through the Forest: New and Selected Poems*. New York: Atlantic Monthly, 1987.

Wehr, Wesley. "Elizabeth Bishop: Conversations and Class Notes." *Antioch Review* 39.3 (Summer 1981): 319–28.

Weiskel, Thomas. *The Romantic Sublime: Studies in the Structure and Psychology of Transcendence*. Baltimore: Johns Hopkins University Press, 1976.

Whitman, Walt. *Leaves of Grass*. Edited by Emory Holloway. Garden City, N.Y.: Doubleday, Page, 1926.

Williams, William Carlos. "Belly Music." *Others* 5.6 (July 1919): 25–32.

———. *The Collected Poems*. Vols. 1 and 2. Edited by A. Walton Litz and Christopher MacGowan. New York: New Directions, 1986.

———. *Selected Essays*. New York: New Directions, 1954.

Woolf, Virginia. *A Room of One's Own*. New York: Harcourt, Brace and World, 1957.

———. *To the Lighthouse*. New York: Harcourt Brace Jovanovich, 1927.

Wordsworth, William. *The Poetical Works*. 6 vols. Edited by E. de Selincourt and Helen Darbishire. Oxford University Press, 1946.

Wright, Elizabeth. "The Uncanny and Surrealism." Collier and Davies 265–82.

Yaeger, Patricia. *Honey-Mad Women: Emancipatory Strategies in Women's Writing*. New York: Columbia University Press, 1988.

Index

trix, 210, 215; and mother's body, 194, 206, 210; and succor/orality, 205–7, 212 (*see also* Body, issue of: and eating/feeding); tied to class, 82–84, 240n.3
"Memories of Uncle Neddy" (prose piece, EB), 20, 128
Memory/remembrance, issue of (in EB's works), 166, 167, 177, 191, 218; and architectonics of, EB's, 165–67; and EB's personal past, 64, 78, 97, 139, 160–61, 181–82, 186, 188–89, 195, 200, 228; and monuments/memorials, 172, 177, 181 (*see also* Monument/statue, as image); and weight/concreteness of, 170–71, 172
Mermaid: EB's identification with, 35–40; and infertile love, 36–37
Merrill, James: on EB, 1, 45, 58
Merrin, Jeredith, 48, 67, 69, 239n.1
Metonymy: and EB's poetics, 217, 242–43n.4, 244–45n.1; EB's use of, 167 (*see also* Longing, EB's: and belongings; Object/souvenir/fetish)
Miller, Margaret, 15, 25, 108, 208
Miller, Nancy K., 209–10
Millier, Brett, 237n.1
Mind, the, 191; as junk-room, 168–71; as whispering gallery, 165–66, 171, 188, 202
Mirror, as trope (in EB's works), 53, 64, 71, 240n.4; and self-image, 58–65; and social order, 57–58
Modernism: and antisentimentality, 84–86, 87, 92, 99, 196–97; EB and literary tradition, 12, 75, 84–94, 103, 181, 188; EB's growing disenchantment with, 88, 90
Monstrosity/monster: and EB's personae, 48; and female body, 203, 238n.4; and surrealism, 173, 175, 186
Montaigne, Michel Eyquem de: "Of the Caniballes," 143, 161
Monument/statue, as image (in EB's works), 177–83; and family, 181–82, 223, 228
"Monument, The" (poem, EB), 178–81, 183, 243–44n.2, 244–45n.1
Moon, as figure (in EB's works), 61, 64, 116, 239n.3; and alienation, 62; EB's identification with, 62–64; and female monstrosity, 61–62
Moore, Marianne, 6, 31, 86, 90, 99,

208; dispute over "The Roosters," 91–93; EB's correspondence with, 127, 128, 178, 229; relationship with/influence on EB, 2, 86, 96, 196, 221; *What Are Years,* 91
"Moose, The" (poem, EB), 218–19, 229–32
Moral sense, EB, 45 (*see also* Observation: ethics of, EB's)
Morbidity: EB's distaste for, 30–31, 44, 102, 103
Mortality, issue of (in EB's works). *See* Body, issue of: and organic process/ mortality
"Mrs. Sullivan Downstairs" (unfinished prose piece, EB), 176–77
Mullen, Richard, 173
Muser, Frani Blough: EB's correspondence with, 25, 53, 104, 132, 222; on EB, 1

Napier, A. David, 184
"Napolean & Hannibal" (unfinished poem, EB), 28
Narrative (in EB's works), 45, 218–19, 229–30; and hysteria (*see* Hysteria: and EB's narrative technique); and nostalgia, 192; and obscurity/ambiguity, 44–48 (*see also* Hermeneutics; Manifest/latent meanings; Opacity; Parable/parabolic)
Narrators/speakers/personae (in EB's works), 40, 49, 65, 176, 192–93; and masks, 184
"Noble Savage, The" (prose piece, EB), 52–53
North & South (EB), 237–38n.1
"North Haven" (poem, EB), 233

Objectification: and writing, 168–71 (*see also* Loss, EB's: and objectification; Visual arts: EB's relation to)
"Objects and Apparitions" (translation, EB). *See* Paz, Octavio
Object/souvenir/fetish (in EB's works), 165–70, 186, 188–91 (*see also* Love, EB: of objects); and animism, 189, 192; and control over pain, 192–93, 217, 244–45n.1 (*see also* Loss, EB's: and objectification); relation to mother's body, 13, 168, 192 (*see also* Metonymy: EB's use of);

Marilyn May Lombardi is an associate professor of English at the University of North Carolina at Greensboro. She is the editor of *Elizabeth Bishop: The Geography of Gender* (1993), a contributor to *Millay at 100: A Critical Reappraisal* (1995), and the author of recent essays for *Twentieth Century Literature* and *Papers in Language and Literature* on Bishop and Mary Shelley.